53.50

CSELLERSJS

J.M Sparrow.
1998

Ex Libris

Ian Sellers

from

Rly. Ian Sellers.
After his sudden death.

Nineteenth-Century
English Religious Traditions

Recent Titles in
Contributions to the Study of Religion

Nineteenth-Century *English Religious Traditions*

Retrospect and Prospect

Edited by
D. G. Paz

Contributions to the Study of Religion,
Number 44

Greenwood Press
Westport, Connecticut • London

1995.

Library of Congress Cataloging-in-Publication Data

Nineteenth-century English religious traditions : retrospect and
  prospect / edited by D.G. Paz.
    p.   cm.—(Contributions to the study of religion, ISSN
  0196–7053 ; 44)
    Includes bibliographical references and index.
    ISBN 0–313–29476–3 (alk. paper)
    1. England—Church history—19th century.   2. Christianity and
  culture—History—19th century.   I. Paz, D.G. (Denis G.)
  II. Series: Contributions to the study of religion ; no. 44.
  BR759.N55   1995
  274.1′081—dc20   95–9665

British Library Cataloguing in Publication Data is available.

Library of Congress Catalog Card Number: 95–9665
ISBN: 0–313–29476–3
ISSN: 0196–7053

First published in 1995

Greenwood Press, 88 Post Road West, Westport, CT 06881
An imprint of Greenwood Publishing Group, Inc.

Printed in the United States of America

The paper used in this book complies with the
Permanent Paper Standard issued by the National
Information Standards Organization (Z39.48–1984).

10 9 8 7 6 5 4 3 2 1

Contents

List of Abbreviations

AHR	*American Historical Review*
CH	*Church History*
EHR	*English Historical Review*
HJ	*Historical Journal*
JBS	*Journal of British Studies*
JEH	*Journal of Ecclesiastical History*
JMH	*Journal of Modern History*
SCH	*Studies in Church History*
TRHS	*Transactions of the Royal Historical Society*

Introduction

D. G. Paz

THE NINETEENTH CENTURY was a time of tension between central tendencies and local independence, between nation and region, between metropolitan and provincial cultures. These tensions were part of the process of constructing the "British" nation and "British" identity, concepts that transcended and subsumed the constituent "countries" of the United Kingdom and that represent more than mere "Englishness" writ large. No doubt the concept of "Britishness" has much analytical utility. Yet, paradoxically, the construction of the "British" national identity also strengthened the sense of identity of the "countries." Keith Robbins, in his nuanced treatment of the subject, observes that although the "British nation" was "made" during the nineteenth century, and England, Scotland, and Wales bound together more closely than ever before, the increased contact also increased the sense of difference.[1] Thus, "Englishness" continues to have utility as an analytical category for understanding the nineteenth century. "English history," Robbins reminds us, "is central to the history of Britain, but is not synonymous with it."[2]

Religious identity also was made during the nineteenth century. That process took the direction of constructing the denomination: an identity that transcended the family, congregation, or community and that was expressed in institutional forms. Although interfaith cooperation was important during the nineteenth century (however, the timing and extent of that cooperation are contested historical problems), differences and conflicts, both institutional and ideological, also were important. This book,

---

[1] Keith Robbins, *Nineteenth-Century Britain: Integration and Diversity* (Oxford, 1988); paperback edition under the title *Nineteenth-Century Britain: England, Scotland, and Wales: The Making of a Nation*, 184.

[2] Ibid., 1.

then, focuses on how religious traditions took those institutional and ideological forms in England during the nineteenth century. (Individual contributors have decided for themselves whether their special subjects warrant moving beyond these bounds.) Each chapter focuses on its religious tradition's social, economic, and political identity, rather than on more purely theological and liturgical issues, although the latter are not neglected.

A distinguished group of scholars comes together in this book. John Wolffe examines the contests for the identity of Anglicanism, and Sheridan Gilley considers the emergence of several styles of Roman Catholicism. Richard J. Helmstadter charts the transformation of Orthodox Nonconformity (Congregationalists, Baptists, and Presbyterians) from seventeenth- and eighteenth-century "Dissent" to the "Free Churches" of the late nineteenth century; while R. K. Webb describes the forging of denominational identities on the part of the Quakers and Unitarians. David Hempton reviews Methodism, its forms and contests for identity and authority. In addition, many other institutional expressions of religious identity flourished like green bay-trees during the period: Peter J. Lineham treats the varieties of the Protestant "Sects,"[3] while Edward Royle does the same for the varieties of Freethought. Jeffrey Cox concludes with a chapter on how the making of that distinctly nineteenth-century identity, the missionary, both recapitulated and recast in a new context the themes explored in the earlier chapters.

The intent of this collection is twofold: to draw a picture of the state of research at the end of the twentieth century and to suggest directions for further exploration. No editor's comments can do justice to the rich analyses in each of the contributions to this collection. Readers will see that the contributors bring several methodological approaches to the study of nineteenth-century religion. The family, the cultural community, the community of faith—each provides a fruitful starting point. Some of the contributors use narrative as the vehicle for their analyses; others approach their subject from the perspective of sociology; still others fall somewhere between. All rest their work on empirical research and on tours of the bibliographical horizon.

Readers also will see that historians have yet to explore some interesting questions.

Systematic histories of theological developments among the Methodists, the "Sects," and Orthodox Nonconformity remain to be written, as do systematic institutional histories of those Methodist groups that broke away from the Wesleyan Connexion and of the Presbyterians. Methodist, Nonconformist, and Sectarian theologies surely ought to be no less privi-

---

[3] This label is perhaps the most problematical of all the labels found in this book, but we use it for want of a better one.

leged than Anglican and Roman Catholic intellectual histories. The various Methodist groups, Orthodox Nonconformity, the "Sects," and Freethought are better served by local studies than are either the Church of England or the Roman Catholic Church. Perhaps historians ought to take seriously the parochial and diocesan structures of these last two denominations.

Both episcopal churches, ironically, are short on studies of bishops; the Roman Church especially needs biographical works on other bishops besides the three Victorian Archbishops of Westminster. Likewise, historians need to move beyond priest lists to collective studies of the socioeconomic background of Roman clergy (ideally using computer-aided statistical analyses) to match the studies of Anglican and Nonconformist clergy. More generally, the story of how clerical status became defined as a profession in Roman Catholicism, Methodism, and the "Sects" needs telling. As well, collective studies of female religious, lady missionaries (and missionaries' ladies), and women preachers are lacking. Perhaps the largest group of Victorian women connected with religion is that of the wives, daughters, and sisters of Anglican clergymen, but what is known of them?

Laity as well as clergy are important. We know more about the laity of some traditions than about those of others. Freethinkers, "sectarians," Quakers and Unitarians, Orthodox Dissenters, and Methodists have been studied intensely, and Anglicans with a somewhat lesser degree of intensity. (One has the sense that, in some studies, Anglicans are what is left over after the Dissenting populations have been examined.) The Roman Catholic population has been studied insofar as that population was Irish, but assumptions about the nature and social standing of the Old Catholics remain unexamined. The computer and quantitative methods are appropriate tools for studies such as these.

On a more theoretical level, the problematical relationship of Evangelicalism to the state warrants examination. Abroad, in the British Empire, Evangelicals, both Anglican and Nonconformist, appear to have been highly suspicious of state support and what they considered "undue" state influence on religion. At home, however, they took a different view: Anglican Evangelicals prized the state connection as a bulwark against Catholicism; Nonconformist Evangelicals, although calling for the redress of "Dissenters' grievances," appealed to the power of the state to control popular behavior and to discourage popery. How significant are the differences between Evangelicals who were Anglican and Evangelicals who were not? How did the British, English, Welsh, Scottish, and Evangelical identities play out in the mission field?

Religious journalism is a lively but relatively unexplored aspect of the history of Victorian religious traditions.[4] The origins of the religious periodical press, the relationship between religious and secular journalism, the institutional and ideological links between periodicals and denominations, changes over time in the nature of religious journalism, the personnel of the religious press, local journalistic efforts, and connections between press and readership—all these problems and more await exploration.

The relationship between religion and the arts is another promising area for study. Literature, especially the novel, has been best served in the recent past with studies that link significant literary output with contemporary theological and ideological issues.[5] But the literary images and influences of Anglo-Catholicism, Methodism, the "Sects," and Freethought have not received the attention that they deserve; and although the fiction of empire is a staple of literary history, a more nuanced treatment of missions and missionaries is warranted. Nor have historians availed themselves enough of the evidentiary power of fiction in their research. The visual arts have been less well explored. Art and architecture both reflect religious issues of the day; and they also offer evidence for historians to use.[6] In the cases of both literature and the arts, historians will want to move beyond the so-called canon to consider a broader range of production that illuminates middle-class and working-class mentalities. Literature, art, architecture, and music are cultural artefacts that both reflect and illuminate the society that produced them.

For several reasons, this volume does not deal with non-Christian religious traditions. The history of the Jewish communities in England is well known, and on certain levels Anglo-Jewish history parallels that of the Christian traditions, especially Orthodox Nonconformity, the Quakers, and the Unitarians. The nineteenth century saw the creation of centralized institutions such as the office of Chief Rabbi and the Board of Deputies of British Jews to provide leadership for local congregations and to repre-

[4] The indispensable starting point is Josef L. Altholz's pioneering survey, *The Religious Press in Britain, 1760-1900* (Westport, Conn., 1989).

[5] I especially single out Elisabeth Jay, *The Religion of the Heart: Anglican Evangelicalism and the Nineteenth-Century Novel* (Oxford, 1979), and Valentine Cunningham, *Everywhere Spoken Against: Dissent in the Victorian Novel* (Oxford, 1975). Robert Lee Wolff's compendium, *Gains and Losses: Novels of Faith and Doubt in Victorian England* (New York, 1977), is a good starting point.

[6] See Lindsay Errington, *Social and Religious Themes in English Art, 1840-1860* (New York, 1984); and Susan P. Casteras, "Virgin Vows: The Early Victorian Artists' Portrayal of Nuns and Novices," *Religion in the Lives of English Women, 1760-1930*, ed. by Gail Malmgreen (Bloomington, 1986), 129-160. Also see Clyde Binfield's chapters on architecture and culture in his *So Down to Prayers: Studies in English Nonconformity, 1780-1920* (London, 1977), 145-185.

sent the communities to the state. Yet, like its Nonconformist counter-
parts, Anglo-Jewry was by no means monolithic. The nineteenth century
saw the emergence of Orthodox, Reform, and Liberal denominational
identities related to differing views about the nature of Jewish law. The
socioeconomic backgrounds of Jewish families also suggest parallels with
their Nonconformist counterparts. Other relationships are possible. How
do the effects on Anglo-Jewry of the influx of Russian Jewish immigrants
after 1881 compare with the effects on English Roman Catholicism of the
influx of Irish Roman Catholic immigrants after 1831?[7]

However, there also may be significant differences. Some of the Jewish
denominational identities were related to the Continental European distinctions among Sephardim (those whose ancestors came from Spain and
the Muslim world), Ashkenazim (those whose ancestors settled north of
the Alps and Pyrenees) from the German lands, and Ashkenazim from
Eastern Europe. Of the Christian traditions, perhaps only Roman Catholicism came as close to being so decisively shaped by Continental European conditions. Another apparent difference is that Jewish institutions
from the earliest part of the nineteenth century were British-wide rather
than limited to England. Whatever the case may turn out to be, comparisons and contrasts between the several Christian and Jewish traditions
should prove suggestive.

Adherents of other non-Christian religions—Muslims, Hindus, and
Sikhs in particular—no doubt were present in nineteenth-century England,
but they appear to have left few traces of institutional life.

Another area of enquiry that several contributors to this volume raise
is that of transatlantic comparisons. As will be seen in the chapters below,
some research along these lines already has been published. Transatlantic
relations were especially close among Anglicans, Quakers, Unitarians,
Methodists, and some of the "Sects" (especially Adventists, Plymouth

---

[7] The historical literature on Anglo-Jewry is large and of high quality. See
Geoffrey Alderman, *Modern British Jewry* (Oxford, 1992); Todd M. Endelman,
*The Jews of Georgian England, 1714-1830: Tradition and Change in a Liberal
Society* (Philadelphia, 1979), and his *Radical Assimilation in English Jewish His-
tory, 1656-1945* (Bloomington, 1990); Israel Feinstein, *Jewish Society in Victorian
England: Collected Essays* (London, 1993); *Victorian Jews through British Eyes*,
ed. by Anne and Roger Cowen (New York, 1986); M.C.N. Salbstein, *The Em-
ancipation of the Jews in Britain: The Question of the Admission of the Jews to
Parliament, 1828-1860* (Rutherford, N.J., 1982); Anne Aresty Naman, *The Jew
in the Victorian Novel: Some Relationships Between Prejudice and Art* (New
York, 1980); Harold Pollins, *Economic History of the Jews in England* (London,
1982); and the older but still useful V. D. Lipman, *Social History of the Jews in
England, 1850-1950* (London, 1954), and Cecil Roth, *A History of the Jews in
England*, 3rd ed. (Oxford, 1964).

Brethren, and Mormons). These relations have been touched on, especially
in the context of antislavery, but more extensive research and analyses of
specifically denominational relationships are needed. Much less well explored are the transatlantic comparisons of Roman Catholicism, Congregationalism, the Baptists, and Freethought. For instance, Irish immigrants
appear to have been excluded from power within the English Roman Catholic Church, but across the Atlantic they (and the Germans) dominated
the American Roman Catholic hierarchy. Were English bishops to the Irish laity in England what Irish bishops were to Italian, Slavic, and Mexican
laity in the United States? The question of whether there was a transatlantic missionary community is perhaps more complicated. Were American and English missionaries rivals for spiritual empire, as English and
French missionaries were in Uganda, and English and Scottish missionaries were in southern Africa? Did American and English missionary rivalry
differ according to region (most intense in China; less so in India and the
Middle East; least so in Africa)?

Scholars interested in a transatlantic perspective must include Canada
in their conceptualizations. The United States, it needs reminding, is not
the only English-speaking country in North America. The Anglophone
regions of Canada (above all, Ontario and the Maritime provinces) must
be brought into any transatlantic comparison. That added perspective will
illuminate both sides of the Atlantic.

It is the hope of all the contributors to this volume that its readers will
come away from it ready to ask new questions, look at the sources in new
ways, and make new connections. The history of religion in Victorian
England, we believe, has an exciting future.

1

Anglicanism

John Wolffe

DURING THE LAST twenty years or so, the historiography of the nineteenth-century Church of England has developed in a similar manner to that of other religious groups, in respect of a broadening out from denominational history to place Anglicanism in the mainstream of the period's political, social, and cultural history.[1] However in the case of the Church of England, the point of departure was different from that of other bodies in two major respects.

Firstly, in the Anglican case, "inside" commitments lying behind denominational approaches have been of many different kinds. These can be viewed initially in terms of the taxonomy of "Church parties" delineated by W. J. Conybeare in a sparkling 1853 article in the *Edinburgh Review*, which remains a more readable introduction to the Victorian Church than many modern secondary works. Conybeare divided the clergy of his day into three main parties: High Church, subdivided into "Anglican," Tractarian, and "High and Dry"; Low Church, made up of Evangelical, "Recordite," and "Low and Slow"; and Broad Church, consisting of "theoretical" and "antitheoretical" clergy.[2] Evangelicals and Anglo-Catholics both have presented their distinctive contributions to the historiography of the Church of England.[3] Differences of opinion within other religious groups

---

[1] I am indebted to Edward Royle for his comments on a draft of this chapter.

[2] "Church Parties," *Edinburgh Review* 98 (1853), 273-342. W. J. Coneybeare (1815-1857) was principal of the Liverpool Collegiate Institution, 1842-48, and vicar of Axminster, Devon, 1848-54.

[3] See, for example, G. R. Balleine, *A History of the Evangelical Party in the Church of England* (London, 1908); R. W. Church, *The Oxford Movement: Twelve Years, 1833-1845* (London, 1891); Broad Church attitudes to history are analyzed in D. Forbes, *The Liberal Anglican Idea of History* (Cambridge, 1952).

have of course left their historiographical traces, but in no other case do these approach the same degree of importance and complexity.

Secondly, it is essential in addition to acknowledge the historiographical implications of the national status of the Church of England, which has always raised the problem of where the history of the Established Church ends and general history begins. Accordingly, historians of Anglicanism, if they have taken Establishment seriously, have always had a wider agenda than students of Nonconformity and of Roman Catholicism, and the transition to the "new" religious history has hence been rather less marked.

It should therefore occasion little surprise that a key departure point for all historians of the Church of England during this period, Owen Chadwick's *Victorian Church*,[4] has features reminiscent both of older-style ecclesiastical history and of more recent religious history. This classic work of urbane and sympathetic scholarship provides a synthesis of much of the work done before the 1960s and has been a stimulating pointer to further research, raising many questions that remain largely unanswered two decades later. Chadwick dwells on the Oxford Movement at substantially greater length than on Evangelicalism and has more to say about theological and constitutional developments than about the Church's response to social problems and its ministry on the ground, but he does address a comprehensive agenda.

The procedure adopted in this chapter is an initial examination of the three main "party" groupings in turn, followed by a consideration of the approach of historians to issues that transcend these divisions, relating to the wider national role of Anglicanism, and the social context of religion. It must be acknowledged at the outset that, although some attempt is made to cover the whole of the period from 1789 to 1914, the constraints of space in the face of the enormous literature on the Church of England mean that the focus is on the early Victorian era between the 1830s and the 1860s.

The historiography of Anglican High Churchmanship has traditionally been dominated by a perception of the central importance of the Oxford (or Tractarian) Movement in a process of revival from eighteenth-century somnolence. This view is represented most clearly by Dean Church's classic *The Oxford Movement: Twelve Years, 1833-1845* (1891). Another seminal work from an earlier generation, Yngve Brilioth's *The Anglican Revival* (1925), does, however, give considerable weight to the prehistory of the movement, which included the influence of Evangelicalism and Romanticism as well as development from the old tradition of High Churchmanship. Like Church, however, Brilioth effectively ended with Newman's conversion in 1845, leaving unexplored the relationship of the

4 2 vols. (London, 1966-70).

Oxford Movement to ritualism and later nineteenth-century Anglo-Catholicism. By contrast, the recent short surveys by Nigel Yates and Geoffrey Rowell both give considerable attention to later developments, thus
implicitly playing down the significance of 1845.[5] Nevertheless, the broad
picture painted by Church, with important dividing lines in 1833 and 1845,
has had an enduring influence.

The central question for students of Anglo-Catholicism is thus one of
continuity. Did the Oxford Movement emerge primarily by evolution from
the past or by reaction against it? How much did the movement itself
change between 1833 and 1845? To what extent was ritualism after 1845
a direct result of influence from Oxford? Should the Tractarians be seen
as central in the development of High Churchmanship or as a diversion
from the mainstream? A new synthesis that addresses such questions is
increasingly needed, but it is becoming possible to advance some hypotheses in the light of recent research.

Work on the prehistory of the Oxford Movement continues to under-
line the importance of the context first explored by Brilioth. Moreover, it
is clear that "old-style" High Churchmanship was far from moribund. This
is evident from its intellectual vitality, at least in relation to political theology, and its record in the performance of public worship, which, although patchy in its geographical distribution, provides grounds for arguing that revival occurred "not only by reaction against the existing order
but by evolution from it."[6] The Hackney Phalanx, an informal network
of conservative but conscientious clergy, was of considerable importance.
William Van Mildert[7] was a central figure, and the group had ties with
William Howley.[8] When the activity of conservative High Churchmen in
years contemporary with the Oxford Movement itself is investigated, it
becomes clear that Tractarianism was by no means the only sign of life.[9]
If this picture is to be fully substantiated, further research is needed, which

[5] G. Rowell, *The Vision Glorious: Themes and Personalities of the Catholic
Revival in Anglicanism* (Oxford, 1983); N. Yates, *The Oxford Movement and Anglican Ritualism*, Historical Association pamphlet (London, 1983).

[6] J.C.D. Clark, *English Society, 1688-1832* (Cambridge, 1985), 354; F. C.
Mather, "Georgian Churchmanship Reconsidered: Some Variations in Anglican
Public Worship, 1714-1830," *JEH* 36 (1985), 255-83.

[7] Bishop of Llandaff, 1819-26, and of Durham, 1826-36. See E.A. Varley, *The
Last of the Prince Bishops: William Van Mildert and the High Church Movement
of the Early Nineteenth Century* (Cambridge, 1992).

[8] Bishop of London, 1813-28; Archbishop of Canterbury, 1828-48. See Clive
Dewey, *The Passing of Barchester* (London, 1991), 155 and passim.

[9] P. B. Nockles, *The Oxford Movement in Context: Anglican High Churchmanship, 1760-1857* (Cambridge, 1994).

might center on bishops such as Henry Phillpotts[10] and Christopher Wordsworth[11] or on men who were initially active supporters of the movement, but shortly appeared out of sympathy with it, such as Hugh James Rose and William Palmer.[12]

Evaluation of the character and evolution of the Oxford Movement itself has inevitably, in the past, been subject to the pressures of theological polemic. The central problem here is the conversions to Rome, which have been seen by both Roman Catholics and Evangelicals (for different reasons) as a logical development from the movement's startingpoint, but by Anglo-Catholics as a repudiation of it. In recent years, however, the growth of a more ecumenical spirit has been associated with more rounded appreciations of the career of John Henry Newman, in which his conversion in 1845 can be viewed more objectively. Continuing fascination with his spiritual crisis in the 1840s is apparent, however, both in various articles and in Ian Ker's substantial biography, in which nearly a quarter of the 764 pages are devoted to the years between 1838 and 1845.[13] By contrast, Sheridan Gilley's study, although somewhat shorter, is more chronologically even in its coverage and is perhaps of rather greater value for understanding Newman as an Anglican.[14] Interest in Newman was fanned further by the centenary (in 1990) of his death,[15] and it is, of course, wholly

[10] Bishop of Exeter, 1830-69.

[11] Bishop of Lincoln, 1868-85.

[12] Rose (1795-1838) was the host at the Hadleigh conference in 1833, which was an important incident in the early stages of the Oxford Movement. He was later professor of divinity at Durham and principal of King's College, London. Palmer (1803-1885) was a liturgical scholar and the author of *A Narrative of Events Connected with the Publication of the Tracts for the Times* (Oxford, 1843), which sought to show that the romanizers did not represent the original standpoint of the movement.

[13] A. Brent, "Newman's Conversion, the Via Media, and the Myth of a Romeward Movement," *Downside Review* 101 (1983), 261-80; T. Merrigan, "Newman's Progress towards Rome: A Psychological Consideration of His Conversion to Catholicism," *Downside Review* 104 (1986), 95-112; R. David Cox, "Newman, Littlemore, and a Tractarian Attempt at Community," *Anglican and Episcopal History* 62 (1993), 343-76; Ian Ker, *John Henry Newman: A Biography* (Oxford, 1988).

[14] Sheridan Gilley, *Newman and His Age* (London, 1990). See also Stephen Thomas, *Newman and Heresy: The Anglican Years* (Cambridge, 1991).

[15] *Newman after a Hundred Years*, ed. by Ian Ker and Alan G. Hill (Oxford, 1990); *John Henry Newman: Reason, Rhetoric, and Romanticism*, ed. by David Nicholls and Fergus Kerr (Bristol, 1991). For a review of the literature, see Peter B. Nockles, "Recent Studies of John Henry Newman," *Anglican and Episcopal History* 63 (1994), 73-86.

legitimate on its own terms, but for the student of Anglicanism there is a danger that it can be a distraction from developing a rounded view of the movement as a whole. Work on Keble and Pusey has served to flesh out the picture of these two men as shaken but ultimately firm pillars of loyalty to the Church of England. In particular, Colin Matthew has traced Pusey's development from the liberal of the 1820s into the inflexible dogmatist of the later years, but suggests that his scholarly ossification was the obverse of an ecclesiastical statesmanship that was of central importance in the difficult years after 1841. Subsequently, R. W. Franklin has presented Pusey as the central figure in the movement, which he stimulatingly relates to parallel developments on the Continent.[16] There is a need, however, for further work, not just on the main figures, but also on less prominent Tractarian sympathizers, before historical assessment of the relative importance of the different strands in the movement can have a fully solid evidential base.

The strength of the connection between theological Tractarianism and liturgical ritualism is debateable in view of the relatively "low" practice of the early Tractarians. Furthermore, G. W. Herring has suggested that in their pastoral and liturgical practice Tractarian clergy differed little from their neighbors, and that the ritualists owed more to the movements to restore Gothic architecture and to advance eucharistic doctrine in the 1850s than to the influence of the Oxford Movement; while Nigel Yates has described fully the wider pattern of liturgical and architectural change.[17] In terms of the achievements of Anglo-Catholicism, local studies point to the wide diffusion of moderate ritualism during the second half of the century, while indicating the danger of concentrating on the extremists who attracted public attention in the 1860s and 1870s, but were by no means representative of the group as a whole.[18] There are also pit-

[16] Georgina Battiscombe, *John Keble: A Study in Limitations* (London, 1963); *Pusey Rediscovered*, ed. by P.A. Butler (London, 1983) H.C.G. Matthew, "Edward Bouverie Pusey: From Scholar to Tractarian," *Journal of Theological Studies*, New Ser. 32 (1981), 101-24; R. W. Franklin, *Nineteenth-Century Churches: The History of a New Catholicism in Württemberg, England, and France* (New York, 1987); R. W. Franklin, "The Impact of Germany on the Anglican Catholic Revival in the Nineteenth Century," *Anglican and Episcopal History* 61 (1992), 433-48.

[17] G. W. Herring, "Tractarianism to Ritualism: A Study of Some Aspects of Tractarianism Outside Oxford, from the Time of Newman's Conversion in 1845, until the First Ritual Commission in 1867" (D.Phil. thesis, University of Oxford, 1984); Nigel Yates, *Buildings, Faith, and Worship: The Liturgical Arrangement of Anglican Churches, 1600-1900* (Oxford, 1991).

[18] See Nigel Yates: *The Oxford Movement and Parish Life: St. Saviour's, Leeds, 1839-1929*, Borthwick Papers, No. 48 (York, 1975); *The Anglican Revival in*

also studies of
W.F. Hook.

falls in uncritical acceptance of an "heroic" view of ritualist slum priests, whose numbers and impact should not be exaggerated.[19] An important area that remains relatively unexplored is the emergence of Anglican religious orders. It is curious that the rise of women's history has not led to any resurgence of interest in sisterhoods, on which the existing work seems ripe for revision, although R. M. Kollar has recently recounted the history of Lord Halifax,[20] Aelred Carlyle,[21] and their efforts to establish Benedictine monasticism in the Church of England.[22] In summary, while conventional assessments of Anglo-Catholicism have not necessarily been invalidated, they are coming under closer scrutiny as new avenues of research are being opened up.

The historiography of Anglican Evangelicalism[23] is beginning to come of age, although its emancipation from the condescension of its opponents and the uncritical enthusiasm of its adherents is proving a long and difficult process. A further mixed blessing has been a tendency in recent years for a number of social and cultural historians to treat evangelicalism as fundamental to Victorian intellectual and social life while seldom satisfactorily

Victorian Portsmouth (Portsmouth, 1983); *Kent and the Oxford Movement*, Kentish Sources, No. 7 (Canterbury, 1983); "'Bells and Smells': London, Brighton, and South Coast Religion Reconsidered," *Southern History* 5 (1983), 122-53; R. W. Franklin, "Puseyism in the Parishes: Leeds and Wantage Contrasted," *Anglican and Episcopal History* 62 (1993), 377-95.

[19] See L. E. Ellsworth, *Charles Lowder and the Ritualist Movement* (London, 1982), and the comments by John Kent in *The Unacceptable Face: The Modern Church in the Eyes of the Historian* (London, 1987), 89.

[20] Sir Charles Lindley Wood, second Viscount Halifax (1839-1934), was president of the English Church Union, 1868-1919 and 1927-34, and a leading lay Anglo-Catholic (*DNB, 1931-40*, 919-21).

[21] (1874-1955), abbot of Caldey Island from 1906; converted to Roman Catholicism in 1913.

[22] The most penetrating research on the subject so far takes the perspective of sociology: M. Hill, *The Religious Order* (London, 1973). See also A. M. Allchin, *The Silent Rebellion* (London, 1958); P. Anson, *The Call of the Cloister* (London, 1958); T. J. Williams, *Priscilla Lydia Sellon* (London, 1950). See also R. M. Kollar: "The Oxford Movement and the Heritage of Benedictine Monasticism," *Downside Review* 101 (1983), 281-90; "Archbishop Davidson, Bishop Gore, and Abbot Carlyle: Benedictine Monks in the Anglican Church," *SCH* 22 (1985), 377-96.

[23] In this chapter the convention of using a capital "E" for Anglican Evangelicals and lower case for the wider evangelical movement is followed. This reflects the author's perception that Anglican Evangelicalism was a distinctive movement and party.

defining their terms or examining the structure of the movement itself.[24] However, D. W. Bebbington's important recent synthesis provides the student with a solidly based general interpretation of evangelicalism on an interdenominational basis. Bebbington's work marks a clear break from traditional styles of religious historiography in that his understanding and definition of evangelicalism are couched more in terms of style than of content, and he argues strongly that it was a movement that reflected, more than it defied, broader contemporary cultural trends.[25] It is no adverse criticism of Bebbington to say that such judgements are likely further to stimulate existing debates rather than to end them. There is still a need for exploring the definition of evangelicalism: should it be viewed in terms of a scheme of ideas, of a conversionist spirituality, or in relation to individuals and institutions? To what extent should Anglican Evangelicalism be viewed as a movement distinct from evangelical Nonconformity? In addition, there is a problem of continuity parallel to that relating to Anglo-Catholicism: how did the strident Evangelicalism of the Victorian period relate to the more "moderate" Evangelicalism of the early nineteenth century?

Much research has been concentrated on the years from 1820 to 1835, which are generally perceived as marking an important watershed in Evangelical history.[26] This can partly be seen in generational terms, as a transition from the late eighteenth and early nineteenth centuries, the era of William Wilberforce[27] and Charles Simeon[28] to the early and middle

[24] These difficulties are evident, for example, in Ian Bradley, *The Call to Seriousness* (London, 1976), and in Leonore Davidoff and Catherine Hall, *Family Fortunes: Men and Women of the English Middle Class, 1780-1850* (London, 1987).

[25] D. W. Bebbington, *Evangelicalism in Modern Britain: A History from the 1730s to the 1980s* (London, 1989). Kenneth Hylson-Smith's *Evangelicals in the Church of England, 1734-1984* (Edinburgh, 1989) is a largely narrative account in the tradition of Balleine and offers little new evidence or analysis.

[26] See especially D. N. Hempton, "Evangelicalism and Eschatology," *JEH* 31 (1980), 179-94; W. H. Oliver, *Prophets and Millenialists* (Auckland, 1978); I. S. Rennie, "Evangelicalism and English Public Life, 1825-1850" (Ph.D. thesis, University of Toronto, 1968); S. C. Orchard, "English Evangelical Eschatology, 1790-1850" (Ph.D. thesis, University of Cambridge, 1968); W.J.C. Ervine, "Doctrine and Diplomacy: Some Aspects of the Life and Thought of the Anglican Evangelical Clergy, 1797-1837" (Ph.D. thesis, University of Cambridge, 1979).

[27] (1759-1833); see J. C. Pollock, *Wilberforce* (London, 1977).

[28] (1759-1836); see H. E. Hopkins, *Charles Simeon of Cambridge* (London, 1977).

Victorian years, the era of Lord Shaftesbury[29] and Hugh McNeile.[30] In the careers of men of intermediate age, such as William Marsh[31] and Edward Bickersteth,[32] can the associated changes of outlook be most clearly discerned. In theological terms, the most important shift was from postmillennialist to premillennialist eschatology, associated with a more pessimistic view of human potential and deeper opposition to Roman Catholicism and "infidelity." It is important to note that this development originated before the emergence of a recognizable "Oxford Movement," and it is therefore misleading to see Evangelical theology in the mid-nineteenth century as primarily "a response to Tractarianism." Nevertheless, during the middle years of the century, antagonism to Catholicism in both its Roman and Anglican forms undoubtedly led to stronger definitions of Evangelical belief on the nature of authority, salvation, and the Sacraments.[33]

The broad outline of these changes is evident enough, but their significance remains unclear. It should be noted that in 1853 Conybeare judged that there were still 3,300 moderate Evangelicals as opposed to only 2,500 "Recordite" extremists, while the *Christian Observer*, the literary organ of the older group, survived until 1877, albeit with the loss of something of its former prominence.[34] It would seem, therefore, that, with "Recordites" as with ritualists, historians have been in danger of assuming that the most noisy groups were automatically the most influential. It may be, too, that the "Recordite"-"moderate" dichotomy is better understood as pointing to tendencies rather than to clearly defined groups of people. Before firm conclusions can be drawn, much further research on the Victorian period is required, examining the careers and religious ideas of Evangelical clergy

[29] (1801-1885); see G.F.A. Best, *Shaftesbury* (London, 1964), and Geoffrey B.A.M. Finlayson, *The Seventh Earl of Shaftesbury, 1801-1885* (London, 1981).

[30] (1795-1879); rector of Albury, 1822-34, incumbent of St. Jude's, Liverpool, 1834-48, St. Paul's, Prince's Park, Liverpool, 1848-67, and dean of Ripon, 1868-75. *DNB*, 35, 246; J. A. Wardle, "The Life and Times of the Rev. Dr. Hugh McNeile, 1795-1879" (M.A. thesis, University of Manchester, 1981).

[31] William ("Millennial") Marsh (1775-1864) held the livings of St. Peter's, Colchester, 1814-29, St. Thomas's, Birmingham, 1829-39, and St. Mary's, Leamington, 1839-60. *DNB* 12, 1103-4.

[32] (1786-1850); secretary of the Church Missionary Society, 1816-30; rector of Watton, Herts, 1830-50. *DNB* 5, 3; M. Hennell, *Sons of the Prophets: Evangelical Leaders of the Victorian Church* (London, 1979), 29-49.

[33] Cf. P. Toon, *Evangelical Theology, 1833-1856: A Response to Tractarianism* (London, 1979); *Religion in Victorian Britain*, ed. by G. Parsons, vol. 1, *Traditions* (Manchester, 1988), 34.

[34] Conybeare, "Church Parties," 338; John Wolffe, "The First Century of *The Churchman*," *Churchman* 102I (1988), 199.

who, while seldom if ever leaving personal papers, have made significant traces in the printed records, above all in the pages of local newspapers.[35]

The wider cultural context of Evangelicalism has been addressed in two important books. Doreen Rosman's work is informed by the development of cultural history and indicates that the austerity and distinctiveness of the mores of Evangelicals in the first third of the nineteenth century should not be exaggerated, although at a later date they were prone to withdraw more emphatically into a subculture.[36] Boyd Hilton approaches Evangelicalism from the standpoint of intellectual history, but tends to a similar conclusion in that he emphasizes the congruence between Evangelical modes of thought and those operative in relation to political economy, social issues, and even science.[37] His argument suffers, however, from a failure to distinguish sufficiently rigorously between Evangelical writers and non-Evangelicals who shared certain Evangelical forms of expression.

While such studies go some way to answer the concern voiced earlier regarding a current tendency to make glib generalizations about the social impact of Evangelicalism, a significant agenda still requires investigation before their conclusions can be regarded as firmly established. In particular, more systematic analysis is required of the network of Evangelical voluntary societies and the role of Exeter Hall and the London May meetings. Hitherto, these have been viewed largely in relation to specific objectives, whether in overseas missions, Sunday observance, or anti-Catholicism.[38] Study of these numerous organizations as social institutions in their own right would reveal much about the personal networks associated with Evangelicalism and provide a means to evaluate more systematically than hitherto the nature and extent of its impact on Victorian life Leslie Howsam's important study of the Bible Society serves to indicate the potentialities of such an approach.[39]

There is a need for continuing exploration of the tension within Anglican Evangelicalism between loyalty to the Church of England and association with a wider evangelical community of faith. In the late eigh-

---

[35] This process should be assisted by the publication of Blackwell's *A Dictionary of Evangelical Biography,* ed. by Donald Lewis (Oxford, 1995).

[36] D. Rosman, *Evangelicals and Culture* (London, 1984).

[37] B. Hilton, *The Age of Atonement: The Influence of Evangelicalism on Social and Economic Thought, 1795-1865* (Oxford, 1988).

[38] On these topics, see, respectively, B. Stanley, "Home Support for Overseas Missions in Early Victorian England, c. 1838-1873" (Ph.D. thesis, University of Cambridge, 1979); John Wigley, *The Rise and Fall of the Victorian Sunday* (Manchester, 1980); John Wolffe, *The Protestant Crusade in Great Britain, 1829-60* (Oxford, 1991).

[39] Leslie Howsam, *Cheap Bibles: Nineteenth-Century Publishing and the British and Foreign Bible Society* (Cambridge, 1991).

teenth century, this was expressed in the divergence between Evangelicals
who remained loyal to the Church of England and those who ultimately
moved into Methodism. From the early nineteenth century, there was a
range of attitudes to evangelical cooperation in voluntary societies. During
the 1820s, interdenominational evangelicalism became strained in the face
of current political pressures, and by the 1830s constitutional crisis had
driven many Evangelicals to a more forceful articulation of loyalty to the
Establishment.[40] Somewhat different views of the early Victorian period
emerge from the work of Donald Lewis, who emphasizes the extent of
evangelical cooperation in the London City Mission, and that of John
Wolffe, who points to the lack of Anglican support for the Evangelical
Alliance in the later 1840s.[41] The two perspectives can, however, be rec-
onciled if one acknowledges that the explicit efforts towards broad Christian union undertaken by the alliance were naturally liable to face greater
obstacles than was the limited collaboration for specific objectives in the
home missionary movement or in relation to moral reform.

Related to this issue is the need to see Evangelicalism in an interna-
tional context. Irish-born clergy such as Hugh McNeile and Richard
Blakeney[42] played an important part in England, and concern for the
Church of Ireland and for missions to the Roman Catholics are crucial for
understanding the roots of the vigorously Protestant stance of midcentury
Evangelicals.[43] The Scottish perspective, too, is an important one: Thomas
Chalmers had a seminal influence on Evangelical thought south of the
border on social matters and on the nature of Establishment.[44] The Scott-
ish Disruption of 1843 raised important questions for English Evangelicals

[40] W. D. Balda, "Ecclesiastics and Enthusiasts: The Evangelical Emergence in
England, 1760-1800," *Historical Magazine of the Protestant Episcopal Church*
49 (1980), 221-31; R. H. Martin, *Evangelicals United: Ecumenical Stirrings in
Pre-Victorian Britain, 1795-1830* (London, 1983); G.F.A. Best, "The Evangelicals
and the Established Church in the Early Nineteenth Century," *Journal of Theological Studies* 10 (1958), 63-78.

[41] D. M. Lewis, *Lighten Their Darkness: The Evangelical Mission to Working-Class London, 1828-1860* (Westport, Conn., 1986); John R. Wolffe, "The
Evangelical Alliance in the 1840s," *SCH* 23 (1986), 333-46.

[42] Richard Paul Blakeney (1820-1884) was educated at Trinity College, Dublin,
and became incumbent of Christ Church, Claughton, Birkenhead, and later of
Bridlington. He was a founder of the Church Association. (*DNB* 5, 186.)

[43] Desmond Bowen, *The Protestant Crusade in Ireland, 1800-70* (Dublin,
1978).

[44] On Chalmers's influence on social thought, see esp. Hilton, *Age of
Atonement*. His *Lectures on the Establishment and Extension of National
Churches*, delivered in London in 1838, attracted great interest. See S. J. Brown,
Thomas Chalmers (Oxford, 1982), esp. 269-71.

about the nature of their future relationship to an Establishment that, like the Church of Scotland, seemed corrupt and restrictive of spiritual freedom. For some, the Gorham Case in the later 1840s, which arose from the refusal of Bishop Phillpotts of Exeter to institute the Calvinist G. C. Gorham[45] to the living of Brampford Speke, seemed to replicate some aspects of the Scottish Church struggles. In the event, the decision of the Privy Council meant that Tractarians, rather than Evangelicals, were left with practical cause to resent the influence of the State over the Church, but it is not inconceivable that, had the judgement gone the other way, English Evangelicals might have found the example of the Free Church of Scotland an inspiring one to follow. Yet another perspective worth exploring is the transatlantic one. It is interesting that the strong antipathy of Americans at this period to religious establishments did not prevent English Evangelicals such as Edward Bickersteth and Baptist Noel (the latter even while still an Anglican) from being considerably respected in the United States. Conversely, Bishop McIlvaine of Ohio[46] was well known in England.[47]

A further important question in the history of Anglican Evangelicalism relates to the assessment of the party's state in the latter half of the Victorian period. The conventional wisdom is that the rising intellectual tide of moral and scientific criticism weakened the foundations of uncompromising biblicism, while Evangelical mores were further weakened by wider cultural reaction against the "seriousness" of the middle of the century.[48] There is a good deal of truth in this; and it must further be acknowledged that the polemical temper of Evangelical anti-Catholicism, perpetuated up to the 1890s in the largely sterile resistance to ritualism, did much to damage the image of the school when such a cause was becoming more unfashionable.[49] Nevertheless, the case for decline should not be overstated: in the first issue of the *Churchman*, a successful new Evangelical

[45] (1787-1857); held several curacies before his appointment as vicar of St. Just-in-Penwith in 1846. He was eventually instituted to Bramford Speke in 1851. (*DNB* 22, 243; J.C.S. Nias, *Gorham and the Bishop of Exeter*, London, 1951.)

[46] Charles Pettit McIlvaine (1799-1873), Bishop of Ohio, 1832-73. W. Carus, *Memorials of C. P. McIlvaine* (London, 1882).

[47] W. B. Sprague, *Visits to European Celebrities* (Boston, 1855).

[48] For an effective recent statement of this perspective, qualified by judicious acknowledgement of the limitations of current understanding, see D. Englander, "The Word and the World: Evangelicalism in the Victorian City," *Religion in Victorian Britain*, vol. 2, *Controversies* (Manchester, 1988), 14-38. See also Bebbington, *Evangelicalism*, 141-50.

[49] Wolffe, *Protestant Crusade*, ch. 8.

monthly that began publication in 1879, J.C. Ryle,[50] shortly to become Bishop of Liverpool, could argue effectively for the continuing strong influence of Evangelicals in the Church.[51] It may well be more helpful to adopt the implication of the title of an important unpublished study and to think more in terms of "transformation" than of decline; of generational change, and the assumption of a more positive role within the Church of England at a time when the evangelical character of Nonconformity was weakening and the penumbra of evangelical tone in society as a whole becoming more diffuse.[52] At all events, such hypotheses need to be tested against further research on the years after 1860.

The third major grouping in the Church of England, the Broad Churchmen, is of its very nature much more difficult to categorize or identify. They were not a party in the sense that the Evangelicals or Anglo-Catholics were, eschewing the institutional and literary bases of independent organization. They tended to be individualists, united only in their critical attitude to the other groupings and in an emphasis on the comprehensiveness of the Church of England. Further apparent complexity arises from the extent to which the Broad Churchmen have been studied from the three perspectives of intellectual history, theology, and politics, without a clear synthesis having yet emerged. In relation to Evangelicals and Anglo-Catholics, one may criticize the limitations of partisan history, but in connection with the Broad Church one begins to long for a similar point of reference. Conybeare in his 1853 *Edinburgh Review* article made a useful distinction between "theoretical" and "antitheoretical" Broad Churchmen. Historians of religious ideas have understandably concentrated on the former, who included some of the most fertile thinkers of the century, but it is worth remembering that Conybeare estimated their numbers at only a thousand or so among the clergy, while he calculated that there were 2,500 of their "antitheoretical" brethren.[53] These latter Conybeare defined as those who believed in the comprehensiveness of the Church of England without espousing the liberal theological views that the "theoretical" school presented as the intellectual legitimation for the rejection of strictly enforced dogma.

---

[50] John Charles Ryle (1816-1900), a leading Evangelical, was rector of Helmingham from 1843, vicar of Stradbroke from 1861, and Bishop of Liverpool from 1880 (*DNB*, Suppl. 3, 334).

[51] J. C. Ryle, "Where Are We?" *Churchman* 1 (1879), repr. in ibid., new ser. 54 (1940), 91-100; Wolffe, "*Churchman*."

[52] A. Bentley, "The Transformation of the Evangelical Party in the Church of England in the Later Nineteenth Century" (Ph.D. thesis, University of Durham, 1971).

[53] "Church Parties," 333, 338.

If the Broad Churchmen are to be viewed in this framework, it would seem profitable to dwell on the role of Thomas Arnold, who lacks a modern biography and whose influence has yet to be systematically evaluated. Arnold was not an original theologian, but his pamphlet, *Principles of Church Reform*, written in 1833, was a manifesto of "antitheoretical" Broad-Churchmanship. Arnold's call for a comprehensive National Church was reminiscent of the position adopted by the latitudinarians of the previous century, but the affinity was political rather than spiritual. Arnold was a passionate Erastian and English nationalist, believing in the role of the Church as the moral and spiritual arm of the State. His sense of moralizing mission and social reform could, in practice, be worked out directly only in the limited arena of Rugby School, but its impact on younger men such as A. P. Stanley,[54] J. M. Ludlow, and Thomas Hughes[55] was profound.[56]

Another route to the investigation of the Broad Churchmen is through an examination of the two discernible intellectual schools, Oriel Noetics, such as Renn Dickson Hampden[57] and Richard Whately,[58] and Coleridgeans, including Julius Charles Hare[59] and Frederick Denison Maurice.[60] As in relation to Arnold, who had some affinities with both groups, an important question arises about the nature of their relationship to the liberal religious thought of the eighteenth century. The general outline of the

[54] Arthur Penrhyn Stanley (1815-1881) was dean of Westminster from 1864 to 1881 (*DNB* 54, 44).

[55] John Malcolm Ludlow (1821-1911) and Thomas Hughes (1822-1896) were leaders of Christian Socialism (*DNB, 1901-11*, 487-89; Suppl. 3, 7).

[56] A. P. Stanley, *Life and Correspondence of Thomas Arnold* (London, 1844); E. R. Norman, *The Victorian Christian Socialists* (Cambridge, 1987), 11-12, 59, 83-84; David Randell Boone, "Appearing to Conspire: An Episode in the Broad Church Historiography of Nineteenth-Century Britain," *Anglican and Episcopal History* 61 (1991), 493-503.

[57] (1793-1868); regius professor of divinity at Oxford from 1836 and Bishop of Hereford from 1848, both of which appointments stirred considerable controversy because of his allegedly heretical views (*DNB* 24, 264).

[58] (1787-1863); principal of St. Alban Hall, Oxford, 1825-31, and thereafter Archbishop of Dublin (*DNB* 60, 423; D. H. Akenson, *A Protestant in Purgatory*, Hamden, Conn., 1981).

[59] (1795-1855); incumbent of Herstmonceaux from 1832 and Archdeacon of Lewes from 1840 (*DNB* 24, 369; M. Distad, "Julius Charles Hare and the 'Broad Church' Ideal," *The View from the Pulpit*, ed. by P. T. Phillips, Toronto, 1978, 45-65).

[60] (1805-1872); professor of English literature and history at King's College, London, 1840-53, and a seminal theological influence on Christian Socialism (*DNB* 37, 105).

developments of the early nineteenth century is clear enough from the
work of V. F. Storr and, more recently, of Bernard Reardon, who dwell
particularly on the rise of the critical spirit epitomized by Whately and the
influence of Romanticism as mediated through the seminal genius of Coleridge.[61] Key points, however, require further elucidation, notably, the relationship of "liberal" thought to the prehistory of the Tractarian Movement and the interrelationship of religious and political influences. John
Gascoigne and Richard Brent have begun to open up this second area
from different chronological perspectives, but further attention to the period from 1789 to 1830 is needed.[62]

The "theoretical"-"antitheoretical" model is also helpful in considering
the impact of the Broad Churchmen. The somewhat pathetic figures cut
by both Hare and Maurice in some practical situations[63] suggest that the
Coleridgeans at any rate had a significant gulf to bridge between theology
and church life, one that even Maurice's enigmatic alter ego Charles
Kingsley was not wholly able to cross.[64] Whately appears to have been
rather happier as an archbishop than Hare was as an archdeacon, but it
would be interesting to know more about the transition of other Noetics
from academics to prelates. This applies particularly to Edward
Copleston[65] and to Hampden, whose twenty years as an apparently unre-
markable Bishop of Hereford were an intriguing apotheosis to his earlier
controversial career.

The publication of *Essays and Reviews* in 1860 revived hostile perceptions of Broad Churchmen as theological radicals. However, H. B.
Wilson's essay showed a continuity with the position adopted by Arnold
in his *Principles of Church Reform* in 1833. There was a similar emphasis
on a comprehensive National Church in which wide freedom of opinion
would be permitted, thus suggesting that the anxiety to accommodate
modern thought was stimulated by concern for the credibility of the An-

---

[61] V. F. Storr, *The Development of English Theology in the Nineteenth Century
1800-1860* (London, 1913); B.M.G. Reardon, *From Coleridge to Gore: A Century
of Religious Thought in Britain* (London, 1971; 2nd ed., 1980, pub. as *Religious
Thought in the Victorian Age*).

[62] J. Gascoigne, "Anglican Latitudinarianism and Political Radicalism in the
Late Eighteenth Century," *History* 71 (1986), 22-38; R. Brent, *Liberal Anglican
Politics: Whiggery, Religion, and Reform, 1830-1841* (Oxford, 1987).

[63] Distad, "Hare," 54; Chadwick, *Victorian Church*, 1, 249-50.

[64] On Kingsley (1819-1875), novelist and incumbent of Eversley from 1844, see
DNB 31, 175, and S. Chitty, *The Beast and the Monk: A Life of Charles Kingsley*
(London, 1974); and John C. Hawley, "Charles Kingsley and the Book of
Nature," *Anglican and Episcopal History* 61 (1991), 461-79.

[65] (1776-1849); fellow of Oriel from 1795 and provost from 1814 to 1828, when
he became Bishop of Llandaff (*DNB* 12, 174).

glican Establishment as well as by intellectual responses to biblical criticism.[66] The reaction to *Essays and Reviews* was strong, reflecting the continuing influence of eighteenth-century concepts of evidential theology and a view of Scripture that could offer no middle ground between orthodoxy and infidelity.[67] However, during the remainder of the century the position of the essayists of 1860 gradually received more acceptance. This was symbolized by the career of Frederick Temple, whose appointment in 1869 to succeed Henry Phillpotts as Bishop of Exeter excited considerable controversy, but who was subsequently translated to London in 1885 and to Canterbury in 1896. At the same time, the tacit recognition of both Anglo-Catholics and Evangelicals that their quarrels had been fought to stalemate left the Church constituted on a de facto Broad Church basis.

The early and mid-Victorian years of intense party conflict had seen a variety of alignments. Broad Churchmen and Evangelicals could show sympathy with each other against Romanizers; Evangelicals and Anglo-Catholics could both attack "liberalism"; while Broad Churchmen and High Churchmen had a shared antipathy to Evangelical "irregularity."[68] It should be stressed, however, that organized campaigns were generally founded by Evangelicals and Anglo-Catholics on a limited party basis. Such struggles within the Church raise two kinds of questions that require further research. On the one hand, areas of conflict still have to be investigated: for example, no systematic work has been done on antagonism to Evangelicals, while there is scope for further study of the antiritualist campaigns of the 1860s, 1870s, and 1880s.[69] On the other hand, it is important to bear in mind that conflict naturally leaves more traces in the historical record than does consensus, and it should not be assumed that interparty disputes were the general experience of all Churchmen in the period. In the early nineteenth century, there were considerable signs of crosscurrents between ecclesiastical groups that must not be obscured by

[66] H. B. Wilson, "The National Church," *Essays and Reviews* (London, 1860), 145-206, esp. 196-98; B. G. Worrall, *The Making of the Modern Church* (London, 1988), 101. Henry Bristow Wilson (1803-1888) was vicar of Great Staughton, Hunts, from 1850 (*DNB* 62, 97).

[67] J. L. Altholz, "The Mind of Victorian Orthodoxy: Anglican Responses to *Essays and Reviews*, 1860-1864," *CH* 51 (1982), 186-97; Altholz, *Anatomy of a Controversy: The Debate over "Essays and Reviews," 1860-1864* (Aldershot, 1994).

[68] An instance of this last alignment was criticism of the Evangelical Alliance in the later 1840s.

[69] The archives of the Church Association have become available to scholars and are housed in the Lambeth Palace Library.

the teleological tendencies inherent in an awareness of later party spirit.[70] Moreover, even at a much later date, the lines of party were never wholly exclusive: when Queen Victoria died, the editor of the Evangelical *Churchman* was William MacDonald Sinclair, who, though a member of a prominent Evangelical family, was himself regarded as more of a "crossbencher."[71] In addition, more work is needed at the local level in order to clarify the extent to which national rivalries found echoes there.

In his survey of writing on church history, John Kent stresses the negative effects of party conflict on the Victorian Church. Far from being revived through the successive impact of Evangelicalism and Anglo-Catholicism, it was left divided between two irreconcilable extremes and ill-equipped to face the twentieth century. Kent thus sees the concept of Anglican revival in the nineteenth century as a myth generated by the committed positions of historians.[72] This seems an unduly negative view and does not do full justice to the tendency of some recent historians of both Anglo-Catholicism and Evangelicalism to revise previously accepted positions. However, much certainly remains to be done, and Kent is right to emphasize the need to evaluate the implications of conflict and to see the Church in its wider social context.

Church parties represent only one dimension of the problems of role and identity facing the Church in the Victorian era as the nature of its national role was being redefined. In part, the tensions within Anglicanism can be related to this wider problem: all church parties felt that the triumph of their viewpoint within the Established Church would best equip it to pursue its historic role. Hence, they were prone to view Anglican opponents as threats to the whole status of the Church as well as to their own party viewpoint. Tractarians saw salvation in the recovery of true Catholic identity; Evangelicals, in a pure and uncompromising proclamation of the gospel that would outflank Dissent; Broad Churchmen, in a comprehensiveness that would accommodate both existing Nonconformity and current criticisms of theological orthodoxy. In general, however, consideration of the place of Anglicanism in English religion and society has been pursued by historians in a manner that somewhat plays down the distinctions between church parties. In the remainder of this chapter, the approach of scholars to a range of such issues will be considered. Attention will be directed first to the political position of the Church; secondly, to

[70] G.F.A. Best, "Church Parties and Charities: The Experience of Three American Visitors to England, 1823-1824," *EHR* 77 (1963), 243-62. The implications of this article still await due exploration.

[71] Wolffe, "*Churchman*," 201. Sinclair was the nephew of Sir George Sinclair of Ulbster, on whom see *DNB* 52, 295 (*Burke's Peerage and Baronetage*, 1938, 2253).

[72] Kent, *Unacceptable Face*, 96.

the practical response to population growth, industrialization, and urbanization; thirdly, to social thought and practice; and finally, to the character
and role of the clergy. Cutting across all these issues are questions of the
relationships of the Church to class and to national identity, which will
be considered in the conclusion.

The Church of England has naturally been a central focus of the
growing attention given by historians to the place of religion in nineteenth-century politics. Two avenues of approach can be discerned. Firstly,
there has been a significant body of work, notably by G.I.T. Machin in
his two-volume survey of the period from 1832 to 1921, on the political
dimensions of specifically religious issues, which naturally usually related
closely to the position of the Church of England. The field of investigation
includes not only parliamentary politics, but also the executive action of
government in such matters as patronage and the administration of the
Ecclesiastical Commission.[73] Secondly, there is an increasing tendency to
argue that religious attitudes in general and Anglican ones in particular
were of key importance in the wider formulation of government policy.
Proponents of this view, notably P. A. Butler and J. P. Parry, have found
their most fertile soil in the career of Gladstone, but Richard Brent has
recently attempted to apply a similar technique to the politics of the
1830s.[74] The most ambitious work of this kind has been J.C.D. Clark's
English Society, 1688-1832,[75] in which it is argued that Anglicanism was
fundamental to the defense of the pre-1832 constitution and its redefinition
central to the "revolutionary" changes of 1828 to 1832. There is a degree
to which work of this kind is overstated, from the natural tendency of
scholars to accumulate evidence consonant with their own hypotheses,
while playing down material less consistent with them. Nevertheless, even
when allowance is made for this, it is apparent that the political ramifications of religion were substantially greater than was supposed by earlier
twentieth-century scholars.

Equally, however, more work on the period is needed if this interpretation is to be firmly established. In particular, further attention might

[73] G.I.T. Machin, *Politics and the Churches in Great Britain, 1832 to 1868*
(Oxford, 1977); *Politics and the Churches in Great Britain, 1869-1921* (Oxford,
1987). See also D.W.R. Bahlman, "Politics and Church Patronage in the Victorian Age," *Victorian Studies* 22 (1978-9), 253-95; William T. Gibson, "Disraeli's
Church Patronage, 1868-1880," *Anglican and Episcopal History* 61 (1992), 197-
210.

[74] P. A. Butler, *Gladstone: Church, State and Tractarianism: A Study of His
Religious Ideas and Attitudes, 1809-1859* (Oxford, 1982); J. P. Parry, *Democracy
and Religion: Gladstone and the Liberal Party, 1867-1875* (Cambridge, 1986);
Brent, *Liberal Anglican Politics.*

[75] (Cambridge, 1985).

usefully be given from this perspective to the Conservative Party after 1832. The ideal of the Anglican Protestant constitution did not disappear overnight, but survived among the rump of Ultras and later, in modified form, in the National Club, founded in 1845. The dynamics of the later relationship of this ideology to the firm but pragmatic Anglicanism of Peel and Wellington and to the grandiloquent posturings of the Disraeli of the 1840s and 1850s are worthy of further exploration. Key questions of identity both for the Church of England and for Conservatism were at stake.[76]

The relationship between Anglicanism and Conservatism not only operated on the ground of high politics, but also appears to have been important at the bases of popular Toryism. In general, historians have hitherto associated external lobbying of Parliament more with Nonconformity than with Anglicanism, but, in fact, activity by the supporters of the Church of England on this front had a long history that can be traced back at least to the early days of the Oxford Movement. This had its immediate origins in political protest against the Irish Church Act of 1833, a genesis that is all too often obscured by preoccupation with theological emphases. In the later 1830s, the initiative lay with Evangelical bodies, the Protestant Association, and the Christian Influence Society, which sponsored Thomas Chalmers's influential lectures on Establishments in 1838.[77] This impulse was, to some extent, combined with that of Conservative High Churchmen in the National Club from 1845 and the Church Institution from 1859.

Anglicans were temperamentally less ready to engage in popular agitation than were Nonconformists, and in the rural anticlericalism of the early 1830s and the confrontation with Chartism in the late 1830s and early 1840s, the gulf between Anglicanism and working-class politics was very apparent.[78] On other occasions, however, Anglicanism could strike a ready chord in popular political consciousness, as in the radical Toryism of the 1830s and in the strong Lancashire Conservatism of the last third of the century.[79] The relationship depended, to some extent, especially in the earlier period, on the continuing appeal of a romantic paternalism, but it also interacted with forms of popular anti-Catholicism. Evaluation of the

[76] See Wolffe, *Protestant Crusade.*

[77] Lewis, *Lighten Their Darkness,* 154-55.

[78] E. J. Evans, "Some Reasons for the Growth of English Rural Anticlericalism," *Past and Present,* No. 66 (1975), 84-109; E. Yeo, "Christianity in Chartist Struggle, 1838-1842," ibid., No. 91 (1981), 109-39.

[79] J. C. Gill, *The Ten Hours Parson* (London, 1959); H. J. Hanham, *Elections and Party Management: Politics in the Time of Gladstone and Disraeli* (London, 1959), ch. 14; Patrick Joyce, *Work, Society, and Politics: The Culture of the Factory in Later Victorian England* (London, 1982), ch. 7.

political significance of Anglicanism might well thus be helped by application to England of the constructs of political culture developed by historians of France and of the United States. In his *Political Culture of the
American Whigs*,[80] Daniel Walker Howe portrays Evangelicalism as central
to Whig support and consciousness in the midcentury years. It would seem
useful to adopt a similar approach to the relationship between Conservatism and Anglicanism, both in its conservative High Church and Evangelical forms.

Political pressures combined with social and economic change to lead
to considerable reform of the structures of the Church of England during
the nineteenth century. Historians have generally concentrated their attention on the reforms initiated by the Ecclesiastical Commission appointed by Sir Robert Peel in 1835,[81] but recent work has increasingly indicated that this needs to be placed in a wider context. In some respects,
the Church had already begun to put its house in order before the 1830s,
and the administration of Queen Anne's Bounty, together with more recent government grants, was alleviating the worst extremes of clerical poverty.[82] Conversely, much remained to be done after the 1830s, and there
were significant further developments later in the Victorian period, notably, the new bishoprics set up by the Conservative government of 1874 to
1880.[83] Reform of the Church, as of the electoral system, was a recurrent
issue throughout Victoria's reign. Indeed, further reform was widely discussed in the later years of the century, and by some was felt to be an essential prerequisite for effective resistance to disestablishment.[84]

Attention should also be given to the contemporary critics of reform.[85]
Trollope's fictional diocese of Barchester should not be uncritically ac-

[80] (Chicago, 1979).

[81] Olive J. Brose, *Church and Parliament: The Reshaping of the Church of
England, 1828-1860* (London, 1959); Kenneth A. Thompson, *Bureaucracy and
Church Reform: The Organizational Response of the Church of England to Social
Change, 1800-1965* (Oxford, 1970); Norman Gash, *Reaction and Reconstruction
in English Politics, 1832-1852* (Oxford, 1965).

[82] P. Virgin, *The Church in an Age of Negligence: Ecclesiastical Structure and
Problems of Church Reform, 1700-1840* (Cambridge, 1989); Mather, "Georgian
Churchmanship."

[83] P. S. Morrish, "County and Urban Dioceses: Nineteenth-Century Discussion
on Ecclesiastical Geography," *JEH* 26 (1975), 279-300; "The Struggle to Create
an Anglican Diocese of Birmingham," *JEH* 31 (1980), 59-88; "History, Celticism,
and Propaganda in the Formation of the Diocese of Truro," *Southern History* 5
(1983), 238-66.

[84] *Churchman* 12 (1885), iii-iv, 14; ibid. 14 (1886), i and passim.

[85] A classic critique of the reforms of the 1830s was offered by Sydney Smith
in his *Letter to Archdeacon Singleton* (London, 1837).

cepted as a portrait of the Church at mid-century, but the conflicts there portrayed and the cynicism directed towards the new order raise important questions.[86] The real-life opponents of the Dean and Chapter Act of 1840, which progressively stripped the cathedrals of much of their endowment, could muster some compelling arguments that might well have commanded greater respect had the political pressure for concrete reform been less.[87] Historians of the urban Church of England have focused their attention on the industrial towns, but a rounded assessment would require much more extensive attention to the implications of reform for the cathedral cities.[88] Moreover, it is by no means self-evident that the division of large town parishes in pursuit of a rurally inspired parochial ideal necessarily strengthened the Church, and it may well be that the money spent on the new bishoprics of the 1870s and '80s would have been better expended on the lower clergy.[89]

Reform of the Church obviously involved implementation on the ground as well as legislative and administrative action, and evaluation of this process must await the accumulation of more local research. The situation in one district, the Vale of York, is indicated by a rural dean's notebook of 1845, showing both the growing zeal for reform in the Church and the considerable improvements still needed in a diocese under the lax rule of the aged Archbishop Harcourt.[90] The York evidence also illustrates the underlying dilemma posed by finance: pluralism continued an economic necessity for many clergy, and, even without the redistribution of the cathedral revenues, resources remained unequal to the demands placed upon them. A valiant effort was made to square the circle through church extension campaigns, particularly in the newer urban areas, which raised

[86] See esp. *The Warden* (London, 1855), *Barchester Towers* (London, 1857), *Framley Parsonage* (London, 1861), and *The Last Chronicle of Barset* (London, 1867).

[87] Chadwick, *Victorian Church* 1, 130-33, 523; R. Jupp, "'Nurseries of a Learned Clergy': Pusey and the Defence of Cathedrals in the Nineteenth Century," *Pusey Rediscovered*, 139-61.

[88] On the internal development of cathedrals, see P. Barrett, "English Cathedral Choirs in the Nineteenth Century," *JEH* 25 (1974), 15-37; D. M. Greenhalgh, "The Nineteenth Century and After," *Wells Cathedral: A History*, ed. by L. S. Colchester (West Compton, 1982), 179-203. For a study of a cathedral city, see Edward Royle, *The Victorian Church in York*, Borthwick Papers, No. 64 (York, 1983); and for the networks centered on a major cathedral (Canterbury), Dewey, *Passing of Barchester*.

[89] D.E.H. Mole, "The Victorian Town Parish: Rural Vision and Urban Mission," *SCH* 16 (1979), 361-71.

[90] "Report upon the State of the Rural Deanery of the City and Ainsty of York," December, 1845, Borthwick Institute, York, RD.AIN.2.

large sums of money through public subscription and resulted in the building of numerous new churches.[91] The scale of such efforts implies the existence of a considerable fund of public sympathy for the Church, which would repay further historical investigation.

Nevertheless, the Church of England did not succeed in gaining the regular support of more than a minority of the working classes. This is the indisputable conclusion to be drawn from the Census of Religious Worship of 1851, although it must be qualified by acknowledgement of the unpredictable nature of local variation. A crude dichotomy between town and country can be dangerously misleading. While the model can be refined by recognizing the differences between cathedral cities and industrial towns, arable and pastoral farming areas, considerable allowance must still be made for the particular conditions in a given parish and for personal factors.[92] For example, in the face of the general strength of Methodism in Leeds, there were 3,000 worshippers in the Parish Church on the evening of Census Sunday, drawn by the ministry of W. F. Hook.[93] Other similar instances might be cited, particularly from the other side of the Pennines.[94] The Church could thus make a considerable, if localized, impact even on unpromising ground, while in the smaller towns of the south and in closed villages it could well be dominant.

Furthermore, it is one thing to acknowledge that the count of bodies on a particular wet English spring day implies that the core of committed Anglican worshippers was less than a quarter of the population, but quite another to use this statistic as a general index to the fortunes of the Church of England in the Victorian period. It should be noted that 1851 was probably rather early to measure the impact of the remarkable upsurge in energy in the Church of England associated with spiritual revival and reforming zeal. Preoccupation with the failure of the Church to gain significantly in support proportionately to total population should not be allowed to obscure the substantial absolute growth in communicants evident

[91] A. D. Gilbert, *Religion and Society in Industrial England: Church, Chapel and Social Change, 1740-1914* (London, 1976), 27-29, 126-31.

[92] B. I. Coleman, *The Church of England in the Mid-Nineteenth Century: A Social Geography*, Historical Association Pamphlet, General Ser., No. 98 (London, 1980).

[93] "1851 Religious Census Returns," Public Record Office (Kew), H.O. 129/501/7, St. Peter's, Leeds; E. Rose, "W. F. Hook and the Dark Satanic Mills," *View from the Pulpit*, 117-41. Walter Farquhar Hook (1798-1875) was vicar of Leeds, 1838-59, and dean of Chichester, 1859-75 (*DNB* 27, 276).

[94] On Salford, see J. B. Marsden, *Memoirs of the Life and Labours of the Rev. Hugh Stowell* (London, 1868); on Oldham, M. A. Smith, *Religion in Industrial Society: Oldham and Saddleworth, 1740-1865* (Oxford, 1994).

for much of the century.[95] With regard to continuing absenteeism, on prima facie grounds it would seem probable that insofar as those who did not attend church or chapel had any religious allegiance, it was more likely to be to the national church than to Nonconformity, with its tendency to a "gathered Church" discipline. This was a connection expressed at least in residual acceptance of the Church's role in providing the rites of passage and participation in such folk Anglicanism as harvest festivals and watch-night services.[96]

Evaluations of the impact of the Church of England in the Victorian era must still, however, be somewhat tentative in the absence of systematic work at the local level, although the quantity of available relevant research is gradually increasing. The work of Diana McClatchey and James Obelkevich has shown clearly the limits of the Church's strength in the countryside, and the latter's work on South Lindsey draws important connections between religious dissent and class formation.[97] Studies by Hugh McLeod and Jeffrey Cox on later nineteenth- and early twentieth-century London suggest that by this period, the attitude of the working class to the Church was more one of apathy than of active hostility.[98] The picture is broadened by a growing number of short studies in local and regional history journals and by the publication of the 1851 Religious Worship returns for a number of counties, including Bedfordshire, Buckinghamshire, Lincolnshire, and Oxfordshire.[99] There remains, however, a

[95] Gilbert, *Religion and Society*, 24. This growth, in part, reflected changing devotional practice, but it can be interpreted to suggest that levels of active commitment were increasing.

[96] James Obelkevich, *Religion and Rural Society: South Lindsey, 1825-1875* (Oxford, 1976), 158-61; John Kent, "Feelings and Festivals: An Interpretation of Some Working-Class Religious Attitudes, " *The Victorian City: Images and Realities*, ed. by H. J. Dyos and Michael Wolff, 2 vols. (London, 1973), 2, 864-66.

[97] Obelkevich, *Religion and Rural Society*, esp. 313-31; Diana McClatchey, *Oxfordshire Clergy, 1777-1869: A Study of the Established Church and of the Role of Its Clergy in Local Society* (Oxford, 1960).

[98] H. McLeod, *Class and Religion in the Late Victorian City* (London, 1974); J. Cox, *The English Churches in a Secular Society: Lambeth, 1870-1930* (Oxford, 1982).

[99] B. I. Coleman, "Southern England in the Census of Religious Worship, 1851," *Southern History* 5 (1983), 154-88; D. P. Pugh, "The Strength of English Religion in the 'Nineties': Some Evidence from the North West," *Journal of Religious History* 12 (1983), 250-65; *A Social History of the Diocese of Newcastle*, ed. by W.S.F. Pickering (London, 1982); D. W. Bushby, "The Ecclesiastical Census, Bedfordshire, March 1851," *Bedfordshire Historical Record Society* 54 (1975), 109-200; *Buckinghamshire Returns of the Census of Religious Worship, 1851*, ed. by Edward Legg, Buckinghamshire Record Society, No. 27 (1991); R.

continued need for further research, above all on urban Anglicanism in the classic Industrial Revolution period of the late eighteenth and early nineteenth centuries. Mark Smith, *Religion in Industrial Society: Oldham and Saddleworth, 1740-1865* (Oxford, 1994), is a significant recent addition to the literature.[100] *also Simon Green on Halifax & Keighley.*

Anglican thinking on social issues reflected a blending of pastoral responses with the influence of theological and other intellectual trends. Norman and Hilton in their substantial books on the subject have tended to view it in terms of the history of ideas, giving considerable attention to the impact of the prevailing orthodoxy of political economy.[101] However, as Hilton himself acknowledges, some Evangelicals did become interventionist in a paternalist sense.[102] This should probably be explained as much in terms of social background, predisposition, and response to circumstances, as in relation to different eschatological frameworks. This was preeminently the case for Lord Shaftesbury, the leading lay Evangelical social activist of the period, who came to perceive social amelioration as a prerequisite for evangelism.[103]

Recent elucidation of the complexities of Evangelical social thought may well serve as a basis for reevaluation of the wider Anglican picture. On the one hand, there is a tendency to regard the ambivalent radicalism of the Christian Socialists, together with the activities of slum ritualists such as A. H. Stanton,[104] as the only chinks in the armor of strong social conservatism. Those who make such a judgement, however, run the risk of imposing anachronistic categories. The Victorian Christian Socialists themselves would have been at odds with modern collectivist socialism, and they unambiguously rejected a materialist world view. More important for understanding the Christian Socialists is the need to explore rather than simply to assume the existence of a link between ritualist sacramentalism

---

W. Ambler, *Lincolnshire Returns of the Census of Religious Worship, 1851*, Lincoln Record Society 72 (1979); K. Tiller, *Church and Chapel in Oxfordshire, 1851: The Return of the Census of Religious Worship*, Oxfordshire Record Society 55 (1987).

[100] E. R. Wickham's *Church and People in an Industrial City* (London, 1957), on Sheffield, is an important pioneering study, but reflects the concerns of Churchmen rather than historians.

[101] E. R. Norman, *Church and Society in England, 1770-1970* (Oxford, 1976); Hilton, *Age of Atonement*.

[102] Ibid., 15-16.

[103] Finlayson, *Shaftesbury*, 183-84.

[104] Arthur Henry Stanton (1839-1913), curate of St. Alban's, Holborn, 1862-1913 (*DNB, 1912-21*, 506-7).

Recent writers like

and social radicalism.[105] As a writer on the controversial Christian Socialist Stewart Headlam[106] has observed: "Although Headlam worshipped like the disciples of Pusey, it was the God of Maurice to whom he prayed."[107] On the other hand, moderate High Church and Evangelical responses to the "condition of England" require sympathetic evaluation on their own terms if we are to understand the impact of incarnational theology after 1860 and, ultimately, the development of widely based support for a "social gospel" at the turn of the century.[108]

Two social issues can be highlighted for more specific comment. Firstly, Anglican involvement in education, although the subject of a significant body of literature, is, in some respects, imperfectly understood in the face of a tendency to adopt a Whiggish view of the development of the modern school system. Nineteenth-century Anglican attitudes are thus often merely made to appear obstructive rather than evaluated on their own terms.[109] On the political front, education represented a crucial strand in the Church's counterattack against Dissent in the 1830s, with the revitalization of the National Society, the establishment of Anglican colleges for teacher training, and largely successful resistance to the Whig education program of 1839.[110] In intellectual terms, education attracted wide Anglican interest, and further attention needs to be directed to the thinking on education of such figures as Thomas Arnold, J. H. Newman, and J. B.

[105] Norman, *Christian Socialists*, 12-13, 183. P. d'A. Jones, in *The Christian Socialist Revival, 1877-1914* (Princeton, 1968), is superficial in his treatment of links between the Oxford Movement and "sacramental socialism" (85-98). R. W. Franklin makes a stronger case for the link in "Pusey and Worship in Industrial Society," *Worship* 57 (1983), 386-412, and in "Puseyism in the Parishes."

[106] (1847-1924); a curate at Bethnal Green from 1873 until he was dismissed in 1878, and the leading figure in the Guild of St. Matthew, which originated in 1877 (Norman, *Christian Socialists*, 98-120).

[107] J. R. Orens, "Christ, Communism, and Chorus Girls: A Reassessment of Stewart Headlam," *Historical Magazine of the Protestant Episcopal Church* 49 (1980), 221-31.

[108] Jones, *Christian Socialist Revival*, 164-224; cf. G. Parsons, "Social Control to Social Gospel," *Religion in Victorian Britain*, 2, 59.

[109] Cf. John Hurt, *Education in Evolution: Church, State, Society and Popular Education, 1800-1870* (London, 1971).

[110] D. G. Paz, *The Politics of Working-Class Education in Britain, 1830-50* (Manchester, 1980), 62-65, 79-95, 98-104; J. L. Alexander, "Collegiate Teacher Training in England and Wales: A Study in the Historical Determinants of Educational Provision and Practice in the Mid-Nineteenth Century" (Ph.D. thesis, University of London, 1977), 59-75.

Sumner,[111] who, in their different ways, were passionately committed to the provision of education, seeing this as central to the mission of the national Church.[112] At the parochial level, the erection and development of schools was a central part of the Church's defence against Dissent and of its offensive on working-class irreligion. Much information about their effectiveness remains to be gleaned from visitation returns and the records of the schools themselves.[113]

Secondly, the growth of interest in women's history raises an important agenda of questions for historians of the nineteenth-century Church of England. To what extent was Anglicanism "feminized"? Why was the Church attractive to women? How did Anglican attitudes differ from those of the Nonconformists and of the wider society? To date, the study of women in nineteenth-century religion has reflected more the preoccupations of students of gender roles and the family than those of historians of the churches. Consequently, there is a danger of oversimplifying religious attitudes and failing to explore the distinctive characteristics of Anglican traditions.[114] A distinguished exception to this has been the pioneering work of the late Brian Heeney, who gave particular attention to the development of women's ministry and participation in the consultative structures of the Church of England.[115] Prochaska's work on women's in-

---

[111] John Bird Sumner (1780-1862) was Bishop of Chester from 1828 and Archbishop of Canterbury from 1848 (*DNB* 4, 168; R. S. Dell, "Social and Economic Theories and Pastoral Concerns of a Victorian Archbishop," *JEH* 16, 1965, 196-208).

[112] Some advance on this ground was made in R. A. Soloway, *Prelates and People: Ecclesiastical Social Thought in England, 1783-1852* (London and Toronto, 1969), chs. 10, 11; and G. Kitson Clark, *Churchmen and the Condition of England, 1832-1885* (London, 1973).

[113] M. Sanderson, "The National and British School Societies in Lancashire, 1803-1839: The Roots of Anglican Supremacy in English Education," *Local Studies in the History of Education*, ed. by T. G. Cook (London, 1972), 1-36, shows the value of a local perspective and underlines the importance of education in Anglican resistance to Dissent. J. L. Alexander, "Endangered Source Material for the History of Teacher Training in England and Wales," History of Education Society, Occasional Publication No. 1, *Archives and the Historian of Education* (London, 1975), 1-12, identifies and describes local Anglican records.

[114] Cf. E. Trudgill, *Madonnas and Magdalens: The Origins and Development of Victorian Sexual Attitudes* (London, 1976); Davidoff and Hall, *Family Fortunes*.

[115] B. Heeney: *The Women's Movement in the Church of England, 1850-1930* (Oxford, 1988); "The Beginnings of Church Feminism: Women and the Councils of the Church of England, 1897-1919," *JEH* 33 (1982), 89-109; "Women's Struggle for Professional Work and Status in the Church of England,

volvement in philanthropy also includes significant Anglican material.[116] However, later Victorian women's organizations remain largely unstudied. These included the Mothers' Union and the Girls' Friendly Society, both with memberships of well over 100,000 in 1900.[117] In general, little is known about the participation of women at the grass roots of church life, but much could be gleaned from visitation returns and parish records.[118] A further dimension is suggested by the work of female Anglican writers such as Charlotte Elizabeth Tonna,[119] Frances Ridley Havergal,[120] and Charlotte Mary Yonge,[121] which is by no means merely a topic of literary interest. There is also an extensive body of contemporary religious literature that explicitly or implicitly considers the place of women in Church and family life and that still awaits serious scholarly analysis.[122]

In the Anglican context it is necessary to relate investigation of the place of women in the Church to the wider issue of the involvement of the laity of both genders. This was a divisive matter in relation to the use of lay agency by Evangelicals in the Victorian period, while, at a higher social level, the role of laymen as patrons, ecclesiastical agitators, and political

1900-1930," *HJ* 26 (1983), 329-47. See also C. M. Prelinger, "The Female Diaconate in the Anglican Church," *Religion in the Lives of English Women*, ed. by Gail Malmgreen (London, 1986), 161-92.

[116] F. K. Prochaska, *Women and Philanthropy in Nineteenth-Century England* (Oxford, 1980). A chapter in Hill's *The Religious Order*, 271-93, discusses the social significance of sisterhoods.

[117] *Mothers' Union Journal*, No. 51 (July 1900), 68; *The Girls' Quarterly*, XXI (Jan. 1900), 1. Brian Harrison, "For Church, Queen, and Family: The Girls' Friendly Society, 1874-1920," *Past and Present*, No. 61 (1973), 107-38, indicates the subject's importance, but by no means treats it exhaustively.

[118] My own article, "The End of Victorian Values? Women, Religion, and the Death of Queen Victoria," *SCH* 27 (1990), 481-503, indicates some of the possibilities. See also J. S. Reed, "'A Female Movement': The Feminization of Nineteenth-Century Anglo-Catholicism," *Anglican and Episcopal History* 57 (1988), 199-208, and his book-length study, *Revolt against Common Sense: The Cultural Politics of Victorian Anglo-Catholicism* (Vanderbilt University Press, forthcoming).

[119] (1790-1846); edited the *Protestant Magazine* and wrote numerous anti-Catholic and other tracts and novels (*DNB* 57, 34).

[120] (1836-1879); a writer of hymns and verses (*DNB* 25, 180).

[121] (1823-1901); a prolific novelist and religious journalist who was strongly influenced by John Keble (*DNB, 1901-11*, 717-19). The subtitle of Georgina Battiscombe's *Charlotte Mary Yonge: The Story of an Uneventful Life* (London, 1943), implies too deprecating a view of its subject.

[122] A brief survey of Anglican literature on women's roles is given in Heeney, *Women's Movement*, 5-18.

representatives raises questions about the nature of leadership. These were also explored in the Church Congresses and in the moves towards lay participation in Parochial Church Councils, Diocesan Conferences, and, after 1919, in the Church Assembly.[123]

Accordingly, as we turn finally to consider the character and role of the clergy, it must be emphasized that, while the ordained ministry was the most public manifestation of the Church of England, it did not, on its own, present a more than partial view of Anglican identity. This became more apparent by the end of the nineteenth century than it had been at the beginning, as the clerical order became more conscious of its own distinctiveness from the laity, a process stimulated, in part, by the diffusion of a Catholic conception of the priesthood, and, in part, by the general trend to professionalization in Victorian society. This was mediated through the development of theological colleges, manuals of pastoral theology, and clerical societies.[124] At the end of Victoria's reign the clergy were still carrying out a wide range of functions other than the strictly spiritual, but these were mostly generated by the voluntary social institutions of the Church itself; a century earlier the clergy had dominated the education of the laity and exercised considerable influence in local government and the administration of justice.[125]

The Victorian clergy have recently attracted considerable scholarly attention, most notably from Alan Haig in his detailed analysis of backgrounds and career patterns. He shows clearly that the clergy were generally men of the "middling sort": younger sons of the gentry and aristocracy were more likely to be drawn to the law and the army, while a lower limit in the social scale was effectively set by the costs of training, even when the nongraduate colleges of St. Bees and St. Aidan's are taken into account. Numbers of ordinations remained high until the 1880s, although in the 1860s and 1870s the proportion of nongraduates steadily increased, and the intellectual calibre of the graduates, as measured by the proportion of Firsts among them, fell. The clergy faced varied later careers, suffering from the erratic workings of the patronage system, the necessity for long cura-

[123] Lewis, *Lighten Their Darkness*, 35-37; Finlayson, *Shaftesbury*, 111-12; M.J.D. Roberts, "Private Patronage and the Church of England, 1800-1900," *JEH* 32 (1981), 199-223; M.J.D. Roberts, "The Role of the Laity in the Church of England" (D.Phil. thesis, University of Oxford, 1974).

[124] Chadwick, *Victorian Church*, 2, 151-81; Brian Heeney, *A Different Kind of Gentleman: Parish Clergy as Professional Men in Early and Mid-Victorian England* (Hamden, Conn., 1976).

[125] Cox, *English Churches in a Secular Society*, 48-89; R. E. Chadwick, "Church and People in Bradford and District, 1880-1914" (D.Phil. thesis, University of Oxford, 1986); J. V. Beckett, *The Aristocracy in England, 1660-1914* (London, 1986), 386-87; Virgin, *Church in an Age of Negligence*, 109-30.

cies, inadequate stipends that bore little relation to the responsibilities of a post, and a lack of satisfactory provision for the superannuated. These difficulties were somewhat alleviated during the later nineteenth century, but were by no means removed.[126] Haig's work is complemented by that of Heeney, who uses the work of pastoral theologians to build up a picture of the clergy's parochial work, and by a collection of essays edited by P. T. Phillips, which achieves a similar end through the study of a number of prominent individuals. Several articles on individual clergy and parishes serve to fill out the picture further.[127]

The complexity of the picture suggested by the analysis of church parties in the first half of this chapter has been compounded by examination of the political and social contexts of Anglicanism. The theological divisions between Evangelical and Anglo-Catholic, Broad Churchman and biblical conservative, were paralleled by the tensions between ecclesiastical reformers and defenders of the pre-Victorian status quo, implicit disagreement on social attitudes between interventionists and advocates of laissez faire, and the perceived distinctions between clergy and laity, well-endowed rectors and struggling curates, men and women. For many, these rivalries served to raise more pressing questions about the identity of the Church than the "party spirit" delineated by Conybeare.

In the face of such diversity, it would be tempting to conclude by reiterating truisms about the incoherence of the Church of England and consequently to despair of identifying a distinctively "Anglican" tradition. However, a more positive note can be struck by dwelling on the position of the Church of England as the national church. This should not be understood purely in relation to its technical constitutional fortunes as an Establishment, which clearly changed very substantially between 1789 and 1914, even though links between Church and State have survived throughout the twentieth century. It is worth remembering that the founders of the Free Church of Scotland in 1843 believed that a national church did not necessarily have to be established in a formal sense, but did require a presence in every corner of the land and a sense of identity with the nation.[128] Judged by these criteria, the Church of England succeeded quite well in the Victorian era.

---

[126] A. Haig, *The Victorian Clergy* (London, 1984).

[127] Heeney, *Different Kind of Gentleman*; Phillips, *View from the Pulpit*; C. Beardsley, "Frederick William Robertson of Brighton: Prince of Preachers," *Studies in Sussex Church History*, ed. M. J. Kitch (Brighton, 1981), 157-71; R. Dunhill, "The Rev. George Bugg: The Fortunes of a Nineteenth-Century Curate," *Northamptonshire Past and Present* 7 (1983), 41-50; T. Ireson, "A Victorian Rector and His Parish: J. H. Holditch at Bulwick," *Northamptonshire Past and Present* 7 (1984-5), 106-13.

[128] Brown, *Chalmers*, 337-49.

Viewed in terms of its relationship to class, the Church of England had proved itself well able to respond to the structural changes of the Victorian era. Never as aristocratic as the stereotype suggests, it attracted numerous clergy who reflected and reinforced the identity of the middle classes. Its vigorous efforts in the cities may well have met with limited success in the slums, but they could be very effective in the "respectable" suburbs. Just as, in a closely related process, the Conservative Party gained in the late nineteenth century substantial middle-class support at the expense of the Liberals,[129] the Church could strengthen its relative position in face of Nonconformity. At the same time, the reform of the Establishment's most conspicuous abuses and the manifestation of increasing social concern took the sting out of the working-class hostility of the 1830s and 1840s. The lasting attitude of the majority of the population was neutrality rather than active support, but this was sufficient to ensure that the Church of England declined rather less catastrophically in the twentieth century than the Free Churches have done.

A sense of national role was the thread that united all Anglicans, with the exception of extreme Anglo-Catholics and hyper-Calvinist Evangelicals, groups both small in number and liable in the long term to accept the logic of their positions in departure for Rome or Nonconformity, respectively. Whatever the limitations of Anglican Church reform, it did maintain the credibility of the Church as a national institution by ensuring its presence in all corners of the land from the Tweed to the Scillies. In political terms, the Church of England still maintained a sufficient fund of popular support for English disestablishment seldom to look practicable. In the long term, even Nonconformists came to a de facto acceptance of the validity of the Church's place in national life. Furthermore, the rising standard of sacred music and the development of the grand public rituals of state and monarchy, in which the Church played a key part, all served to widen its appeal for aesthetic and nationalist reasons.[130]

As a counterpoint to these developments, however, this was the era in which Anglicanism established itself as an international creed as well as redefining its position as the English national church. The widespread connections of Evangelicalism, which have been discussed before, often

[129] J. P. Cornford, "The Transformation of Conservatism in the Late Nineteenth Century," *Victorian Studies* 7 (1963-4), 35-66.

[130] J. Obelkevich, "Music and Religion in the Nineteenth Century," *Disciplines of Faith: Studies in Religion, Politics, and Patriarchy*, ed. by J. Obelkevich, Lyndal Roper, and Raphael Samuel (London, 1987), 550-65; David Cannadine, "The British Monarchy and the 'Invention of Tradition', c. 1820-1977," *The Invention of Tradition*, ed. by E. J. Hobsbawm and Terence Ranger (Cambridge, 1983), esp. 130-32; John Wolffe, "Secular Saints: Church and Civic Commemoration in the United Kingdom, 1847-1910," *Hispania Sacra* 42 (1990), 435-43.

all the local government ritual.

implied a looseness to specifically Anglican loyalties, but High Church linkages were also important. An obvious point of departure here is the consecration of Samuel Seabury[131] in 1784 by Scottish Episcopalians, as the first bishop in the United States. It is anachronistic to see this as the beginning of the Anglican Communion, but it did signify the beginnings of rapprochement between the Church of England and the Episcopal Church in Scotland.[132] The interaction of English, Scottish, and Irish influences was further apparent in the early Victorian years.[133] Meanwhile, the Episcopal Church in the United States continued to cultivate its English links.[134] Above all, the flowering of the missionary movement led to the establishment of overseas bishoprics and eventually to independent Anglican churches.[135] The deposition for heresy of Bishop John William Colenso[136] of Natal in 1863 is conventionally seen primarily as an episode in the mid-Victorian conflict over liberal doctrine, but it was equally significant in revealing the problems of jurisdiction and identity that expansion raised for the Church as a whole.[137] Within the British Isles, disestablishment in Ireland in 1871 and in Wales in 1920 weakened the transnational institutional coherence of the Church, while the maturing of overseas churches, first in the United States and then in the colonies, again reduced the obvious links. On the other hand, the commencement of the Lambeth Conferences in 1867 has served during the last 100 years to preserve a residual broader Anglican identity. The detailed exploration of the relationship of such centrifugal and centripetal forces lies outside the geographical scope of the present chapter, but they do serve to suggest a further and somewhat neglected dimension to the history of the Church in England.

It may well be, therefore, that the best prospect for understanding nineteenth-century Anglicanism as a whole is to view it in the context of

[131] (1729-1796); Bishop of Connecticut, 1784-96, and Presiding Bishop, 1789-92 (*Dictionary of American Biography* 7, 528-30).

[132] G. White, "The Consecration of Bishop Seabury," *Scottish Historical Review* 83 (1984), 37-49.

[133] Nockles, "Continuity and Change," 346-426, 529-600.

[134] Best, "Church Parties and Charities"; Esther deWaal, "John Henry Hobart and the Early Oxford Movement," *Anglican Theological Review* 65 (1983), 324-31.

[135] Stephen Neill, *A History of Christian Missions*, 2nd ed. (London, 1986), 392-95 and passim.

[136] (1814-1883); Bishop of Natal, from 1853 (*DNB* 11, 290). Colenso's deposition in December 1863 by Bishop Gray of Cape Town was declared null and void by the Judicial Committee of the Privy Council in March 1865. A minor schism in Natal ensued.

[137] Chadwick, *Victorian Church*, 2, 90-97.

the curiously neglected history of English nationalism.[138] This is a perspective that will serve to explain and illuminate differences between the Anglican experience and that in Wales and Ireland, as well as that of the Episcopal Church in Scotland, while producing a key insight into the dynamics of the relationships between the constituent parts of the United Kingdom.[139] The visionary scheme of a formally comprehensive Church of England that Thomas Arnold sketched out in 1833 could never be realized, but in his aspiration that it would become a focus of national unity, he was being by no means unrealistic:

> The Church of Christ is indeed far beyond all human ties; but of all human ties that to our country is the highest and most sacred: and *England*, to a true Englishman, ought to be dearer than the peculiar forms of the *Church of England*.[140]

A generation later, Matthew Arnold graphically wrote of the receding tide of faith, but like his father he held to a conviction of the value and defensibility of the Church of England as a national institution. Both father and son were helping to articulate the framework in which the Church could endure.[141]

---

[138] John Wolffe, *God and Greater Britain: Religion and National Life in Britain and Ireland, 1843-1945* (London, 1994); John Wolffe, "Evangelicalism and Nationalism in Nineteenth-Century England," *Patriotism: The Making and Unmaking of British National Identity*, ed. by R. Samuel, vol. 1, *History and Politics* (London, 1989), 188-202; Desmond Bowen, *The Idea of the Victorian Church: A Study of the Church of England, 1833-1889* (Montreal, 1968), 341-93; Distad, "Hare," 63-65. Cf. *Englishness: Politics and Culture, 1880-1920*, ed. by R. Colls and P. Dodd (London, 1986).

[139] Cf. K. Robbins, *Nineteenth-Century Britain: Integration and Diversity* (Oxford, 1988); paperback edition under the title *Nineteenth-Century Britain: England, Scotland, and Wales: The Making of a Nation*.

[140] Thomas Arnold, *Miscellaneous Works*, ed. by A. P. Stanley (London, 1845; Farnsborough, 1971), 316.

[141] R. apRoberts, *Arnold and God* (London, 1983), 257-66. Cf. G. Parsons, "Reform, Revival, and Realignment: The Experience of Victorian Anglicanism," *Religion in Victorian Britain*, 1, 63-64.

scathing about academics, popularisers and journalists; yet witches are always handled gently, even when criticised. In Hutton's eyes, modern paganism is a distinct religion in its own right, a (thankfully rather selective) revival of ancient paganisms rather than a wing of the New Age movement. He is also concerned to stress its benevolence; the resulting view is perhaps too rosy. Most strikingly, he insists on taking pagans' religious claims seriously, and refuses to arbitrate between rival claims of natural and supernatural causation. His own beliefs are never spelt out, but he does not disguise his contempt for the trite rationalism of most academic discourse. As he hints in his carefully worded introduction, his willingness to take such a view in print entails a lowering of the academic's normal shield of dispassionate detachment. It may be questioned whether this can be sustainable. Hutton's achievement, however, is that this approach has not compromised his scholarship; and it has allowed him to write a passionate, important and consistently fascinating book.

UNIVERSITY OF BIRMINGHAM

ALEC RYRIE

The silent revolution and the making of Victorian England. By Herbert Schlossberg. Pp. x + 405. Columbus, OH: Ohio State University Press, 2000. £54·95 (cloth), £21·50 (paper). 0 8142 0843 6; 0 8142 5046 7
JEH (53) 2002; DOI: 10.1017/S0022046902324254

Forty years ago Ford K. Brown's attempt to demonstrate that the Hanoverian evangelicals should take the blame as the *Fathers of the Victorians* encountered

Walkowitz. Yet while few would dispute the claim that evangelicalism helped transform English society and culture, one suspects even fewer would accept Schlossberg's simplistic characterisation of that transformation, of which the main engine was evangelical preaching, as 'making almost all things better' (p. 314),' replacing a 'rough, uncouth, brutal society' by 'a kinder, more decent one' (pp. 287–8). The thesis thus emerges as virtually the antithesis of Brown's, and equally *parti pris*. It is founded on a crude portrayal of the eighteenth century as violent, drunken, corrupt and depraved. If the author knows his Hogarth, he appears to have no acquaintance with the very different eighteenth centuries which emerge from the work of Brewer, Clark or Langford; indeed coffee-houses are here presented not as a characteristic eighteenth-century cultural form, but as a feature of the transition to the sober Victorian period (p. 242). His account of the Hanoverian Church is equally uninformed by recent scholarship. Schlossberg is fiercely critical of the work of Victorianists whose 'antinomianism' renders them incapable of a sympathetic reading of the nineteenth century, but it is clear that he has a similar blind spot when it comes to the eighteenth, which prevents him from properly evaluating non-evangelical theological and secular contributions to the fashioning of Victorian England. As a result this account of the evangelical impact on the nineteenth century ultimately fails to convince.

KING'S COLLEGE,
LONDON

ARTHUR BURNS

memorable critical fire, and few have since essayed the synoptic treatment that the theme invites. It is all the riper for fresh investigation in the wake of recent work illuminating central dimensions of the evangelical contribution to the Victorian world-view. Herbert Schlossberg sets out to fill this gap. He argues that the evangelical revival inaugurated a 'silent revolution' which transformed the culture, institutions and structures of English life. If evangelicals led the way, both the Oxford Movement and Arnoldians made distinctive contributions reflecting their affinities with evangelicalism; so did the cultural 'prophets' Coleridge and Carlyle, if not the utilitarians. The 'revolution' was manifest in new moral understandings of the 'Condition of England' and, of poverty, provoking remarkable initiatives in philanthropy; a massive educational project fuelling a significant rise in literacy; a new, morally and doctrinally informed, high culture in literature, music and the visual arts; a moralisation of the working classes marked by declining illegitimacy, a new domesticity in family life and Sunday observance; and indeed a similar moralisation of the political classes, manifest in parliamentary behaviour and early nineteenth-century reform projects. If the 'silent revolution' created Victorian England, however, by the end of the reign 'a gathering putrescence' (p. 314) was apparent as the evangelical impulse was diluted in the cultural mainstream and paid the price for its theological undervaluation of the creation and incarnation. The chief strengths of *The silent revolution* lie in the author's informed concern for theological themes; but the focus is on the many faces of Romanticism, which coupled the language and imagery of ancient paganism with a wholly idealistic view of nature – undeterred by the highly cultivated quality of the English 'natural' landscape. He traces this tradition through literary heavyweights – Keats, Hardy, Kenneth Grahame, D. H. Lawrence and Yeats – and through the nineteenth-century folklorists who insisted, in the teeth of the evidence, that the oral traditions they were recording were timeless. In the twentieth century these threads come together with the neatness and cohesion of an origin myth. Romanticism's elitist contempt for real peasants (underpinned by shoddy scholarship which Hutton exposes mercilessly); its love of ancient traditions, real or invented; its enjoyment of ritual; and its undercurrent of hostility to Christianity, fostered something more than a mere interest in ancient paganisms. Finally, the chaotic change and barbarity of the modern age allowed this to crystallise into a real religion. Its claim to be ancient belies (if it does not betray) its modernity; one of Hutton's achievements is to demonstrate how closely the ideological world of paganism has been related to 'mainstream' western culture, including academic culture. If nothing else, this survey should settle for good the myth that we live in a secular age.

The second half of the book traces modern paganism's history since the 1940s, from the early covens in the New Forest to a movement which Hutton estimates to be some 100,000 strong in Britain today. As a kind of mystery religion,

2

Roman Catholicism

Sheridan Gilley

THE NINETEENTH CENTURY, when England was mistress of the seas and workshop of the world, also was the great century of English Protestantism, the era of the Evangelical and Nonconformist Revivals, when the religion of the Reformation moulded the lives of the population at as deep a level as in any other era of English history.[1] To Britons of the time, these two facts were connected: Britain was great because in adopting the Reformation, she had become a favored nation like the Jews of old, a people blessed by Providence and chosen by God to do his will. Britain was great because Britain was Protestant; and even Protestants who sat lightly to their religion believed devoutly in the congruity between the Protestant ethic of industry, sobriety, and thrift and the heroic spirit of progress and enterprise that carried British goods and soldiers and sailors as well as missionaries to the remotest corners of the earth. Moreover, the mass of Englishmen defined these national virtues as the antithesis of Roman Catholic poverty and dirt, summed up as "popery and wooden shoes." Protestantism was patriotism, and popery was the religion of England's enemies, France and Spain, and of the despised sister-kingdom of Ireland. Moreover, popery was tyranny, and Protestantism was liberty. Popery was bound up with passionate historic memories of Mary's burnings, of the defeat of the Armada, of the expulsion of James II at the Glorious Revolution, and with a whole internal history of national liberation from Rome, in which a popish England had become Protestant and free.[2]

[1] I wish to express my gratitude to my colleague Colin Crowder for his proof-reading and suggestions and to Professor John Dickson for the statistics in note 65.

[2] E. R. Norman, *Anti-Catholicism in Victorian England* (London, 1968); G.F.A. Best, "Popular Protestantism in Victorian England," *Ideas and Insti-*

In the twentieth century, however, Protestant nationalism has faded, and Britain has ceased to be great as she has ceased to be Protestant. Even the Church Establishment has been partly Catholicized from within, while the largest English church as measured by the number of its worshippers is now the Roman Catholic.[3] It is true that since 1960, after a long period of eclipse, the Evangelical element in the Church of England's constitution has undergone a considerable revival. It is equally true that despite the catastrophic decline in the mainstream liberal Nonconformist churches, popular Protestantism has extended its appeal in quiet ways of which educated public opinion is hardly conscious: with 100,000 full members, there may well be in a decade as many practicing Jehovah's Witnesses as Methodists. But the transformation of English public religion in 200 years has been extraordinary. England in 1800 was becoming more Protestant, not less so, and its Catholic population of rather less than 100,000 people was an inconsiderable minority—a minority regarded with superstitious awe. When the convert Augustus Pugin crossed himself on a railway journey, a lady passenger cried out, "You are a Catholic, sir; Guard, Guard, let me out—I must get into another carriage."[4] "No Popery" was renascent, as the liberal tradition of the eighteenth century suffered eclipse in the face of a new Evangelical fervor, and the radical Evangelicals revived in the national imagination the old Protestant apocalyptic images of Rome and the pope as the Beast and Scarlet Woman of Revelation, as the Antichrist and Man of Sin of St. John and St. Paul. By 1900, this Protestant apocalyptic tradition was in eclipse. Catholicism was clearly on the march, and for most of this century it has enjoyed a better fortune than its Protestant rivals. This chapter is an attempt to show why this was so from the church's nineteenth-century history.[5]

tutions of Victorian Britain: Essays in Honour of George Kitson Clark, ed. by Robert Robson (London, 1967), 115-42; Walter Ralls, "The Papal Aggression of 1850: A Study in Victorian Anti-Catholicism," Religion in Victorian Britain, ed. by Gerald Parsons, 4 vols. (Manchester, 1988), 4, 115-34 (originally published in CH 43, 1974, 242-56); John R. Wolffe, The Protestant Crusade in Great Britain, 1829-1860 (Oxford, 1991); D. G. Paz, Popular Anti-Catholicism in Mid-Victorian England (Stanford, 1992). See also note 41.

[3] Kenneth Thompson, "How Religious Are the British?" The British: Their Religious Beliefs and Practices, 1800-1986, ed. by Terence Thomas (London, 1988), 227. The preponderance of Catholics over Anglicans in Britain is still larger if the statistics for Scotland and Wales are included.

[4] Kenneth Clark, The Gothic Revival: An Essay in the History of Taste (London, 1962), 110. Benjamin Ferrey, Recollections of A. N. Welby Pugin (London, 1861), 262.

[5] There is a complete detailed narrative of the ecclesiastical history of Catholicism for this period in the works by Bernard and Wilfrid Ward. See Bernard

For the origins of the Catholic Revival, however, it is necessary to go back, however briefly, to the sixteenth century.[6] When Elizabeth re-Protestantized the Church of England after 1558, she and her advisors thought and hoped that the old Catholic faith of medieval England would simply die away. They were confounded by the conversion to the Catholicism redefined and reaffirmed at the Council of Trent of scores of Oxford and Cambridge graduates who left the country to found and staff and train in new Continental Catholic seminaries at Douai in Flanders, at Lisbon, Seville, Valladolid, Paris, and Rome itself. From 1570, these priest-manufactories despatched a new generation of missionaries to England, bringing the good news from Trent and dying for the work of bringing it. Within a century, English Catholics could claim hundreds of martyrs, priests and layfolk, men and women. One northern lady, Margaret Clitherow of York, was crushed to death under weights for harboring priests, and it was arguably devotion to the memory of their sacrifice that, above anything else, preserved the Catholic faith in England.

Catholic historians, stimulated by John Bossy's stimulating and trail-blazing *English Catholic Community*,[7] have debated whether the modern Roman Catholic Church in England was a medieval survival or a modern revival. The new Church undoubtedly looked back with nostalgia to the medieval Church; one restored religious order, the Benedictine, still bestowed on its members some of the titles to the English cathedrals now in

Ward, *The Dawn of the Catholic Revival in England, 1781-1803*, 2 vols. (London, 1909); *The Eve of Catholic Emancipation, 1803-1829*, 3 vols. (London, 1911-12); *The Sequel to Catholic Emancipation, 1830-1850*, 2 vols. (London, 1915). See Wilfrid Ward, *The Life and Times of Cardinal Wiseman*, 2 vols. (London, 1897), and *The Life of John Henry Cardinal Newman*, 2 vols. (London, 1912). This sequence is weakest in the area of social history, on which see notes 7, 21, and 22. Other histories covering part or all of the period are *The English Catholics, 1850-1950*, ed. by G. A. Beck (London, 1950); from a modern Anglo-Gallican viewpoint, J. Derek Holmes, *More Roman than Rome: English Catholicism in the Nineteenth Century* (London and Shepherdstown, W.Va., 1978); and Edward Norman's sparkling *The English Catholic Church in the Nineteenth Century* (Oxford, 1984). For a good local study, see Judith F. Champ, "Assimilation and Separation: The Catholic Revival in Birmingham, 1650-1850" (Ph.D. thesis, University of Birmingham, 1984).

[6] For good general histories of post-Tridentine English Catholicism, see E. I. Watkin, *Roman Catholicism in England from the Reformation to 1950* (London, 1957); J.C.H. Aveling, *The Handle and the Axe: The Catholic Recusants in England from Reformation to Emancipation* (London, 1976); and Edward Norman, *Roman Catholicism in England from the Elizabethan Settlement to the Second Vatican Council* (Oxford, 1986). See also note 7.

[7] John Bossy, *The English Catholic Community, 1570-1850* (London, 1975).

Protestant hands. But the new church was a very different organization from the old. It was an underground, illegal, evangelistic and missionary body. Papal authority was remote, and the disastrous papal initiatives of the sixteenth century—above all, Pius V's excommunication of Elizabeth as a heretic and usurper—bred a Gallican reserve towards Rome. The Church's form of government was barely even episcopal. Apart from a brief period in the 1620s, it had no bishops before 1685; and when the pope appointed four bishops for England during the brief reign of James II between 1685 and 1688, these bishops were not diocesans in ordinary but were merely Vicars Apostolic to the Holy See.[8]

From 1688 until 1840, the Vicars Apostolic nominally ruled a Church divided up into four vicariates, the London, Northern, Midland, and Western Districts; the last also included Wales. But the Vicars Apostolic counted for little in the Church. A disproportionate number of the missionary clergy were members of religious orders answerable to their own superiors, the largest of these orders being the Jesuits[9] and Benedictines.[10] Moreover, the same spirit of independence from episcopal authority developed among the secular clergy, who had their own separate organization, the Old Chapter, set up by a bishop in the 1620s but largely independent of the bishops thereafter, so that the government of large parts of the Church was virtually Presbyterian.

The Counter-Reformation Church was a battleground of competing jurisdictions, and any delver into Roman Catholic archives will be impressed at the energies that English Catholics have devoted to fighting one another. Yet, there is a certain especial impressiveness to the evidences of warfare and bad feeling between the Vicars Apostolic, on the one hand, and the regular and secular clergy, on the other, and between the seculars and regulars. These animosities lasted for centuries, and only in the course of the nineteenth century did the bishops get the upper hand and bring their clergy under their control. The Apostolic Constitution "Romanos Pontifices" was to curb the independence of the religious orders, especially the most powerful, the Jesuits, in 1881, at the behest of Archbishop

---

[8] Basil Hemphill, *The Early Vicars Apostolic of England, 1685-1750* (London, 1954).

[9] Bernard Basset, *The English Jesuits from Campion to Martindale* (London, 1967); Francis Edwards, *The Jesuits in England: From 1580 to the Present Day* (London, 1985).

[10] The only critical history of the Benedictines for the whole period is the unprinted Dom Athanasius Allanson, "History of the English Benedictine Congregation," in the archives of Ampleforth Abbey and available on microfilm. For the earlier period there is David Lunn's excellent *The English Benedictines, 1540-1688* (London, 1980).

Manning,[11] but over the years, the Sacred Congregation for the Propagation of the Faith, which had England under its jurisdiction as a missionary territory, found all this conflict sadly puzzling.

The real power in the Church was in the hands of the laity. Early modern England was a society in which wealth and influence depended on the ownership of land, and the persecuted missionary priest tended to build his congregation around the secret chapel and the estate of a gentry or aristocratic family. These families paid the chaplain, sent their sons and daughters into the ministry or the religious life, and maintained an extensive network of colleges, convents, monasteries, and schools upon the Continent. But as they paid the piper, so they called the tune, hiring and firing the chaplains without reference to the bishop and sustaining a kind of neofeudal family religion. Again, Catholics were distinguished from Protestants by the observance of a cycle of feasts and fasts controlled not so much by the bishops and clergy as from the kitchen.

The faith survived on this basis best in some of the remoter, what the Puritans called the darker, corners of the kingdom, especially in parts of northeast England and Lancashire, where one village, Little Crosby, remained wholly Catholic and one town, Preston, remained disproportionately so. The Penal Laws against Catholics were designed to beggar them by recusancy fines for avoiding the parish church, but Catholicism survived the early modern period as the religion of the quality. As Charles II might have said, but did not, Catholicism is the only religion fit for a gentleman, and that has given popery a certain social chic that has lasted in England ever since.

That upper-crust lay element in Catholicism became less important in the eighteenth century, with the lightening of persecution and the growth of urban missions outside gentry control. Many English Catholic country folk migrated to the towns; but this was only one aspect of the transformation of a rural upper-class institution into a wholly different kind of church. The Evangelical Revival among Nonconformists had its Roman Catholic parallel in a new political activism and middle-class religious seriousness, and the laity in their anti-episcopal Catholic Committees agitated for the Emancipation Act of 1791, which legalized Catholic worship. Many of them acquired the taste for politics, and the failure of the Jacobite cause and the hostility of anti-Catholic High Church Tories shifted Catholic politics to the left.[12] In their claim for emancipation from the An-

---

[11] Henry Edward Manning (1808-1892); archdeacon of Chichester, 1840-50. After his conversion in 1851, he rose rapidly in the ranks, serving as provost of Westminster Cathedral and as superior of the Oblates of St. Charles, 1857-65, and Archbishop of Westminster, 1865-92; made a cardinal, 1875.

[12] Leo Gooch, "The Durham Catholics and Industrial Development, 1560-1850" (M.A. thesis, University of York, 1984).

glican confessional state, Catholics were allied to the radicals and Whigs, and Bossy has suggested that around 1800, English Catholics formed with the Quakers and the Unitarians the radical non-Protestant wing of English religious Dissent. In the 1780s, the influential Birmingham priest and writer Joseph Berington[13] was a good friend to the leading English Unitarian, Joseph Priestley. The first passenger railway line in the world, the Stockton-Darlington line, was a Catholic-Quaker enterprise, with two priests present at the laying of the first rail.[14]

Indeed, some radical Catholics wanted a semi-democratized church; but the days of lay power were passing. The new model bishop was the intransigent John Milner,[15] Vicar Apostolic of the Midland District, a writer, fighter, and biter, christened the English Athanasius by Newman. Where most of the Old Catholics wanted good relations with tolerant Protestants, Milner signalled the rise of a more militant Catholicism by smiting the Protestants hip and thigh; his work, *The End of Religious Controversy*, turned out to be its beginning. Milner also wanted clerical power over the laity, episcopal power over the clergy, and papal power over the bishops. He fought the tendency to ecclesiastical democracy, and, in the event, the French Revolution was to bring about a conservative reaction in Catholicism that resulted in a far more clerical, episcopal, and papal church, a church asserting its own authority over its faithful as well as against its enemies.

The immediate consequence of the Revolution was to send to Albion 7,000 French priests and religious, who became, with thousands of lay émigrés, pensioners on English charity and the English state. The first refugee bishop, of St. Pol de Léon, arrived in a cargo of brandy, and when the emigration was at its height, there were 1,000 priests in the King's House in Winchester who raised the roof every night with their singing of "God Save the King." The Church of England deplored their popery yet gave them charity as ministers in a sister church, and the Protestant University of Oxford printed their Latin Vulgate Bibles.[16] French Trappists established a monastery at Lulworth, French Carthusians went to Ward-

---

[13] (1743-1827), an Anglo-Gallican and liberal, active in pressing for civil liberties; author of numerous controversial works. See Eamon Duffy, "Joseph Berington and the English Catholic Cisalpine Movement, 1772-1803" (Ph.D. thesis, University of Cambridge, 1973).

[14] Leo Gooch, "From Jacobite to Radical: The Catholicism of North East England, 1688-1850" (Ph.D. thesis, University of Durham, 1989).

[15] (1752-1826), opposed Anglo-Gallicanism and all attempts to give the government a voice in church affairs as the price for Catholic Emancipation.

[16] Dominic Aidan Bellenger, *The French Exiled Clergy in the British Isles after 1789: An Historical Introduction and Working List* (Downside Abbey, 1986), with an introductory essay and a full bibliography (including thirty-four essays in the

our, and one French nunnery, complete with a Bourbon princess, put down its roots into English soil and was still keeping its records in French a century later.[17] Most of the Gallican clergy returned to France after Napoleon had restored the French church in 1801, but some remained to found missions and to do work of lasting pastoral effectiveness. They brought to England devotion to the Blessed Sacrament and to the Sacred Heart of Jesus and were to be the first of an invasion of England by Continental Catholic priests, who were to play an important role in the internal transformation of English Roman Catholicism.

Even more important was the flight back to England of around thirty English Catholic convents, monasteries, and seminaries from the Continent. Benedictine monks from Douai and Dieulouard and the prince-abbey of Lambspring in Germany eventually established new houses at Downside and Ampleforth. The Carmelites of Lierre received a pension from the Bishop of Durham at Bishop Auckland; the English Benedictine convents of Brussels, Cambrai, Ghent, Paris, and Dunkirk were ultimately reestablished at Stanbrook, Oulton, Colwich, and Teignmouth.[18] The only medieval religious order to have survived the Reformation intact, the Bridgettine nuns of Sion, ended in Devon their three centuries of exile in Antwerp, Rouen, and Lisbon. The surviving ex-Jesuits settled at Stonyhurst, while the seminary at Douai gave rise to new Catholic colleges at Ware and Ushaw.[19] With freedom of worship and a new institutional vitality on English soil, Catholics saw the dawn of a Catholic Revival in England.

What transformed the Church's fortunes, however, was the influence of Catholic Ireland. The parliaments of both countries and their Protestant Church establishments were united in 1800, at a time when the population of Ireland was 5 million and the population of England and Wales was about 9 million, a far closer ratio than today. Three-quarters of the Irish population were poor Catholic peasants, who were organized in the 1820s by their priests into a Catholic Association, the first democratic mass movement in the modern world, under the leadership of a Catholic lawyer,

area by Dom Aidan himself). On the wider émigré problem, see Margery Weiner, *The French Exiles, 1789-1815* (London, 1960).

[17] Dominic Bellenger, "The French Revolution and the Religious Orders: Three Communities, 1789-1815," *Downside Review* 98 (1980), 25-41.

[18] Denis Agius, "Benedictines under the Terror," *English Benedictine History Symposium, 1982,* 14-21. A number of these institutions have histories: see, e.g., *A History of the Benedictine Nuns of Dunkirk now at St. Scholastica's Abbey, Teignmouth, Devon* (London, 1957).

[19] The best of the seminary histories is David Milburn, *A History of Ushaw College* (Ushaw, 1964).

Daniel O'Connell.[20] In scenes reminiscent of 1989 Poland or Czechoslovakia, O'Connell's association forced the English Tory administration in 1829 to pass the third Emancipation Act, admitting Roman Catholics to the British Parliament and to most public offices under the Crown. From 1829-30, there was a body of Irish Catholic M.P.s at Westminster, and a small but significant number of English Catholic peers occupied seats in the Lords, so that the Catholic interest had henceforth a definite say in the government of Protestant England.

The Irish economy, however, was already in crisis and was subject to periodic famine. Even by 1790, Irish peasants were beginning to migrate in large numbers to England, some as seasonal harvesters, some to come and remain in the poorest and most squalid quarters of the English towns. There were three main routes of emigration, from Ulster to western Scotland, from Cork to London direct by sea or via Bristol, and from Dublin to Liverpool. But while the three largest concentrations of Irish settlement developed at the end of these routes in London, Liverpool, and Glasgow, there were a great many smaller centers of Irish settlement, and by the 1830s, the Catholic Church in much of northern England was in a state of crisis, as young priests shortened their lives in ministering to huge new Catholic populations for whom no proper pastoral provision was yet possible.

Irish immigration was a trickle in the 1790s. It was a stream in the 1820s, but by the 1840s it had become a flood, as the Irish potato failed, a million people died of starvation, and another million emigrated, mostly to North America. Many of the poorest, however, came to Britain, nearly doubling the number of Irish-born people in England from 291,000 to 520,000 between 1841 and 1851, so that by 1850, with the children of the Irish in England, the English church had the task of evangelizing a nominally Catholic population of well over half a million people.[21]

---

[20] (1775-1847), "the Liberator." See Oliver MacDonagh, *Daniel O'Connell*, 2 vols. (London, 1988-90).

[21] Lynn Hollen Lees, *Exiles of Erin: Irish Migrants in Victorian London* (Manchester, 1979); *The Irish in the Victorian City*, ed. by Roger Swift and Sheridan Gilley (London, 1985); *The Irish in Britain, 1815-1939*, ed. by Roger Swift and Sheridan Gilley (London, 1989). Both Swift and Gilley volumes have extensive bibliographies. See also M. Hickman and M. Hartigan, *The History of the Irish in Britain: A Bibliography* (London, 1986); Roger Swift, *The Irish in Britain, 1815-1914: Perspectives and Sources* (Historical Association, 1990); Graham Davis, *The Irish in Britain, 1815-1914* (Dublin, 1991); Sheridan Gilley, "Irish Catholicism in Britain," *Religion, State, and Ethnic Groups*, ed. by D.A. Kerr (Aldershot, 1992), 229-60; Gerard P. Connolly, "Catholicism in Manchester and Salford, 1770-1850: The Quest for 'Le Chrétien Quelconque'," 3 vols. (Ph.D. thesis, University of Manchester, 1980); K. I. Ziesler, "The Irish in Birmingham,

This was, moreover, a Catholic population with a rather different understanding of Catholicism. The immigrants were much more willing than the English Catholic gentry to defer to the priest in matters of religion and so reinforced the rise of English Catholic clericalism, but it was unwise for an English priest to foist his political views upon them. The English priest, unlike his Irish brethren, was disqualified from becoming a political leader by appealing to the Irish blend of radical nationalism and religion and by invoking the intermingled loves of faith and fatherland. Where the Irish were Gaelic speakers, the English clergy were ignorant of their language, and some English bishops were reluctant to import Irish-speaking priests from Ireland. The Irish were still attached to customs like the wake for the dead, and their religion was permeated by an ancient pre-Christian folklore driven underground by the Counter-Reformation in much of Catholic Europe. Moreover, in parts of rural Ireland, especially in the West, perhaps as little as 40 percent of the population went to Mass every Sunday, and the practice of the faith was centered not on the scattered priesthood and weekly Mass attendance at a distant chapel, but on family prayer and the local shrine or holy well and the pattern or pilgrimage, in a rural landscape that had not yet lost its sacred character. Weekly Mass-going was a habit that some of the immigrants in England would have to acquire, together with a religion centered on the priest, the Mass, and the chapel, for the chapel would be the only holy place in an English urban slum.[22]

Thus, the English Catholic Church had several overwhelming pastoral tasks on its hands, the provision of priests and churches for the immigrant Irish and the reeducation of at least some of them in the modern norms of English Catholicism.

However, the church's leaders had still bigger fish to fry, in the opportunities opened up by the dramatic impact of Romanticism on the English cultural stance towards the Catholic Church. The novels and poetry of Sir Walter Scott created a new fascination with the religion of the Middle Ages, as well as with its history, while Wordsworth wrote a sonnet teaching the doctrine of the Immaculate Conception:

> MOTHER! whose virgin bosom was uncrost
> With the least shade of thought to sin allied;
> Woman! above all women glorified,
> Our tainted nature's solitary boast;

1830-1970" (Ph.D. thesis, University of Birmingham, 1989); W. J. Lowe, *The Irish in Mid-Victorian Lancashire: The Shaping of a Working-Class Community* (New York, 1989).

[22] See esp. Gerard Connolly, "Irish and Catholic: Myth or Reality? Another Sort of Irish and the Renewal of the Clerical Profession among Catholics in England, 1791-1918," *Irish in the Victorian City*, 225-54.

Purer than foam on central ocean tost;
Brighter than eastern skies at daybreak strewn
With fancied roses, . . .[23]

There was a new Catholic mood abroad in Anglicanism, apparent in the devotional poetry on the Christian Year by Reginald Heber and John Keble. The study of Anglo-Saxon and medieval history aroused a new interest in the ancient English Church in communion with Rome. A young historian from Ushaw, John Lingard,[24] wrote first on the Anglo-Saxon Church and then a restrainedly Catholic history of England, to challenge the preeminence of Hume and later of Macaulay.[25] The most virulently pro-Catholic work came from the pen of a great Protestant radical journalist, William Cobbett, who extolled the loving charity of the medieval monks and described the Reformation as the plunder of the patrimony of the poor by violent and unprincipled barbarians. Antiquarian-minded architects like Thomas Rickman identified the various styles in medieval building, and when the Houses of Parliament burned down in 1834, they were rebuilt in true Gothic style by a brilliant young architect, Augustus Pugin,[26] the son of a Swiss Protestant émigré and a convert to Catholicism.

Pugin was a revolutionary of genius. He insisted that as there is an intrinsic connection between a religion and the culture it produces, so classical architecture was pagan, and only Gothic was Christian. He was accused of calling St. Peter's in Rome the upas tree of Christendom, a pagan building that should be pulled down and rebuilt in a Christian style. Pugin found two great church-building patrons, the Earl of Shrewsbury,[27] whose strangest public production expresses his enthusiasm for two young north Italian ladies with the stigmata, and a Leicestershire squire called Ambrose Phillipps, later Phillipps de Lisle,[28] who had been converted to Catholicism

[23] "The Virgin," 25, *Ecclesiastical Sonnets*, in *The Poetical Works of Wordsworth*, ed. by Thomas Hutchinson (Oxford, 1956), 341-42.

[24] (1771-1851), the son of a carpenter, he studied at Douai, 1782-93, when he fled to England; after teaching at Ushaw, he was a missioner at Hornby, Lancs, 1811 to his death.

[25] J. P. Chinnici, *The English Catholic Enlightenment: John Lingard and the Cisalpine Movement, 1750-1850* (Shepherdstown, W.Va., 1980); Sheridan Gilley, "John Lingard and the Catholic revival," *SCH* 14 (1977), 313-27.

[26] (1812-1852); after his conversion in 1835, he prepared the detail drawings for the new Houses of Parliament, designed the cathedrals of Southwark, Killarney, and Enniscorthy, and published many books of design.

[27] John Talbot, 16th earl (1791-1852). Denis Gwynn, *Lord Shrewsbury, Pugin and the Catholic Revival* (London, 1946).

[28] (1809-1878); converted in 1824. E. S. Purcell, *Life and Letters of Ambrose Phillipps de Lisle*, ed. and finished by Edwin de Lisle, 2 vols. (London, 1900).

by a divine revelation that it was the Turk and not the pope who was
Antichrist. Pugin designed hundreds of churches, gave away a fortune in
charity, married three times, and died of madness and exhaustion at the
age of forty, having accomplished in two decades the work of several life-
times, but his circle produced one of the profoundest revolutions in English religion, out of the belief that the only proper religious atmosphere is
one created by stained glass, pointed arches, pipe organs, all-male choirs,
central marble altars, stone fonts, and all the other paraphernalia of neo-
medieval devotion:

> The Catholic Church, she never knew—
>   Till Mr. Pugin taught her,
> That orthodoxy had to do
>   At all with bricks and mortar.[29]

At its most successful, as in Pugin's gorgeous church at Cheadle, the
Puginesque church is a riot of light and color and makes worship as much
a matter of the eye as of the ear. Pugin also taught the ritually illiterate
religion of the English its love of ritual:

> The stoups are filled to the brim; the rood is raised on high; . . . the lamps
> of the sanctuary burn bright; the saintly portraitures in the glass windows
> shine all gloriously; and the albs hang in the oaken ambries, and the cope
> chests are filled with orphreyed baudekins; and pix, and pax, and chris-
> matory are there, and thurible and cross.[30]

The most enthusiastic converts to his principles were the clergy of the
Church of England. In 1839, the Cambridge Camden Society, later the
Ecclesiological Society, was founded to popularize Pugin's neomedieval-
ism by two undergraduates, John Mason Neale and Benjamin Webb, so
successfully that almost every Anglican church either constructed or restored during the century from 1840, including the great new cathedrals at
Truro and Liverpool, was built in some sort of Gothic,[31] though under the
influence of Ruskin, there was a plethora of Christian Gothic schools,
villas, banks, and railway stations as well. *And few church chapels!*
Medieval Catholic art and architecture had been widely considered
barbarous: the word "Goth" was close cousin to "Vandal." Now, it was
the only Christian style. Catholic chapels built before 1840 were generally
plain, rectangular, ballroom-type buildings, and even when they had ar-

---

[29] Ferrey, *Pugin*, 115. See also Michael Trappes-Lomax, *Pugin: A Mediæval Victorian* (London, 1932); and Phoebe Stanton, *Pugin* (London, 1971). All these studies are necessary for a full view.

[30] Clark, *Gothic Revival*, 120; Ferrey, *Pugin*, 163.

[31] James F. White, *The Cambridge Movement: The Ecclesiologists and the Gothic Revival* (Cambridge, 1962).

chitectural pretensions, these were usually classical, not Gothic.[32] The music, if available, as in the Catholic Embassy Chapels in London, was provided by a very unmonastic operatic choir containing women from the Italian opera, and one London chapel was called the shilling opera house. To Pugin, this was pure secularity. The zeitgeist was clearly moving in a Catholic direction, in an interest in forms of worship, and in an artistic and architectural symbolism invested with a sense of awe, tenderness, mystery, and wonder, qualities lacking in the eighteenth-century preaching of a reasonable religion and in the emotional but aesthetically barren presentation of the Atonement theology of popular Protestantism. There was a sense of the need for a symbolism of the spirit that neither Protestantism nor rationalism could command, and that symbolism was Catholic.

Some of the most radical Protestants felt this. One of the premillennial sects of the 1830s, the ex-Presbyterian Edward Irving's Catholic Apostolic Church, adopted a hierarchy of angels and apostles and an externally splendid liturgy, at the very time that the same enthusiasm for a higher doctrine of church, ministry, and sacrament appeared among the High Churchmen of the Church of England. Some of these, like Robert and Henry Wilberforce, sons of William Wilberforce, the great emancipator of the slaves, were ex-Evangelicals.[33] Their theology at first appeared in 1833 as a reassertion of their church's religious authority against the radicals, Dissenters, and Roman Catholics who were attacking the power, privileges, and properties of the Church as an establishment controlled and supported by the state, so that the High Church reaction began by being bitterly anti-Roman Catholic. By 1838, however, the leading High Churchmen were calling themselves Anglo-Catholic, were denouncing the Church of England's Protestant tradition, and were actually accused by the liberals and Evangelicals in the church of being secret Roman Catholics themselves.[34]

By 1845, however, the Anglo-Catholics were dividing into two groups. One party, under Edward Bouverie Pusey and John Keble, remained Anglicans and set out, with considerable effect and under Protestant and liberal persecution, to Catholicize the worship, doctrine, and devotion of the Church of England. The other group followed the lead of the only great theologian whom modern England has produced, John Henry

[32] On Catholic architecture, see Bryan Little, *Catholic Churches since 1623* (London, 1966).

[33] David Newsome, *The Parting of Friends: A Study of the Wilberforces and Henry Manning* (London, 1966).

[34] Geoffrey Rowell, *The Vision Glorious: Themes and Personalities of the Catholic Revival in Anglicanism* (Oxford, 1983).

Newman, and became Roman Catholics.[35] The result was a considerable influx of educated men and women into the Roman Catholic Church, most of them the refined and genteel offspring of the landed aristocracy and gentry where the High Church revival was strong. It is notable that Newman, another ex-Evangelical from the commercial middle class, converted no one in his family, reminding one of the remark that one only need be worried when the shopkeepers showed signs of becoming Catholics. Gordon Gorman's work on Roman Catholic converts indicates that about 450 nineteenth-century Anglican clergy became Catholics,[36] and Vicary Gibbs's appendix in *Cokayne's Complete Peerage* suggests that there were over seventy convert peers and peeresses, though some of these were in traditionally Catholic families.[37] As W. H. Auden said, Baptists were people who came to the back door, but conversion to Catholicism was a disaster that might happen in the best of families, so that Catholicism remained as it had always been, a religion fit for ladies and gentlemen.

The nineteenth century was, however, the golden age of the ecclesiastical gypsy of no fixed abode, and not all the converts stuck. There was Richard Waldo Sibthorp, a member of an old Lincoln family that also produced his mad M.P. brother Colonel Sibthorp, a man who opposed the Great Exhibition as calculated to attract wicked foreigners to England. Richard Waldo Sibthorp figures as a saintly radical Evangelical in Newman's early history. He became a Roman Catholic, went back to the Church of England, and then became a Roman Catholic again.He died a cleric of Nottingham Cathedral, having asked for the Prayer Book service at his grave.[38] Another clerical convert was the American Episcopalian Pierce Connelly. As he wanted to become a priest, he persuaded his wife to become a nun. Reverting to Protestantism, he unsuccessfully sued in the courts for the restoration of his conjugal rights, but did recover custody of his children. His wife remained true to her vows and is now venerated as the foundress of the Society of the Holy Child Jesus.[39]

[35] (1801-1890). See Ian Ker, *John Henry Newman: A Biography* (Oxford, 1988); and Sheridan Gilley, *Newman and His Age* (London, 1990).

[36] W. Gordon Gorman, *Converts to Rome* (London, 1892). The fullest and most useful edition is that of 1910.

[37] *The Complete Peerage of England, Scotland, Ireland, Great Britain, and the United Kingdom*, ed. by Vicary Gibbs, 13 vols. repub. in 6 vols. (London, 1982), 3, 639-40.

[38] J. Fowler, *Richard Waldo Sibthorp: A Biography* (London, 1880).

[39] *The Life of Cornelia Connelly (1809-1879): Foundress of the Society of the Holy Child Jesus*, by a member of the Society [i.e., Mary Catherine Gompertz] (London, 1922); Radegunde Flaxman, *A Woman Styled Bold: The Life of Cornelia Connelly, 1809-1879* (London, 1991); D. G. Paz, *The Priesthoods and*

A significant number of the converts were women. Many of these became nuns, and not the least of the attractions of Catholicism was the fact that it gave women's work a degree of autonomy in its religious orders, which initiated massive new works in the realm of education, nursing, and charity.[40] It is notable that Florence Nightingale was attracted to Catholicism, and the converts included some Protestant women who had gone with her to the Crimea and had worked there with Catholic nursing nuns. Again, Catholicism was a sanction for both outraging and defying the authority of the Victorian paterfamilias; there was no more dramatic way of breaking free from parental authority than converting to Catholicism.[41] One old naval captain settled in Brompton in order to combat the sinister influence of its Roman Oratory; his son was to become its superior. Many fashionable conversions owed nothing to Roman missionary enterprise. Newman knew hardly any Roman Catholics before he became one himself, and Rome's puzzlement about these odd convert "Inglesi" is reflected in Pope Pius IX's remark that Pusey was like the bell that calls the faithful to church but never enters it himself.

The well-known conversions were not typical of converts as a whole. Most Roman converts were humble folk who were converted on marrying a Catholic as poor as themselves. But the movement attracted visionaries, and one of these, a member of the Shrewsbury circle, the Honourable and Reverend George Spencer,[42] the nephew, brother, and uncle of successive Earls Spencer, began in 1838 a Crusade of Prayer among both foreign and British Catholics for the conversion of England. Spencer was opposed by the more conservative Old Catholics, even by as imaginative a man as

Apostasies of Pierce Connelly: A Study of Victorian Conversion and Anticatholicism (Lewiston, N.Y., and Queenston, Ont., 1986).

[40] J. N. Murphy, *Terra Incognita; or, the Convents of the United Kingdom* (London, 1873). Of the older histories of the new orders, the most useful is Mother Austin Carroll, *Leaves from the Annals of the Sisters of Mercy*, 2 (New Orleans, 1883), on England and the Antipodes. There are many good convent biographies (e.g., Maria Winowska, *Pioneer of Unity: The Life of Caroline Sheppard, the first English Little Sister of the Poor*, London, 1969), but there is no modern overall critical study. An excellent beginning has, however, been made by Susan O'Brien. See her "*Terra Incognita*: The Nun in Nineteenth-century England," *Past and Present*, No. 121 (1988), 110-40. Michael Hill's *The Religious Order: A Study of Virtuosi Religion and its Legitimation in the Nineteenth-Century Church of England* (London, 1973) has some interesting suggestions and ideas.

[41] On convents and anti-Catholicism, see Walter L. Arnstein, *Protestant versus Catholic in Mid-Victorian England: Mr. Newdegate and the Nuns* (Columbia, Mo., 1982).

[42] (1799-1864); converted in 1830; a Passionist known as "Father Ignatius."

Bishop Peter Augustine Baines,[43] a renegade Benedictine who had converted the old mansion of Prior Park above Bath into a Catholic college with nearly a quarter of a mile of facade, through grand arcades connecting the main house to two pavilions.[44] In quite correctly pouring contempt on the prospects of converting England, Baines did not recognize that Rome now had the fascination of forbidden fruit and was again an influence on the national culture.

The outcome of the Catholic cultural influence in the long term was a succession of conversions of novelists, poets, and painters to Catholicism: Gerard Manley Hopkins, Coventry Patmore, Edward Caswall, Lionel Johnson, Aubrey de Vere, Frederick Rolfe, and Robert Hugh Benson, the last a priest-novelist with two equally distinguished literary brothers and son of an Archbishop of Canterbury. The more wayward or eccentric left conversion to their deathbeds, like Robert Hawker of Morwenstow, Aubrey Beardsley, and Oscar Wilde. It is especially notable how many literary figures, not all of whom remained Catholic, received in the later Victorian period a Catholic education: Alfred Austin, Wilfrid Scawen Blunt, and George Moore at Oscott; Arthur Conan Doyle at Stonyhurst; Lafcadio Hearn and Francis Thompson at Ushaw. This was in spite of the failure of Newman's Catholic University in Ireland to attract English Catholics, the defeat of his plan (in part because of Manning's hostility) to found an Oratory in Oxford, and the failure in turn (because of the hostility of Newman and the Jesuits) of Manning's Catholic University at Kensington.[45]

Catholicism had an intellectual cutting edge; and the pattern established itself whereby the public defense of Christianity to the literate English public increasingly fell into Roman or Anglo-Catholic hands. The best-known Christian apologists in this century were to be Anglo-Catholic poets and novelists like T. S. Eliot, C. S. Lewis, Charles Williams, Dorothy L. Sayers, John Betjeman; and Roman Catholics like Chesterton and Belloc, Monsignor Ronald Knox, Wyndham Lewis, Edith Sitwell, Evelyn Waugh, Graham Greene, and J.R.R. Tolkien. There are no professional theologians in the list, but then they have been generally marginal to English culture anyway. The historiography of the Catholic Revival in its English aspect was put on a sound footing by the members of a single fa-

[43] (1787-1843); Benedictine at Lamspring, Hanover, 1798-1803, Ampleforth, 1803-17, and Bath from 1817; coadjutor Vicar Apostolic of the Western District, 1823; succeeded to the vicariate and received papal permission to leave the Benedictine Order in 1829.

[44] J. S. Roche, *A History of Prior Park College and Its Founder Bishop Baines* (London, 1931).

[45] Vincent Alan McClelland, *English Roman Catholics and Higher Education, 1830-1903* (Oxford, 1973).

... Was Lewis an Anglo C.

mily, Bernard, Wilfrid, and Maisie Ward.[46] The odd result has been a twofold Catholic culture in England: an aristocratic, convert, and literary culture on the one hand, and an Irish proletarian culture on the other. Here, then, were the two strands to the Church's mission, to reclaim the Irish Catholics and to convert the English Protestants, to convert Protestants who were mostly educated or rich and to reclaim papists who were mostly poor.

There were some odd encounters in consequence. One convert, W. G. Ward, recalled a priest who read his pauper parishioners the French court sermons of Bourdaloue. Ward and a fellow-convert Grafton were the only gentlemen in the midst of a rough Irish congregation as the priest thundered out, "Hear this, you young voluptuary! Hear this, you butterfly of fashion! Hear this, you that love to haunt the antechambers of the great!" "I looked at Grafton," the burly Ward added, "to see how we could divide the parts—which was the butterfly and which the voluptuary. For myself, I didn't think I looked much like a butterfly."[47] There was the fastidious Newman encountering bugs for the first time in the confessional while hearing the confessions of "dirty Paddies"; an aristocratic novelist, Lady Georgiana Fullerton, practicing holy poverty by wielding a crossing sweeper's broom; the Countess de Stacpoole founding the poor Battersea mission in the teeth of opposition from the Bishop of Southwark by pulling rank to get at the Pope, and gravitating between a caravan on the site of the new chapel and the Cadogan Hotel.[48] Many poor missions were founded out of just such an accident of upper-crust charity, and while weak in the middle class, who were the backbone of English religion, Romanism in England enjoyed something of the advantage of a poor following below and a rich leadership above.

One thing, however, was clear at an early date to Rome, that there was a boom in Catholicism in England. The pope doubled the numbers of Vicars Apostolic from four to eight in 1840. In 1850, he restored the hierarchy proper, with twelve bishops of full territorial dioceses under the primatial authority of the Cardinal Archbishop of Westminster. The measure was announced to a startled nation by the new Primate, Nicholas Wise-

[46] On Wilfrid and Bernard, see notes 5, 47, 56. Maisie Ward's writings include, on the Catholic world of her father Wilfrid, *The Wilfrid Wards and the Transition*, vol. 1, *The Nineteenth Century* (London, 1934), and vol. 2, *Insurrection versus Resurrection* (London, 1937); and *Young Mr. Newman* (London, 1948).

[47] Wilfrid Ward, *William George Ward and the Catholic Revival* (London, 1893), 75-76.

[48] The countess was also a foundress of the Salesians in England. William John Dickson, *The Dynamics of Growth: The Foundation and Development of the Salesians in England* (Rome, 1991).

man,[49] in a flamboyant pastoral letter from out the Flaminian Gate of Rome, which produced the last great outbreak of popular "No Popery" sentiment in England over the "Papal Aggression," fuelled by a letter to the Bishop of Durham by the Prime Minister, Lord John Russell, who as a Whig had always supported the Catholic claims, but now seemed to be opposing them. Out of the furor came a last piece of anti-Catholic legislation, the Ecclesiastical Titles Bill of 1851, denying the new Catholic bishops the right to use the names of their sees; but the act was a dead letter and was quietly repealed by a later Liberal prime minister, Gladstone, in 1871. Indeed, just as Lord John Russell conceded in his Durham Letter the Roman Church's right to minister to its Irish poor, so the decades from 1850 saw a kind of official endowment of Catholicism, an increase in government aid to Catholic schools, and the appointment of Catholic chaplains in the army, which was about a third Catholic, and to the workhouses and prisons, which contained many Irish paupers and criminals, together with the concession of their right to worship as they pleased, a right for long denied to them.

Wiseman was the architect of the new church. A flamboyant purple figure, born to be a cardinal, he was the son of an Irish merchant family long settled in Seville, but was educated at Ushaw and then in Rome, where he became an internationally famous Syriac scholar in his twenties and then Rector of the English College.[50] Rome has a weakness for clever English aristocrats—there were several English curial Cardinals in the nineteenth century: Weld, Acton, and Howard—but Wiseman was determined to return to England to push forward the English Catholic revival, and in the 1840s he made Oscott College near Birmingham, where he was the Bishop-President, the center of the English Catholic world. Wiseman was incredibly facile in everything except administration and even wrote a popular novel, *Fabiola* (1855), about an early girl-martyr of the Roman Church; at one time the prize possession of every Catholic schoolchild, this work has included among its twentieth-century schoolgirl readers such famous lapsed Catholics as Mary McCarthy and La Pasionaria. Wiseman's combination of personal friendliness and doctrinal intransigence made possible the Anglican conversions, and he was the patron of those converts who followed his lead in making the English Catholic Church more Roman than Rome.

The heart of the matter was the transformation of English Catholic devotion. English Catholics used as their manual of prayer the eighteenth-century Bishop Richard Challoner's *Garden of the Soul*, a work instinctive with a sober piety stemming from the English medieval mystical

---

[49] (1802-1865).

[50] Richard J. Schiefen, *Nicholas Wiseman and the Transformation of English Catholicism* (Shepherdstown, W.Va., 1984); also Wilfrid Ward in note 5.

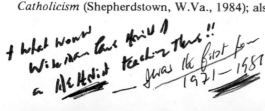

tradition.[51] This was in keeping with a reserve of feeling natural to an intensely private faith that had of necessity dispensed with the public ritual and extravagant aids to worship of the Counter-Reformation Baroque. Until the nineteenth century, the Mass was called "prayers." Priests were plain "Mr.," not "Father," and had nothing intrinsically sacerdotal in their demeanor and dress. They were a sad disappointment to poor Pugin: "What's the use of decent vestments with such priests as we have got? a lot of blessed fellows! Why, sir, when they wear my chasubles, they don't look like priests, and what's worse, the chasubles don't look like chasubles."[52]

English Catholic decorum was reinforced by Augustan formalism, but it succumbed to the religious excitements of the age. Wiseman wanted nothing less than the full Roman ritual, including Roman architecture, vestments, and art, to the fury of Pugin and his Goths. Wiseman introduced the Roman devotion of the *Quarant' Ore* or Forty Hours adoration of the Blessed Sacrament,[53] and in his enthusiasm for warm Italianate devotions to the Sacrament, the Virgin, and saints, he was seconded by the new revivalist religious orders of Italian origin, Rosminians, Redemptorists, and Passionists. Newman himself preferred Italian classical to Gothic, as a style better suited to the modern church, and introduced into England the Oratory of St. Philip Neri, the Apostle of Counter-Reformation Rome. The spiritual leader of Wiseman's devotional revolution was one of Newman's followers, the son of a Bishop of Durham's secretary, Frederick William Faber,[54] brought up at Auckland Palace. Like Newman he was of Huguenot descent and had been an Evangelical in his youth, and as a Roman Catholic, he pioneered the new kind of Catholic revivalism. He also called the Virgin Mary "Mamma," and liked nothing better than a procession with a Madonna in petticoats. He is, however, a great and now greatly neglected spiritual writer, and his works *The Creator and the Creature* (1858) and *Growth in Holiness* (1855) are two of our spiritual classics. Newman himself came to prefer the restraint and reserve of the

---

[51] Edwin Burton, *The Life and Times of Bishop Challoner*, 2 vols. (London, 1909); *Challoner and His Church: A Catholic Bishop in Georgian England*, ed. by Eamon Duffy (London, 1981).

[52] Ferrey, *Pugin*, 112.

[53] A devotion "in which continuous prayer is made for forty hours before the Blessed Sacrament exposed." *The Catholic Encyclopedia* (New York, 1913), 6, 151.

[54] (1814-1863); converted in 1845; superior of the Brompton Oratory, 1850 to his death.

older English Catholics, but Faber made the spirituality of the younger generation more Roman than Rome.[55]

Faber was, in part, responsible for the tension and conflict between the Old Catholics and the new Roman converts, boiling over in the 1850s into a celebrated row between, on the one hand, Wiseman and his loyal convert assistant, Henry Edward Manning, and on the other, the predominantly Old Catholic Westminster Cathedral Chapter, of which Manning was Provost, and Wiseman's coadjutor Archbishop George Errington. Wiseman accused his enemies of Gallicanism and got Errington dismissed by Rome, and when Wiseman died in 1865, he was succeeded by Manning as Archbishop of Westminster. Here was speed indeed: Manning had gone from being an Anglican archdeacon to a Roman archbishop in fourteen years, and he set out to complete the ultramontanization and Romanization of the church in England. Manning had influenced Wiseman to wind up a joint Anglican-Roman Catholic prayer organization, the Association for Promoting the Unity of Christendom. Manning was also a leading proponent of the measure to define papal infallibility at the Vatican Council in 1870, where he was described as the whip of the infallibilist majority among the bishops.

In this, he was assisted by the sharpest mind whom Newman converted, one of the ablest philosophers of his generation, William George Ward. The son of the owner of Lord's Cricket Ground and himself the owner of most of the Isle of Wight, Ward was an intellectual extremist, with the blundering body of a rhinoceros and the mind of an archangel. His solution to the problem of religious doubt was an infallible papal encyclical on the breakfast table with his *Times* every morning. Yet he was regarded with enormous respect by T. H. Huxley and John Stuart Mill, who declared Ward's reply to him on the subject of free will as the best that could be said and whose death in the midst of the controversy Ward described as a severe controversial disappointment. In Ward one can see most clearly the attraction to minds, beset by the characteristic forms of Victorian doubt, of an infallible pope and church and the especial attraction of this idea to former members of the Church of England.[56]

Newman's theology is the greatest of nineteenth-century responses to the problem of doubt, but he found himself in the odd position of be-

[55] John Edward Bowden, *The Life and Letters of Frederick William Faber* (London, 1869); Ronald Chapman, *Father Faber* (London, 1961); *Faber: Poet and Priest: Selected Letters by Frederick William Faber, 1833-1863*, ed. by Raleigh Addington (London, 1974).

[56] Wilfrid Ward, *William George Ward and the Oxford Movement* (London, 1889); also note 47.

coming the totem and figurehead of the more reserved and liberal[57] or Gallican Old Catholics against the fiercer neoultramontanes like Ward and Manning. Manning and Ward thought Newman a heretic, and Manning seems to have tried to prevent the grant of Newman's cardinal's hat by a none-too-clever piece of trickery. The personal dispute, however, reflected a conflict of international importance. The Roman Catholic Church was confronted in the Latin nations, especially in Italy, by liberal anticlerical movements intent on secularizing education, public morality, and charity and on seizing the monastic lands and properties of the church. The result was Pope Pius IX's condemnation in the Syllabus of Errors in 1864 of "progress, liberalism and modern civilization." The neoultramontane movement to define papal infallibility was the church's response to liberalism, especially to the seizure by Italian nationalists of the Papal States themselves. Of course, the reaffirmation of church authority in the face of liberalism also took place in some Protestant churches, but to Newman, Manning's ultramontane crusade was a refusal of the intellectual challenge and opportunities of the age.

Manning, however, also has his greatness.[58] Much more effectively than Wiseman, the old parson, as Manning was called, threw himself into the crusade to reclaim the Irish for the church, by building up a chain of poor schools in his diocese, by his temperance crusade, the League of the Cross, and by identifying himself, with some reservations, with the moderate expression of Irish political aspirations to Home Rule for Ireland. In the 1870s, Manning's social activism expanded into an attempt to reclaim the English working class for Christianity by placing the Catholic Church at the forefront of the movement for social and political reform. Conservative Catholics shuddered when Manning appeared on a Protestant platform to endorse the Primitive Methodist Joseph Arch's Agricultural Workers' Union, when he denounced the pogroms against Russian Jews, when he applauded the social activism of the Salvation Army, when the notorious journalist W. T. Stead arrived at Archbishop's House to apprise the car-

[57] On Newman's connection with the Liberal Catholic movement of Sir John Acton and Richard Simpson, see Josef L. Altholz, *The Liberal Catholic Movement in England: The 'Rambler' and Its Contributors, 1848-1864* (London, 1962); and *The Correspondence of Lord Acton and Richard Simpson*, ed. by Josef L. Altholz, Damian McElrath, and James C. Holland, 3 vols. (Cambridge, 1971-75).

[58] E. S. Purcell, *Life of Cardinal Manning, Archbishop of Westminster*, 2 vols. (London, 1895), on which see Sheridan Gilley, "New Light on an Old Scandal: Purcell's Life of Cardinal Manning," *Opening the Scrolls: Essays in Catholic History in Honour of Godfrey Anstruther*, ed. by Dominic Aidan Bellenger (Downside Abbey, 1987), 166-99; Vincent Alan McClelland, *Cardinal Manning: His Public Life and Influence, 1865-92* (London, 1962); Robert Gray, *Cardinal Manning: A Biography* (London, 1985).

dinal of the horrors of the white slave trade in underage girls, and when leading labor agitators like Tom Mann and Ben Tillett advised him on the progress of the dock strike, in which his successful mediation won him a place beside Marx on the trade union banners in the world's first May Day procession.[59]

Manning's archiepiscopate did something to bridge the gap between the English Catholic bishops and their Irish flocks, and it was a loss to the church when his social policies were abandoned by his successor, Herbert Vaughan.[60] Vaughan was one of the ten children of a Welsh border gentry family to become priests or monks or nuns. He was as ultramontane as Manning, and he placed the keystone on the arch of Catholic triumphalism in building Westminster Cathedral, but as a strong Tory, he was probably nearer the politics of most of the higher clergy in England. English priests were opposed to revolutionary Irish nationalism and were even uneasy about the involvement of their Irish faithful in a succession of Nationalist organizations that supported the Irish M.P.s in the Commons, and sent to Westminster one Catholic Nationalist M.P., T. P. O'Connor ("Tay Pay"), Member for more than forty years from 1885 for the Scotland Road division in Liverpool.[61] The only other social activist and militant Hibernophile among the English Victorian bishops was Edward Bagshawe,[62] who tried to ban Catholics from joining Disraeli's Tory Primrose League on the ground that it was a secret society of the type condemned by the Holy See.

Yet most nineteenth-century English priests were probably Liberals, like their flocks, and in the twentieth century blessed the departure of those flocks into the Labour Party, which formed some of its great redoubts in the Catholic strongholds of northern England and western Scotland, where the collective faiths of Socialism and Catholicism have reacted on and reinforced each other.[63] The most extraordinary example of such Irish Ca-

[59] *Manning: Anglican and Catholic*, ed. by John Fitzsimons (London, 1951), 145.

[60] (1832-1903); founded the missionary college at Mill Hill, 1866; Bishop of Salford, 1872-92, and Archbishop of Westminster, 1892-1903; Cardinal, 1893. J. G. Snead-Cox, *The Life of Cardinal Vaughan*, 2 vols. (London, 1910); Arthur McCormack, *Cardinal Vaughan* (London, 1966); *Remembered in Blessing (The Courtfield Story)*, by a Mill Hill Father (London, 1955).

[61] L. W. Brady, *T. P. O'Connor and the Liverpool Irish* (London and Rutherford, N.J., 1983).

[62] (1829-1915); Bishop of Nottingham, 1874-1901.

[63] James E. Handley: *The Irish in Scotland* (Cork, 1943); *The Irish in Modern Scotland* (Cork, 1947); *The Celtic Story: A History of the Celtic Football Club* (London, 1960); *The Navvy in Scotland* (Cork, 1970). Also, *Modern Scottish Catholicism, 1878-1978*, ed. by David McRoberts (Glasgow, 1979); Tom Gal-

tholic political influence was in interwar Stepney, where an Irish-Jewish condominium in local government was ruled by an Orthodox Jewish-Socialist crook, Morry Davis. The general ecclesiastical approval of the Irish Catholic alignment with Labour rather contradicts the impression of political conservatism given by Cardinal Bourne's condemnation of the General Strike in 1926, and it is difficult to say how far the conservatism of many of the Roman clergy alienated some of the Irish laity.[64] More Irish bishops might have made a difference. There were only two in England in the 1870s and only two in the 1920s, though some parishes continued to import Irish priests even when the Irish-born had become a small element in the congregation. England was never wholly part of the Irish ecclesiastical empire that embraced millions of Catholics in North America and Australasia, an empire that has decisively shaped Rome's power in the twentieth century, and many Irish Catholics may have failed to identify with English Catholicism in consequence.

The number of Irish-born in England peaked at 602,000 in 1861, and the English Church's mission was assisted by the steady rise in the number of priests and churches after 1860 as immigration from Ireland fell away. From 392 in 1771, the number of priests had more than doubled to 826 by 1851, but it then underwent an astonishing near fourfold increase to 3,298 by 1901.[65] The increase in the size of the largest of the orders, the Society of Jesus, formally restored in 1829, is nearly as remarkable: from 100 members, including novices, in the unrestored society in 1826 to 507 in 1885 and 807 in 1925.[66] This steady growth in clerical manpower permitted the steady consolidation of congregations. In 1850, the Redemptorist missioners were preaching to the unchurched poor; by 1900, their role was to strengthen church attendance in existing parishes in which the Catholic population had settled down to a steady pattern of religious

lagher, *Glasgow: The Uneasy Peace: Religious Tension in Modern Scotland* (Manchester, 1987).

[64] Stuart Mews, "The Churches," *The General Strike*, ed. by Margaret Morris (London, 1976), 318-37. On a late phase of Irish nationalism in Britain, see Stuart Mews, "The Hunger-Strike of the Lord Mayor of Cork, 1920: Irish, English and Vatican Attitudes," *SCH* 25 (1989), 385-400.

[65] Bossy, *English Catholic Community*, 392; Alan Gilbert, *Religion and Society in Industrial England: Church, Chapel, and Social Change, 1740-1914* (London, 1976), 46. The figure for 1901 may include some French religious, refugees from anti-Catholic legislation in France. Godfrey Anstruther, *The Seminary Priests*, 4 vols., 1 (Gateshead, 1968), 2-4 (Great Wakering, 1975-77); Dominic Bellenger, *English and Welsh Priests, 1558-1800: A Working List* (Downside Abbey, 1984); Charles Fitzgerald Lombard, *English and Welsh Priests, 1801-1914: A Working List* (Downside Abbey, 1993).

[66] Edwards, *Jesuits in England*, 171, 242.

practice and nonpractice.[67] The church seems to have held on to the active allegiance of only about a third of the nominal Catholics in secularist London. This figure rose to over 60 percent in sectarian Liverpool,[68] which reproduced the sectarian antagonisms of Belfast, and erupted in 1909-10 in some spectacular sectarian rioting over the setting up of a street altar for a public procession.[69] The Irish had higher rates of churchgoing than the English working class, but these compared poorly with the very high rates of practice among the native English Catholics. What helped the Church in the long term was the emergence of partly Irish Catholic neighborhoods, settled peacefully in the midst of the British working class, but with their own pubs, schools, and churches, with a large core of committed churchgoers and a large fringe of "bad Catholics" who might be reclaimed for a time by a mission, who would despatch their children to the Catholic school and send for the priest when dying. By the 1920s, these Catholic neighborhoods were ready for the more public display of their faith, with public street processions like the Corpus Christi procession in Middlesbrough or the Whit walks in Manchester, where the Labour councillors walked behind their priests, so that as the loyalty to Ireland faded, Catholicism provided the social cement for a flourishing communal life.[70]

It was, however, arguably the ultramontanization of the church that made it a success, as the new gaudy shrine chapels with their altars and statues and smells of incense and melted beeswax projected a sense of the sacred with a visual and olfactory power utterly lacking in the tabernacles of Nonconformity. Moreover, ultramontane clericalism gave the church a firm, dogmatic structure that underpinned its pastoral success. The priest, garbed in the Roman collar that was spreading through all the churches, was a figure of authority and the immediate servant of higher authorities, His Lordship the bishop and His Holiness in Rome, whose picture stared or smiled in benediction from hundreds of thousands of domestic, classroom, and presbytery walls. In a sense, that authority was popular and voluntary. Manning not only strengthened Roman authority in England

[67] John Sharp, *Reapers of the Harvest: The Redemptorists in Great Britain and Ireland, 1843-1898* (Dublin, 1989).

[68] For a summary of the statistics, see Connolly, "Irish and Catholic: Myth or Reality?", and Jean Alain Lesourd, *Les Catholiques dans la Société Anglaise, 1765-1865*, 2 vols. (Lille, 1978).

[69] Frank Neal, *Sectarian Violence: The Liverpool Experience, 1819-1914: An Aspect of Anglo-Irish History* (Manchester, 1988).

[70] Steven Fielding, *Class and Ethnicity: Irish Catholics in England, 1880-1939* (Buckingham and Philadelphia, 1993). See also the excellent Alan Bartlett, "The Churches in Bermondsey, 1880-1939" (Ph.D. thesis, University of Birmingham, 1987). In a special class of its own is Dermot Quinn, *Patronage and Piety: The Politics of English Roman Catholicism, 1850-1900* (Stanford, 1993).

over bishop and priest and layman; he also helped to create the ethos of
the priest as the remote and awesome, but compassionate, representative
on earth of the most high God. Manning's most influential work was *The
Eternal Priesthood* (1883), which is notable not only for its high ultramontane doctrine of the authority of the priest, but for its uncompromis-
ingly otherworldly demand that the priest lead a life of utter dedication and
holy poverty like his Lord. Most priests lived better than their parishioners, hence, the not wholly true remark ascribed to the Roman priest that
if Anglicans had better halves, he had better quarters. Yet, the demands
upon the Roman clergy were there, to be available at any hour of the day
or night to console the sick or to administer the last rites to the dying,
whatever the cost. The outcome of this dedication was the only substantial
working-class Church in the country. Outside St. Patrick's Church in
Toxteth, there is a memorial to the ten Liverpool priests who died ministering to the typhus- and cholera-ridden refugees of the great Irish Famine,
in an epidemic in which not a single Anglican incumbent lost his life. The
Church of England did produce many devoted slum priests and pastors,
but they were not so typical of the system that produced them; and the
difference in fortune between the Anglican and Roman Churches for most
of this century arises, in part, from that comparison.

A fine *nurses*.

3

Orthodox Nonconformity

Richard J. Helmstadter

DURING THE FIRST half of the nineteenth century the term "Nonconformist" gradually edged out "Dissenter" as the term most generally used to identify those English Protestants who did not consider themselves part of the Church of England. Nonconformists differed among themselves in a great many ways. There was no common theological bond or sociological uniformity, and political cooperation was achieved only sometimes and always with difficulty.[1] Michael Watts[2] argues that the tendency to fragmentation in English Protestantism generally had at base social and economic causes. This is an argument that is different from, but not necessarily incompatible with, the position that the English tradition of religious separatism has had an ideological continuity from the mid-sixteenth century.[3] While it is clearly difficult to probe the nature of religious Dissent and try to understand its roots, it is even riskier to try to group Victorian Nonconformist denominations and sects into categories that might permit less profound historical generalizations. This categorization is nevertheless necessary, and it makes sense in a rough way to see nineteenth-century English Nonconformity as comprising four divisions. These divisions are largely artificial and analytical. They do not reflect formal institutional realities.

---

[1] D. W. Bebbington, *The Nonconformist Conscience: Chapel and Politics, 1870-1914* (London, 1982); Ian Sellers, *Nineteenth-Century Nonconformity* (London, 1977).

[2] *The Dissenters: From the Reformation to the French Revolution* (Oxford, 1978).

[3] See B. R. White, *The English Separatist Tradition from the Marian Martyrs to the Pilgrim Fathers* (London, 1971).

The four divisions are (1) Baptists[4] and Congregationalists.[5] These denominations traced their roots to the Puritans of the seventeenth century. They shared similar styles of ecclesiastical organization, and they were frequently allied in political and evangelical enterprises. English Presbyte-

[4] For nineteenth-century works on the Baptists, see J. M. Cramp, *Baptist History: From the Foundation of the Christian Church to the Close of the Eighteenth Century* (London, 1868); Joseph Ivimey, *History of the English Baptists*, 4 vols. (London, 1811-30). Among the most useful of modern works are the following: H. Leon McBeth, *The Baptist Heritage: Four Centuries of Baptist Witness* (Nashville, Tenn., 1987); *Cumulative Index for the Transactions of the Baptist Historical Society, 1908-1920*, ed. by Douglas C. Sparkes (University Microfilms, 1966); Robert G. Torbet, *A History of the Baptists* (London, 1966); Ernest A. Payne, *The Baptist Union: A Short History* (London, 1958) and *The Fellowship of Believers: Baptist Thought and Practice Yesterday and Today* (London, 1944); A. C. Underwood, *A History of the English Baptists* (London, 1947); W. T. Whitley, *A History of the British Baptists* (London, 1923). Important collections of records are to be found in both the Baptist Missionary Society Archives and the Heritage Room at Spurgeon's College. The Angus Library in Regents' Park College at Oxford houses all the papers of the Baptist Union. The most helpful journals are the *Transactions of the Baptist Historical Society* and the *Baptist Quarterly*.

[5] For the Congregationalists, see both R. W. Dale, *History of English Congregationalism* (London, 1907), and H. S. Skeats and C. S. Miall, *History of the Free Churches of England, 1688-1891* (London, 1891). See also John Webster Grant, *Free Churchmanship in England, 1870-1940, With Special Reference to Congregationalism* (London, 1955); R. Tudur Jones, *Congregationalism in England, 1662-1962* (London, 1962); Benjamin Albert Millard, *Congregationalism* (London, 1912); William Boothbie Selbie, *Congregationalism* (London, 1927). Ernest Payne's chief contributions to the literature on this subject are *The Free Church Tradition in the Life of England* (London, 1944) and *Free Churchmen: Unrepentant and Repentant, and Other Papers* (London, 1965). See also Albert Peel's authoritative work: *These Hundred Years: A History of the Congregational Union of England and Wales, 1831-1931* (London, 1931), *Essays Congregational and Catholic: Issued in Commemoration of the Centenary of the Congregational Union of England and Wales* (London, 1931), and *Invisible Congregationalism* (London, 1937). Both the *Congregational Historical Society Transactions* and the *Journal of the United Reformed Church Historical Society* contain a large number of useful articles. It is important to stress that a large percentage of the work in this field has taken the form of local congregational histories. For a helpful guide to some of these, see Dr. Williams's Library, *Nonconformist Congregations in Great Britain: A List of Histories and other Material in Dr. Williams's Library* (London, 1973). Dr. Williams's Library also houses the most important collection of archival material for this denomination.

rians, also dating from the seventeenth century, tended to fade into Congregationalism or Unitarianism in the late eighteenth and early nineteenth centuries. The Scottish Presbyterians in England have a different history. Their chapels were offshoots of the Kirk in Scotland and ministered for the most part to Scottish immigrants.[6] (2) Quakers and Unitarians differed much from each other, as R. K. Webb points out in Chapter 4. They differed from the rest of Nonconformity in that they remained a social and intellectual elite for most of the century, never impelled by Evangelical zeal to draw in masses of converts. (3) The various sorts of Methodists, analyzed by David Hempton in Chapter 5, descendants of the followers of John Wesley and George Whitefield. These did not have as strong a sense of grievance against the Church of England as did those who considered themselves heirs of the Puritans. At the beginning of the nineteenth century, Methodists did not think of themselves as Dissenters; as the century progressed they moved clearly into the Nonconformist camp for a variety of reasons. (4) Finally, there was a host of smaller sects and congregations, some of them colorful and eccentric, ranging from small bands gathered around a single prophet, through enthusiastic movements such as the British Israelites, to highly respectable and successful institutions such as the Salvation Army. Peter Lineham takes these up in Chapter 6.

Among these four groupings of Nonconformists, the Congregationalists and Baptists probably have the highest level of similarity and internal cohesion. For much of the nineteenth century, for reasons outlined later, the political leadership of Nonconformity was in the hands of the Baptists and Congregationalists. Arguably, moreover, the Baptists and Congregationalists, with Methodist support, set the styles of chapel and family life and encouraged the narrow, prudish, provincial Nonconformist culture that Matthew Arnold pilloried in *Culture and Anarchy* (1869).

For the Congregationalists and Baptists, the shift in fashion from "Dissent" to "Nonconformity" parallels a massively important transformation of character. In the early eighteenth century, the Congregationalists and the Baptists, descendants of seventeenth-century theological and political turmoil, comprised relatively small, and sometimes shrinking, congregations in which Calvinism was tempered by rationalism, and the doc-

---

[6] See G. C. Bolam et al., *The English Presbyterians: From Elizabethan Puritanism to Modern Unitarianism* (London, 1968); G. C. Cameron, *The Scots Kirk in London* (Oxford, 1979); A. H. Drysdale, *A History of the Presbyterians in England: Their Rise, Decline, and Revival* (London, 1889). See also the *Journal of the Presbyterian Historical Society of England*. The United Reformed Church History Society in London houses important records and papers pertaining to Presbyterian history.

trine of the Trinity became a matter for debate.[7] In the second half of the eighteenth century, the Evangelical Revival had such a major impact on the Congregationalists and many of the Baptists that these denominations were, in effect, reborn into a new life.[8] Increasing interest in the course of the Revival in all corners of Britain has spawned an impressive corpus of works over the past several decades.[9] The character of this impact is a matter of debate among both Victorian Nonconformists and modern historians. Some see the impact of the revival as giving new energy to forms

[7] R. Tudur Jones describes the social character of Congregationalism at this time in *Congregationalism in England, 1662-1962* (London, 1962), p51-68. Tudur Jones deals, as well, with the intellectual debates within orthodox Dissent in the early eighteenth century, as does Michael Watts, *The Dissenters: From the Reformation to the French Revolution.*

[8] See especially, D. W. Bebbington, *Evangelicalism in Modern Britain: A History from the 1730s to the 1980s* (London, 1989). Also helpful are the following list of works: A. Dallimore, *George Whitefield: The Life and Times of the Great Evangelist of the Eighteenth-Century Revival*, vol. 1 (London, 1970); A. D. Gilbert, *Religion and Society in Industrial England: Church, Chapel, and Social Change, 1740-1914* (London, 1976), ch. 3; Boyd Hilton, "The Role of Providence in Evangelical Social Thought," *SCH* 20 (1985), 215-32; G. F. Nuttall, "Methodism and the Older Dissent: Some Perspectives," *Journal of the United Reformed Church Historical Society* 2 (1981), 259-74; B. Semmel, *The Methodist Revolution* (New York, 1973); John Walsh, "Origins of the Evangelical Revival," *Essays in Modern English Church History in Memory of Norman Sykes*, ed. by G. V. Bennett and J. D. Walsh (London, 1966).

[9] M. Bassett, *The Welsh Baptists* (Swansea, 1977); R. Carwardine, "The Welsh Evangelical Community and 'Finney's Revival,'" *JEH* 29 (1978), 463-80; C. B. Turner, "Revivalism and Welsh Society in the Nineteenth Century," *Disciplines of Faith*, ed. by James Obelkevitch (London, 1987), 311-23. David Hempton's contributions to the study of Irish Protestant Evangelical history are substantial. See "Evangelicalism in English and Irish Society, 1780-1840," *Evangelicalism: Comparative Studies of Popular Protestantism in North America, the British Isles, and Beyond, 1700-1900*, ed. by Mark A. Noll, D. W. Bebbington, and George A. Rawlyk (New York, 1994). See also Hempton and Myrtle Hill, *Evangelical Protestantism in Ulster Society, 1740-1890* (London, 1992). For Scottish Evangelicalism, see J. Hunter, "The Emergence of the Crofting Community: The Religious Contribution, 1789-1843," *Scottish Studies* 18 (1974), 95-116; Ned Landsman, "Evangelists and Their Hearers: Popular Interpretation of Revivalist Preaching in Eighteenth-Century Scotland," *JBS* 28 (1989), 120-49; T. C. Smout, "'Born again at Cambuslang': New Evidence on Popular Religion and Literacy in Eighteenth-Century Scotland," *Past and Present*, No. 97 (1982), 114-27; M. J. Westerkamp, *Triumph of the Laity: Scots-Irish Piety and the Great Awakening, 1625-1760* (New York, 1988).

of Dissent that continued to maintain continuity with the past. In the nineteenth century, Robert Vaughan, the Congregational historian and founding editor of the *British Quarterly Review*, Charles Haddon Spurgeon, the great Baptist preacher, and many others, including those who rallied to support the 1862 celebration of the Great Ejectment of 1662, were proponents of the idea that the Baptists and Congregationalists of their own time were the lineal descendants of the Puritans. David Bebbington takes the same point of view: "Dissent gained a new vitality from the infusion of Evangelicalism."[10] While acknowledging that Dissent had entered "a different world" by the end of the eighteenth century, Geoffrey Nuttall, one of the great historians of the Puritans and later Congregationalists, argues that evolving institutions provided a backbone of continuity.[11] Michael Watts also stresses continuity, arguing that the Evangelical Revival was "an attempt to return, after the spiritual lethargy of the late seventeenth century, to the religious fervour of an earlier age."[12]

This position has its opponents. In the late nineteenth century, when the theology of the Evangelical Revival had passed out of fashion, R. W. Dale of Birmingham, one of the preeminent figures in Victorian Nonconformity, attacked the revival as a movement that had weakened the intellectual foundations of orthodox Dissent and diverted its energies towards suspect, emotional ends.[13] In our own time, one of the two most important discussions of the Evangelical Revival as a moment of discontinuity is by Deryck Lovegrove.[14] R. W. Dale long ago emphasized in his *History of English Congregationalism* (London, 1907), that the institutional structure of Congregationalism had changed dramatically under pressure exerted by Evangelical imperatives. The business of saving souls demanded systematic organization on first a regional, then a national basis. This move towards hierarchical organization, in tension with the ideal of congregational independence, took place at roughly the same time among both the Congregationalists and the Baptists.[15] Lovegrove's fine book, a work of great im-

[10] *Evangelicalism in Modern Britain*, 33.

[11] G. F. Nuttall, "Assembly and Association in Dissent, 1689-1831," *SCH* 7 (1971), 289-309. Nuttall's idea of spiritual continuity is examined by Richard L. Greaves in "The Nature of the Puritan Tradition," *Reformation Conformity and Dissent: Essays in Honour of Geoffrey Nuttall*, ed. by R. Buick Knox (London, 1977).

[12] *Dissenters*, 394.

[13] R. W. Dale, *The Old Evangelicalism and the New* (London, 1889).

[14] *Established Church, Sectarian People: Itinerancy and the Transformation of English Dissent, 1780-1830* (Cambridge, 1988).

[15] For useful treatments that highlight these tensions, see Peel's *These Hundred Years*, chs. 3-5, and Payne's *Baptist Union*. (See below for a consideration of the contributions of these two historians.) Ian Sellers, *Nineteenth-Century Noncon-*

portance in the history of Nonconformity, makes the point that the Evangelical Revival provided the Congregationalists and Baptists with a new Evangelical theology, with new forms of organization, and with a new membership that overwhelmed the old in size.[16] He stresses the role of itinerancy and points to the hitherto little noticed similarities between the instruments of the revival among the Methodists and the orthodox Dissenters.

W. R. Ward's important vision of the Evangelical Revival as a major break with the past is presented in *Religion and Society in England, 1790-1850.*[17] Ward, with an approach very different from Lovegrove's, boldly contends that for a time at the end of the eighteenth century the revival had created a "pure" Evangelicalism that existed in the Church of England and in a number of Dissenting bodies. The goal of this "pure" Evangelicalism was the conversion of souls at home and abroad. Towards this end, pan-Evangelical organizations were founded, Evangelical men and women cooperated across ecclesiastical boundaries and across social boundaries, and a genuinely ecumenical and democratic movement flourished for a brief time, roughly from 1790 until 1820.[18] This time of revival was different from what had come before and what was to come afterwards. Ward's argument is basically that differences of social class among Evangelicals, especially Dissenting Evangelicals, had political implications that eventually created splits within the revival and encouraged the emer-

formity; D. M. Thompson, "Denominationalism and Dissent, 1795-1835: A Question of Identity," *Friends of Dr. Williams's Library*, 39th Lecture (London, 1985); Underwood, *English Baptists*, chs. 7-8.

[16] See Robert Currie, Alan Gilbert, and Lee Horsley, *Churches and Churchgoers: Patterns of Church Growth in the British Isles since 1700* (Oxford, 1977), Appendix A4 and 147-52. See also Lovegrove, *Established Church, Sectarian People*, 38.

[17] (London, 1972). See also W. R.Ward, "The Baptists and the Transformation of the Church, 1780-1830," *Baptist Quarterly* 25 (1973), 167-84; and R. Philip Roberts, *Continuity and Change: London Calvinistic Baptists and the Evangelical Revival, 1760-1820* (Wheaton, Ill., 1989).

[18] For Evangelical ecumenism, the most comprehensive study is Roger H. Martin, *Evangelicals United: Ecumenical Stirrings in Pre-Victorian Britain, 1795-1830* (Metuchen, N.J., 1983). See also R. H. Martin, "The Place of the London Missionary Society in the Ecumenical Movement," *JEH* 31 (1980), 283-300; Stuart Piggin, "Sectarianism Versus Ecumenism: The Impact on British Churches of the Missionary Movement to India, c. 1800-1860," *JEH* 27 (1976), 387-402; Howsam, *Cheap Bibles*. For a late manifestation of pan-Evangelical action, largely directed against Roman Catholicism, see John Wolffe, "The Evangelical Alliance in the 1840s: An Attempt to Institutionalize Christian Unity," *SCH* 23 (1986), 333-46.

gence of more socially and politically unified denominations. By the middle of the century, in Ward's view, denominations had replaced the revival.

The emergence of denominational structures of organization has been one of the main themes of Congregationalist and Baptist history written in the twentieth century. Albert Peel is a key figure among Congregationalist historians. His principal book, and in some ways still the best history of Congregationalism in the period he covers, is *These Hundred Years: A History of the Congregational Union of England and Wales, 1831-1931* (1931). Peel's book tells the story (rather Whiggishly) of the central denominational organization from its foundation in 1832, but this is not a dry history of a bureaucracy. Peel brings alive the personalities of the principal figures associated with the denomination, and he, better than anyone else so far, presents an integrated, comprehensive history of the denomination, at least as seen in the view from the center. For the Baptists, Ernest A. Payne has played a role similar to Peel's. Payne's *The Baptist Union: A Short History* (1958) is a contribution towards the general history of the denomination.

The creation of the Congregational Union and the reconstitution of the Baptist Union, both occurring in 1832, were linked both to needs flowing from the Evangelical Revival and to the exigencies of the role of Dissent in national politics. There is no solid, comprehensive study of the place of Dissent in politics during the period of the French Revolution and the Napoleonic Wars.[19] Robert Hole's *Pulpits, Politics, and Public Order in England* is a stimulating survey of Christian political theory, frequently at the practical level of the pamphlet and the pulpit. Hole generally confirms the accepted picture that puts Unitarian ministers at the fore as spokesmen for respectable radicalism, while Baptist and Congregational ministers were much more cautious and ready to support the civil authorities. Hole makes it clear that there were numerous exceptions to this generalization. But the generalization still stands.[20]

One of the important reasons for the difference between the politics of the Unitarians and those of the orthodox Dissenters can be traced to the Evangelical Revival. Those who were caught up in the revival tended towards political quietism in order not to call down upon themselves the wrath of the state, a wrath that might seriously interfere with their ability to carry on the business of salvation as usual. This explanation is forcefully

[19] The most generally inclusive study of the politics of eighteenth-century Dissent before 1789 is James Bradley, *Religion, Revolution, and English Radicalism: Nonconformity in Eighteenth-Century Politics and Society* (Cambridge, 1990).

[20] See Hole, *Pulpits, Politics, and Public Order in England, 1760-1832* (Cambridge, 1989), 27-30, 113; Watts, *Dissenters*, 474-76; David Hempton, *Methodism and Politics in British Society, 1750-1850* (London, 1984), 135, 140-41.

put by Deryck Lovegrove.[21] After 1803, according to Lovegrove, Evangelical Dissent moved from political quietism to active support for the government. Nevertheless, religious Dissent of all types continued to be suspected of subversion by the authorities. The climax of the tension between Dissent and the state came with the furor over Lord Sidmouth's failed bill to stiffen the licensing requirements for itinerant preachers.[22] Lovegrove has shown how important itinerancy was to the Congregationalists and Baptists as well as the Methodists; Sidmouth's bill seemed to strike at one of the principal instruments of the revival. The reaction of orthodox Dissent to the bill was both to retreat into political inactivity once again and also to strengthen their long-term commitment to secure their liberties through repeal of the Test and Corporation Acts, the primary symbols of their inferior status in the state.[23]

Recently, J.C.D. Clark has brought the Test and Corporation Acts back into the mainstream of English historiography. He argues that the repeal of those measures in 1828, along with the passing of Catholic Emancipation the next year and the Reform Act in 1832, constituted a major turning point in the history of England that has been in this century interpreted too much in terms of secular politics.[24] The best account of the role of Dissent in the campaign against the Test and Corporation Acts is in Richard Davis, *Dissent in Politics*. William Smith was a Unitarian, and Davis makes it clear that Unitarians led in this struggle. Orthodox Dissent, however, joined in the campaign and supported the Unitarian

[21] "English Evangelical Dissent and the European Conflict, 1789-1815," *SCH* 20 (1983), 263-76. See also V. Kiernan, "Evangelicalism and the French Revolution," *Past and Present*, No. 1 (1952), 44-56.

[22] Ward, *Religion and Society*, 55-60; Lovegrove, *Established Church, Sectarian People*, 135-37.

[23] See Richard W. Davis, *Dissent in Politics, 1780-1830: The Political Life of William Smith, M.P.* (London, 1971).

[24] J.C.D. Clark, *English Society, 1688-1832: Ideology, Social Structure, and Political Practice During the Ancien Regime* (Cambridge, 1985). For an informative discussion of Clark's work, see Joanna Innes, "Jonathan Clark, Social History, and England's Ancien Regime," *Past and Present*, No. 115 (1987), 165-200. Innes does not agree that heterodoxy necessarily gave rise to political radicalism and she contrasts Clark's argument with that of John Seed ("Gentlemen Dissenters: The Social and Political Meanings of Rational Dissent in the 1770s and 1780s," *HJ* 8, 1985, 299-325), who sugests that changing social circumstances served as a stronger catalyst of reform than did religion. See also the very helpful "Bibliographical Appendix" in Hole, *Pulpits, Politics, and Public Order*.

leadership.[25] Bernard Lord Manning's study of the long established Dissenting political pressure group, *The Protestant Dissenting Deputies*, is still a valuable source for Nonconformist politics at this time.[26]

The tangled story of Dissenting politics in the decades of the 1830s and 1840s has yet to find its historian. For this period, and indeed for the earlier part of the century as well, the impressively well researched and clear-headed works of Elie Halévy remain an important guide. *England in 1815* (1924) contains the famous "Halévy Thesis" that assigns to the Methodist movement a key role in the prevention of revolution in England in the late eighteenth and early nineteenth centuries. The subsequent volumes treat the politics of Dissent with often surprising detail. As a general narrative they remain unchallenged. Norman Gash provides a helpful overview of Nonconformist politics in his Ford Lectures, but his account is distorted, to some extent, by a deeply conservative bias that leads him to exaggerate the radicalism introduced in the 1840s by Edward Miall and the provincial proponents of disestablishment.[27] Richard Brent has explored the relations between Nonconformists and the Whig politicians in the 1830s.[28] In the two decades after the Reform Act, Congregationalists and Baptists took over the political leadership of Nonconformity from the Unitarians. At almost the same time there emerged a struggle between the relatively cautious London-based leadership of those two denominations and a new, more radical and energetic provincial leadership that formed around the Congregationalist Edward Miall.[29] For the serious enquirer, Miall's own

[25] See Richard Davis, "The Strategy of Dissent in the Repeal Campaign, 1820-28," *JMH* 38 (1966), 374-93; and Richard Davis, "The Tories, the Whigs, and Catholic Emancipation, 1827-1829," *EHR* 97 (1982), 89-98.

[26] *The Protestant Dissenting Deputies* (Cambridge, 1952). For the origins of the pressure group, see N. C. Hunt, *Two Early Political Associations: The Quakers and the Dissenting Deputies in the Age of Sir Robert Walpole* (Oxford, 1961).

[27] *Reaction and Reconstruction in English Politics, 1832-1852* (Oxford, 1965).

[28] *Liberal Anglican Politics: Whiggery, Religion, and Reform, 1830-1841* (Oxford, 1987). For a critical comment on Brent's work, set in the context of a spate of recent books on the Whigs, see Richard Davis, "The Whigs and Religious Issues, 1830-5," *Religion and Irreligion in Victorian Society: Essays in Honour of R. K. Webb* (London, 1992), 29-50.

[29] There is no published, modern, full-length study of Miall. The biography by his son, Arthur Miall, *Life of Edward Miall* (London, 1884), is still useful, but it is tinged with hagiography and limited by Victorian reticence. J. S. Newton's University of Durham doctoral thesis, "The Political Career of Edward Miall, Editor of the *Nonconformist* and Founder of the Liberation Society" (1975), is as yet unpublished. By far the best published work on Miall is the chapter "Pacemaker or Crotcheteer?—The Impact of a Strolling Agitator: A Study of

works are the richest source for his ideas and opinions.[30] The *Nonconformist*, the newspaper Miall edited from its foundation in 1840 until 1874, is the best source of all.

Miall and the Baptist leader F. A. Cox were key figures in the establishment of the Liberation Society (called the Anti-State-Church Association when it was created in 1844, and renamed in 1853.) From the middle of the century until near its end, the Liberation Society, replacing the Dissenting Deputies in that role, took over the political leadership of Nonconformity at the national level. Disestablishment and disendowment of the Church of England remained the ultimate goal of the Liberation Society throughout the century.[31] The history of the established Presbyterian Church in Scotland is very different from that of the Established Church in England, but there are several points of close connection. The most important of these is the Great Disruption of 1843. This profound schism in the Church of Scotland helped to encourage English Nonconformists to escalate their attack on the Church of England.[32]

Edward Miall," in Clyde Binfield's *So Down to Prayers: Studies in English Nonconformity, 1780-1920* (London, 1977).

[30] *Religious Equality*, Manchester Nonconformist Association (London, 1873); *The British Churches in Relation to the British People* (London, 1849); *The Nonconformist's Sketch-Book: A Series of Views of a State-Church and Its Attendant Evils* (London, 1845); *The "Liberation Society" and Church Property: Two Lectures* (London, 1860); *What Is the Separation of Church and State?*, in British Anti-State-Church Association Tracts, No. 2 (1846).

[31] There is no sustained study of the Liberation Society in print. It is described well by David M. Thompson, "The Liberation Society, 1844-1868," *Pressure from Without in Early Victorian England*, ed. by Patricial Hollis (London, 1974), 210-238. By far the most thorough study remains A. H. Welch, "John Carvell Williams: The Nonconformist Watchdog" (Ph.D. thesis, University of Kansas, 1968). W.H.Mackintosh, *Disestablishment and Liberation: The Movement for the Separation of the Anglican Church from State Control* (London, 1972), surveys the entire campaign, but his work must be used with caution and it does not adequately place the disestablishment movement in context. For the high-water mark of the disestablishment campaign, see S. M. Ingham, "The Disestablishment Movement in England, 1868-74," *Journal of Religious History* 3 (1964), 38-60; and for the subsequent period, Noel J. Richards, "Disestablishment of the Anglican Church in England in the Late Nineteenth Century: Reasons for Failure," *Journal of Church and State* 12 (1970), 193-211.

[32] There is a voluminous literature on the Great Disruption of 1843. Stewart J. Brown, "Martyrdom in Early Victorian Scotland: Disruption Fathers and the Making of the Free Church," *SCH* 30 (1993), 319-32. See also *Scotland in the Age of the Disruption*, ed. by S. J. Brown and M. Fry (Edinburgh, 1993); R. Buchanan, *The Ten Years' Conflict*, 2 vols. (Glasgow, 1849); *Dictionary of Scottish*

Mid-Victorian Nonconformists, however, both those inside and those outside the Liberation Society, devoted most of their political energy to more practical goals. Those practical political issues are most comprehensively surveyed in authoritative works by G.I.T. Machin.[33] Chief among those practical issues, at least in terms of systematic, organized, sustained effort, was the successful campaign, carried on over three decades, to abolish compulsory church rates. These were rates levied at the parish level of government for the maintenance and repair of the physical structure of the local Anglican church building. Church rates applied to all residents of the parish, whether or not they were Nonconformists, whether or not they wished to support the Established Church. The best study of the church rate controversy is Jacob Ellens's meticulously detailed and stimulating book.[34]

While church rates constituted the most sustained Nonconformist political issue after 1832, state-supported primary education was the most explosive.[35] Nonconformity reacted with surprising vigor against the attempt to increase the educational authority and role of the established clergy in Sir James Graham's Factory Bill of 1843.[36] Passions aroused by that bill led to the foundation of the Anti-State-Church Association in the

Church History and Theology, ed. by Nigel M. de S. Cameron et al. (Edinburgh, 1993); D. Chalmers, "The Church of Scotland's Parochial Extension Scheme and the Scottish Disruption," *Journal of Church and State* 16 (1974), 263-86; A. L. Drummond and J. Bulloch, *The Scottish Church, 1688-1843* (Edinburgh, 1973); *The Church in Victorian Scotland, 1843-1874* (Edinburgh, 1975); G. D. Henderson, *Heritage—A Study of the Disruption* (Edinburgh, 1943); J. G. Kellas, "The Liberal Party and the Scottish Church Disestablishment Crisis," *EHR* 79 (1964), 31-46; G.I.T. Machin, "The Disruption and British Politics, 1834-43," *Scottish Historical Review* 51 (1972), 20-51. P.M.H. Bell's *Disestablishment in Ireland and Wales* (London, 1969) is a first-class treatment of the successful attacks on the Celtic outworks of the Establishment.

[33] *Politics and the Churches in Great Britain, 1832-1868* (Oxford, 1977), and *Politics and the Churches in Great Britain, 1869-1921* (Oxford, 1987). See also Frank Salter, *Dissenters and Public Affairs in Mid-Victorian England* (London, 1967).

[34] *Religious Routes to Gladstonian Liberalism: The Church Rate Conflict in England and Wales, 1832-1868* (University Park, Penna., 1994). Also see Olive Anderson, "Gladstone's Abolition of Compulsory Church Rates: A Minor Myth and its Historiographical Career," *JEH* 25 (1974), 185-98.

[35] The best comprehensive introduction to the vexed education question is J. Murphy, *Church, State, and Schools in Britain, 1800-1970* (London, 1971).

[36] See J. T. Ward and J. H. Treble, "Religion and Education in 1843: Reaction to the 'Factory Education Bill,'" *JEH* 20 (1969), 79-110; and D. G. Paz, *The Politics of Working-Class Education in Britain, 1830-1850* (Manchester, 1980).

following year. The bill also encouraged the younger Edward Baines, proprietor and editor of the *Leeds Mercury*, a great provincial newspaper, to enter national politics and devote a great deal of his time to promoting educational voluntaryism. Edward Baines was one of the great men among the Victorian Congregationalists. He is an excellent example of a rather cautious Whig who became, in the 1840s, a progressive Liberal.[37] Baines helped make the *Leeds Mercury* into one of the important props of the Liberal Party.[38] Baines's life of his father, *The Life of Edward Baines* (London, 1851), is one of the classics of Nonconformist biography. After 1843, the religious question in education experienced major eruptions again with the Minutes of the Committee of Council on Education in 1846, with Forster's landmark Education Act of 1870, and with the Education Act of 1902.[39] In every case, Nonconformists were reacting against what they perceived as an unfair grant of increased privilege by the state to the Established Church. Each of these crisis points was a major event in the political history of Victorian Nonconformity.

Nonconformists had traditionally looked to the Whigs as more friendly to their political aspirations than the Tories. In the third quarter of the nineteenth century, Nonconformity came to play a significant role as part of the loose alliance of interest groups that helped constitute the Liberal Party. J. R. Vincent devotes two chapters of his important study, *The Formation of the Liberal Party*, to supporting the argument that Nonconformity made up one of the most important elements among the Liberal electorate. Fundamental to Nonconformist political influence was its power, or potential power, at the polls. "What it brought to Liberalism," Vincent wrote of Dissent, "was not conscience, which the party was already troubled with, but votes."[40] The number of Nonconformists, growing rapidly until the middle of the century and more slowly thereafter, was the foundation fact of Nonconformist politics. At the beginning of the

[37] Clyde Binfield has a good chapter on him and his family, "Self-Harnessed to the Car of Progress. Baines of Leeds and East Parade: A Church and a Dynasty," in *So Down to Prayers*, 54-100. Derek Fraser, "Edward Baines," *Pressure from Without*, ed. Hollis, 183-209, is excellent and informative but all too brief. James Lowerson, "The Political Career of Sir Edward Baines, 1800-1890" (M.A. thesis, University of Leeds, 1965), remains unpublished.

[38] For this see Donald Read, *Press and People, 1790-1850: Opinion in Three English Cities* (London, 1961); and more directly to the point, J. R. Vincent, *The Formation of the Liberal Party* (London, 1967).

[39] For the 1870 act and subsequent legislation, see Machin, *Politics and the Churches, 1869-1921*, 31-40, 260-73. D. W. Bebbington's chapter, "The Education of the People," in *Nonconformist Conscience*, 127-52, also provides a useful analysis of events.

[40] *Formation of the Liberal Party*, 76.

century, Anglicans in England outnumbered Nonconformists by about three to one. Nonconformity, growing most rapidly in those districts in which the Church of England was weakest, that is, the industrial areas of the North and Midlands, surpassed the Established Church in numbers by 1840 and maintained a small, steady superiority until the decade of the 1890s.

Dissent grew at a rate far outstripping the growth of the population as a whole. While the population of England doubled between 1801 and 1851, Nonconformity increased by a factor of five. The Church of England, in the first half of the century, fell slightly behind the general population growth. During this period of explosive growth for all the Evangelical denominations, Dissent increased its strength everywhere in England, in the countryside as well as the towns.[41] Even in Herefordshire, the county in which Nonconformity had the weakest showing in the Religious Census of 1851, Dissent accounted for 28 percent of the available sittings. In the industrial and seaport towns, however, Nonconformity showed its greatest and politically most significant strength. Patterns of religious affiliation are complex and not yet thoroughly understood, but a few certain general observations can be made on the data gathered in the Religious Census of 1851.[42] The census results show Nonconformity with a preponderance over the Church of England in almost every one of the seventy-three towns with a population over 20,000 for which detailed returns were published. In the industrial districts, in the East Midlands and Yorkshire especially, that preponderance was sometimes dramatic. Bradford Dissenters outnumbered Anglicans on Census Sunday by three to one and in Nottingham by two to one. The Nonconformist superiority in Leeds, 59 percent as against the Anglican 35 percent, or Manchester, 42 percent against 34 percent, was closer to the provincial urban norm.

Was Nonconformist strength tantamount to Liberal strength? Did Nonconformist chapel-goers, at the time of the Religious Census, constitute a solid block of support for the Liberal Party? Beyond question, their pastors were unshakeable in their Liberalism. In his study of Victorian pollbooks, John Vincent discovered that "no other occupation was so

---

[41] Currie, Gilbert, and Horsley, *Churches and Churchgoers*, is the fullest and most authoritative treatment of patterns of religious affiliation in modern England. Also see Alan M. Everitt, *The Pattern of Rural Dissent: The Nineteenth Century* (Leicester, 1972).

[42] The religious census was published in *Parliamentary Papers*, 1852-53, 89. For critical analysis of the religious census, see K. S. Inglis, "Patterns of Religious Worship in 1851," *JEH* 11 (1960), 74-86; D. M. Thompson, "The 1851 Religious Census: Problems and Possibilities," *Victorian Studies* 11 (1967), 87-97; and W.S.F. Pickering, "The 1851 Religious Census—A Useless Experiment?," *British Journal of Sociology* 18 (1967), 382-407.

partisan, so militant, so unfloating as the Dissenting ministers."[43] Vincent's observation that Methodist ministers, including Wesleyans, were as reliably Liberal as their Baptist or Congregational confrères, has been re-affirmed in several recent local studies.[44] The Toryism associated with Wesleyan Methodism in the age of Jabez Bunting seems to have been an aspiration of Wesleyan national leadership rather than a grassroots reality. While it cannot be demonstrated, because pollbooks do not contain direct information on religious affiliation, it seems highly likely that most chapel people, like their pastors, supported the Liberals. The historic tradition of the Whigs as the party of civil and religious liberty, and what Vincent calls the "rigid difference of political culture" that separated church and chapel from early in the nineteenth century, made highly unlikely the possibility that Nonconformists of any denomination would, in any locality, give general support to the Tories.[45] Edward Miall felt throughout his career that the gratitude Dissenters owed Lord John Russell for his part in the repeal of the Test and Corporation Acts in 1828 imposed upon them a perpetual obligation that could not be negated by Russell's unsympathetic Erastianism. Both their vision of history and their consideration of present political advantage helped to bind Nonconformists to the emerging Liberal Party.

Leaders of the Liberal Party appealed to Nonconformist voters by showing sympathy for Dissenting "grievances" and by appealing to what was perceived as their highly developed moral sense. Gladstone's cultivation of Nonconformity has been well documented.[46] Nonconformity and reactions to Nonconformist political objectives play a major part in J. P. Parry's detailed and persuasive analysis.[47] At the national level, however, there is very little evidence of Nonconformist influence on policy outside the important but progressively circumscribed area of religious issues.[48]

[43] J. R. Vincent, *Pollbooks: How Victorians Voted* (Cambridge, 1967), 18.

[44] Vincent, *Pollbooks*, 68-70; John Garrard, *Leadership and Power in Victorian Industrial Towns, 1830-1880* (Manchester, 1983); Gilbert, *Religion and Society in Industrial England*; Bebbington, *Nonconformist Conscience*.

[45] Vincent, *Pollbooks*, 18. *Eclectic Review* (1844),

344-345: "To the Whigs, as a party, the dissenters of England owe much. Whatever we have wrung from the intolerance and bigotry arrayed against us, has been by their help."

[46] G.I.T. Machin, "Gladstone and Nonconformity in the 1860s: The Formation of an Alliance," *HJ* 17 (1974), 347-64; David Bebbington, "Gladstone and the Nonconformists: A Religious Affinity in Politics," *SCH* 12 (1975), 369-82.

[47] *Democracy and Religion: Gladstone and the Liberal Party, 1867-1875* (Cambridge, 1986).

[48] R. T. Shannon, in *Gladstone and the Bulgarian Agitation, 1876* (London, 1963), provides a rare discussion of Nonconformists engaged in a national poli-

Nonconformists tended to distrust state intervention, suspecting that the Established Church would try to exploit any extension of state activity to its own privileged advantage.[49] The record of state support for primary education, particularly since the fiasco of the education clauses of Sir James Graham's Factory Bill in 1843, served as a warning that helped drive Nonconformists into voluntaryism. Nevertheless, there were some areas in which Nonconformists, after the middle of the century, actively supported the powers of the regulatory state in an effort to impose their own moral values on the rest of society. Legal restriction of activities permitted on Sunday was one of these areas. Some Nonconformists campaigned to prevent postal deliveries on Sunday, and to prevent the opening of the British Museum on Sunday or band concerts in the parks.[50] Anglicans loomed large among the Sabbatarians. The Lord's Day Observance Society was controlled by Evangelical clergy of the Church of England. Some free-trading Nonconformists, Edward Miall for example, on principle disapproved of using the law to enforce Sunday as a day for religion and rest. But Miall was among the minority. Edward Baines, one of the most dedicated of Nonconformist voluntaryists, was more typical of the majority. He was a major proponent of using the power of the state to protect his vision of the appropriate Sabbath.[51] By the end of the 1850s, the Sabbatarians had lost most of their battles.

tical issue that did not directly affect their own interests. On this issue see also H.C.G. Matthew, "Gladstone, Vaticanism, and the Question of the East," *SCH* 15 (1978), 417-42. On Gladstone and religion generally, see David Bebbington, *William Ewart Gladstone: Faith and Politics in Victorian Britain* (Grand Rapids, Mich., 1993). Bebbington's book contains a very useful annotated bibliography.

[49] Boyd Hilton's tour de force, *The Age of Atonement: The Influence of Evangelicalism on Social and Economic Thought, 1785-1865* (Oxford, 1988), is a provocative exploration of the impact of the Evangelical frame of mind on prevailing economic and social theory. It deals with Evangelicals generally and not Nonconformists in particular. *9t omits McHdiu~* .

[50] See Brian Harrison, "Religion and Recreation in Nineteenth-Century England," *Past and Present*, No. 38 (1967), 98-125, and "The Sunday Trading Riots of 1855," *HJ* 8 (1965), 219-45. See also G. M. Ellis, "The Evangelicals and the Sunday Question, 1830-1860: Organized Sabbatarianism as an Aspect of the Evangelical Movement" (Ph.D. thesis, Harvard University, 1951); E. W. Bristow, *Vice and Vigilance: Purity Movements in Britain since 1700* (Dublin, 1977); J. Wigley, *The Rise and Fall of the Victorian Sunday* (Manchester, 1980).

[51] See his defense of Sabbatarianism in *On the Performance of Military Bands in the Parks on Sundays* (London, 1856) and *A Letter to the Rt. Hon. Lord Palmerston: On the Attempts Making in Parliament to Secularize the Sabbath* (London, 1856).

Temperance was a much more important political issue than Sabbatarianism. Over the course of the second half of the century, the temperance movement in England was dominated by Nonconformists and represented the most persistent and politically successful effort to impose a neo-Puritan code of behavior through the law.[52] The United Kingdom Alliance, founded in Manchester in 1853 and led by Nonconformists, became the leading temperance organization and one of the best-funded and most effective Victorian political pressure groups.[53] The temperance advocates pressed for local option and for tighter restriction and regulation of public houses. They succeeded, to a degree, in achieving an increased level of regulation of the drink trade, and they brought the temperance issue into the mainstream of politics and pressed the Liberal Party to take up the cause.[54] Temperance served as the central program for the moral reformers in the second half of the century, and it encouraged a number of spin-off groups with their own interests.[55] Temperance advocates and other supporters of moral purity were sometimes in sharp conflict with each other and with other groups within the Liberal Party. For a snapshot of

[52] The standard and still the best study of the temperance movement is Brian Harrison, *Drink and the Victorians: The Temperance Question in England, 1815-1872* (London, 1971). The movement in the last third of the century is treated in Lilian Lewis Shiman, *Crusade Against Drink in Victorian England* (New York, 1988).

[53] The authoritative study is A. E. Dingle, *The Campaign for Prohibition in Victorian England: The United Kingdom Alliance, 1872-1895* (London, 1980). See his "The Agitation for Prohibition in England," (Ph.D. thesis, Monash University, 1974), for detailed biographies of Alliance personnel. The Nonconformist dominance in the temperance is underscored as well in Brian Harrison, "British Prohibitionists, 1853-1872: A Biographical Analysis," *International Review of Social History* 15 (1970), 375-467.

[54] See D. A. Hamer, *The Politics of Electoral Pressure: A Study in the History of Victorian Reform Agitations* (Hassocks, 1977); H. J. Hanham, *Elections and Party Management: Politics in the Time of Disraeli and Gladstone* (London, 1959); David M. Fahey, "The Politics of Drink: Pressure Groups and the British Liberal Party, 1883-1908," *Social Science* (1979), 76-85; and David M. Fahey, "Temperance and the Liberal Party—Lord Peel's Report, 1899," *JBS* 10 (1971), 132-59. For a view from the other side, see David W. Gutzke, *Protecting the Pub: Brewers and Publicans against Temperance* (London, 1989).

[55] For a discussion of some of these groups, see Judith Walkowitz, *Prostitution and Victorian Society* (Cambridge, 1980); Clyde Binfield, *George Williams and the YMCA: A Study in Victorian Social Attitudes* (London, 1973); and Brian Harrison, "Philanthropy and the Victorians," *Victorian Studies* 9 (1966), 353-74.

these conflicts, see Michael Hurst's waspish article, "Liberal versus Liberal."[56]

On the whole, Nonconformity was most successful in national politics, not in the area of moral reform, but when they attacked the privileges, old or new, of the Established Church, especially those privileges that could be construed as directly discriminating against Dissent. These attacks seemed to swim with the Liberal tide and to be in harmony with the Liberal ideals of fairness and individuality. These issues, detailed in G.I.T. Machin's two volumes on *Politics and the Churches* and discussed in B. L. Manning's *Protestant Dissenting Deputies*, were rooted in the emergence of religious pluralism and rested, on the Nonconformist side, on the principle that all citizens, no matter what their religion, should have equal civil rights.[57] The passage of the Burials Laws Amendment Act in 1880 did not end Anglican privilege in English society by any means, but it did effectively settle the last of the Nonconformists' high-profile "grievances" that had dominated their drive for civil equality over the previous fifty years. Discrimination that remained was more social than legal.

Many Evangelical Nonconformists, while foes of religious discrimination and advocates of toleration where Protestants were concerned, did not hesitate to take up an entirely different posture for Roman Catholics. Distrust, even hatred, of papists and the papacy was one of the elements that went into creating the British national identity. This is one of the themes of Linda Colley's acclaimed *Britons: Forging the Nation, 1707-1837* (New Haven, 1992). Britons were free; Roman Catholics were seen as tyrannized. British Catholics were suspected as agents of a foreign power. In the nineteenth century, anti-Catholicism was closely bound up with the Irish question, as well as with the tendency of Protestant Britons of all political parties and all denominations to identify their anti-Catholic venom with a self-satisfied celebration of British liberty. There were, of course, many exceptions to this generalization. The enlightened leadership of Nonconformity was able, in 1829, to swing official Dissenting opinion towards support for Catholic Emancipation.[58] Later on, the London-based leadership of the Liberation Society, with clear-headed logical consistency, maintained staunch support for the principles and practice of religious to-

[56] "Liberal versus Liberal: The General Election of 1874 in Bradford and Sheffield," *HJ* 15 (1972), 669-713.

[57] For the coming of religious pluralism, see Olive Brose, *Church and Parliament: The Reshaping of the Church of England, 1828-1860* (Stanford, 1959); and for a careful discussion of the ideas underlying the early nineteenth-century campaigns against religious discrimination, see Ursula Henriques, *Religious Toleration in England, 1787-1833* (Toronto, 1961).

[58] G.I.T. Machin, *The Catholic Question in English Politics, 1820 to 1830* (Oxford, 1964).

leration for Roman Catholics as well as for Protestant Dissenters. Edward Miall, even in the heat of Protestant outrage against the Papal Aggression of 1850, remained consistently a spokesman for liberty. There is a growing body of excellent work on the history of British anti-Catholicism in the nineteenth century, encouraged, probably, by current concerns for civil liberties, as well as by increasing interest in the newly emphasized illiberalities of Victorian society.[59] Anti-Catholicism as a part of the dark side of Victorian Nonconformity is, however, by no means a new discovery. In 1869, in *Culture and Anarchy*, Matthew Arnold, no admirer of the provincial Nonconformists, whose schools it was his professional duty to inspect, singled out their ugly anti-Catholicism as one of the evidences that they lacked the sweetness and light of the culture he was trying to promote.

At the level of those newly large provincial towns of the Midlands and the North, Nonconformists were even more significant politically than they were in Parliament in Westminster. This was made clear years ago by A. Temple Patterson[60] and Conrad Gill and Asa Briggs.[61] In the provincial towns, especially after the Municipal Reform Act of 1835, the battle for local power was frequently defined as a battle between Churchmen and Nonconformists. In the towns, Tory or Whig, Conservative or Liberal, often implied Churchman or Nonconformist. In some towns—Rochdale is an example—all the Liberals were Dissenters, and all the Tories were Churchmen.[62] While the basic pattern seems unassailable, it would be a mistake to think that it could be applied as a formula to explain the politics of any particular town. There was a considerable variety in social structure, class relations, and religious patterns among Victorian industrial cities.[63] Paul Philips, in his study of the role of religious conflict in the

[59] See D. G. Paz, *Popular Anti-Catholicism in Mid-Victorian England* (Stanford, 1992); John Wolffe, *The Protestant Crusade in Great Britain, 1829-1860* (Oxford, 1991); E. R. Norman, *Anti-Catholicism in Victorian England* (London, 1968); W. L. Arnstein, *Protestant versus Catholic in Mid-Victorian England: Mr. Newdegate and the Nuns* (Columbia, Mo., 1982); Sheridan Gilley, "English Attitudes to the Irish in England, 1780-1900," *Immigrants and Minorities in British Society*, ed. by C. Holmes (London, 1978), 81-110; Walter Ralls, "The Papal Aggression of 1850: A Study in Victorian Anti-Catholicism," *CH* 43 (1974), 242-56. See also Desmond Bowen, *The Protestant Crusade in Ireland, 1800-70: A Study of Protestant-Catholic Relations between the Act of Union and Disestablishment* (Dublin, 1978).

[60] *Radical Leicester: A History of Leicester, 1780-1850* (Leicester, 1954).

[61] *History of Birmingham*, 2 vols. (London, 1952).

[62] John Gerrard, *Leadership and Power in Victorian Industrial Towns, 1830-1880* (Manchester, 1983), 111.

[63] Richard Dennis, *English Industrial Cities of the Nineteenth Century: A Social Geography* (Cambridge, 1984), sums up recent work.

politics of five early Victorian cotton towns, shows both the importance of local diversity and the existence of a clear pattern in which the Church is generally on the Conservative side and Nonconformity is on the Liberal. Phillips argues that religious conflict cut across class lines and tended to dampen the political impact of economic conflict. In his impressive work, R. J. Morris supports Phillips's point of view and presents sectarian division as a major barrier to class formation.[64] No recent work on the politics of Victorian towns disputes the fundamental importance of religious sectarianism, and none suggests that sectarianism is understandable outside the complex local context.[65]

Harold Perkin's observations about the middle-class status of Nonconformity represent the received wisdom.[66] The widely accepted view is that Congregationalists were predominantly of the middle class and that Baptists were also, but less wealthy and with more working-class congregations. This impression accords with the comments of contemporaries. Baptist and Congregationalist leaders made a point of identifying their denominations with the "intelligent" and "wealthy" middle classes. Algernon Wells, the secretary of the Congregational Union, made in 1848 a lengthy statement about the "special mission" of his denomination to the "middle classes." The Baptist C. H. Spurgeon emphasized his middle-class position.[67] These references, however accurate in a general sort of way, are

[64] Paul Phillips, *The Sectarian Spirit: Sectarianism, Society, and Politics in Victorian Cotton Towns* (Toronto, 1982); R. J. Morris, *Class, Sect, and Party: The Making of the British Middle Class, Leeds, 1820-1850* (Manchester, 1990).

[65] See E. P. Hennock, *Fit and Proper Persons: Ideal and Reality in Nineteenth-Century Urban Government* (London, 1973); Neville Kirk, *The Growth of Working-Class Reformism in Mid-Victorian England* (Urbana, Ill., 1985); P. J. Waller, *Democracy and Sectarianism: A Political and Social History of Liverpool, 1868-1939* (Liverpool, 1981); Derek Fraser, *Urban Politics in Victorian England* (Leicester, 1976); *A History of Modern Leeds*, ed. by Derek Fraser (Manchester, 1980); Dennis Smith, *Conflict and Compromise: Class Formation in English Society, 1830-1914: A Comparative Study of Birmingham and Sheffield* (London, 1982); Stephen Yeo, *Religion and Voluntary Organizations in Crisis* (London, 1976); Neil Collins, *Politics and Elections in Nineteenth-Century Liverpool* (Aldershot, Hants, 1994); John A. Gerrard, *Leaders and Politics in Nineteenth-Century Salford: A Historical Analysis of Urban Political Power* (Salford, 1977); Frank Neal, *Sectarian Violence: The Liverpool Experience, 1819-1914: An Aspect of Anglo-Irish History* (New York, 1988); Alan J. Kidd and K. W. Roberts, *City, Class, and Culture: Studies of Social Policy and Cultural Production in Victorian Manchester* (Manchester, 1985).

[66] *The Origins of Modern English Society, 1780-1880* (London, 1969).

[67] See Edward Miall, *The British Churches in Relation to the British People* (London, 1849); A. Wells, "Thoughts on the Need for Increased Efforts to Pro-

so vague that they do not carry precise meaning. As R. J. Morris points out, "middle class," then and now, is a category so broad that it includes a wide array of occupations, incomes, and levels of prestige and power.[68] Congregationalists and Baptists did not draw on the landed aristocracy. Indeed, they thought of themselves as in opposition to the oppressive privileges and the arrogant, sometimes hedonistic style of life enjoyed by that group. While both denominations contained large numbers of men and women from the working classes, the leading families in most congregations and the national denominational leaders, clerical and lay, were of the middle class. Did this middle class, which stretched from small shopkeeper to wealthy merchant or professional man, possess a sufficiently common set of ideals to give significance to the term?[69] That is a difficult question, and one that probably cannot be answered with assurance until the politics and social composition of a number of Baptist and Congregational chapels have been studied with some precision.

Leonore Davidoff and Catherine Hall, like Perkin, take the view that Evangelicalism, especially Evangelical Nonconformity, played an important role in making the middle class.[70] But their work is diminished by a host of inaccuracies, and they pay so little heed to distinctions among denominations or among different status ranks within the middle class that one must use their work with caution. Their discussion of middle-class prescriptive literature on appropriate family behavior is, nonetheless, an important contribution. Much of this literature was written by Evangelical ministers, many of them Baptists and Congregationalists. This aspect of Nonconformist ministerial writing in England has received almost no attention from historians. Davidoff and Hall have pointed the way towards valuable work for the future.

Little has been written about the manners and morals of the Evangelical Nonconformists, especially for the first half of the nineteenth century. Some of the work that has been done on Anglican Evangelicals must

mote the Religious Welfare of the Working Classes in England," *Congregational Year Book* (1848); R. J. Helmstadter, "Spurgeon and Outcast London," *The View from the Pulpit: Victorian Ministers and Society*, ed. by P. T. Phillips (Toronto, 1978), 161-85.

[68] *Class, Sect, and Party*, 11-13.

[69] Harold Perkin certainly thinks so. He argues in *The Origins of Modern English Society* that Nonconformity was a significant factor in nineteenth-century class formation and that the Victorian middle class, broadly defined, shared an identifiable outlook on life.

[70] *Family Fortunes: Men and Women of the English Middle Class, 1780-1850* (London, 1987).

surely apply to the Nonconformists as well.[71] Even for the days of pan-E-vangelical cooperation, however, it is not safe to assume, as do Davidoff and Hall, that there was no significant difference between the culture of Evangelical Churchmen and Evangelical Nonconformists. The social insecurity, the sense of being a people set apart, that even wealthy Nonconformists lived with had no counterpart in leafy, expensive, and Anglican Clapham.[72]

Clyde Binfield has attempted to rescue Nonconformist culture from the attack launched by Matthew Arnold in *Culture and Anarchy*. Much of Binfield's *So Down to Prayers* is couched within this frame, especially his interesting essay on Nonconformist architecture.[73] Another helpful work is James Munson's *The Nonconformists: In Search of a Lost Culture* (London, 1991). Kenneth Young, writing with affection and verve, captures some of the energy of chapel life in *Chapel: The Joyous Days and Prayerful Nights of the Nonconformists in Their Heyday, Circa 1850-1950* (London, 1972). Hardly a work of scholarship, Young's book is very well illustrated and gives some sense of the feel of Victorian Nonconformist life. The much more scholarly and serious collections of documents edited by David M. Thompson[74] and J.H.Y. Briggs and Ian Sellers[75] offer a rich variety of sources on Nonconformist life. For a very good description of what one might call the "church life," as distinct from theology, of the Baptists and Congregationalists, see Horton Davies, *Worship and Theology in England: From Newman to Martineau, 1850-1900* (Princeton, 1962).

Biography is one of the very rich sources for a wide range of aspects of Nonconformist life. Important ministers especially, but many prominent laymen as well, often received biographies in the years following their

[71] See Ford K. Brown, *Fathers of the Victorians: The Age of Wilberforce* (Cambridge, 1961); Standish Meacham, *Henry Thornton of Clapham* (London, 1964); E. M. Forster, *Marianne Thornton: A Domestic Biography* (London, 1956); Ian Bradley, *The Call to Seriousness: The Evangelical Impact on the Victorians* (London, 1976); M.J. Quinlan, *Victorian Prelude: A History of English Manners, 1700-1830* (London, 1941; repr. 1965). Doreen Rosman, in her excellent book, *Evangelicals and Culture* (London, 1984), concentrates on Anglicans but includes much reference to Nonconformists. She deals with family life, fashion, and theology, as well as with music, reading, and painting.

[72] For the sense of insecurity, see R. J. Helmstadter, "The Reverend Andrew Reed (1787-1862): Evangelical Pastor as Entrepreneur," *Religion and Irreligion in Victorian Society*, 7-28.

[73] "The Shores of Philistia: A Perspective of Late Victorian Nonconformity," *So Down to Prayers*, 162-185. See also Binfield's "English Free Churchmen and a National Style," *SCH* 18 (1982), 519-33.

[74] *Nonconformity in the Nineteenth Century* (London, 1972).

[75] *Victorian Nonconformity* (London, 1973).

deaths, and while these books are not works of scholarship, they often contain useful information and a sense of the character and vitality of Nonconformist culture that is not available anywhere else. Many significant Congregational figures were subjects of biographies.[76] Among Baptists, Charles Haddon Spurgeon has attracted the most attention,[77] but others have had their chroniclers as well.[78] There are few studies of Presbyterian figures.[79] Some of these biographies are first-class examples of the

[76] E. R. Conder, *Josiah Conder: A Memoir* (London, 1857); W. S. Fowler, *A Study in Radicalism and Dissent: The Life and Times of Henry Joseph Wilson* (London, 1961); Edwin P. Hood, *Thomas Binney: His Mind, Life, and Opinions* (London, 1874); *A Memorial of the Late Rev. Thomas Binney*, ed. by John Stoughton (London, 1874); J. Kenyon, "R. W. Dale and Christian Worldliness," *View from the Pulpit*, 187-207; C. S. Miall, *Henry Richard, M.P.* (London, 1889); *Alexander Raleigh: Records of His Life*, ed. by M. Raleigh (Edinburgh, 1881); A. Peel and J.A.R. Marriott, *Robert Forman Horton* (London, 1937); Keith Robbins, "The Spiritual Pilgrimage of the Rev. R. J. Campbell," *JEH* 30 (1979), 261-76; W. B. Selbie, *The Life of Charles Silvester Horne* (London, 1920); J. L. Paton, *John Brown Paton: A Biography* (London, 1914); R. W. Dale, *Life and Letters of John Angell James* (London, 1862).

[77] Ernest W. Bacon, *Spurgeon: Heir of the Puritans* (London, 1967); John C. Carlile, *C. H. Spurgeon: An Interpretive Biography* (London, 1933); W. Y. Fullerton, *Charles Haddon Spurgeon: A Biography* (London, 1920); P. S. Kruppa, *Charles Haddon Spurgeon: A Preacher's Progress* (New York, 1982); I. Murray, *The Forgotten Spurgeon* (London, 1966); G. Holden Pike, *The Life and Work of Charles Haddon Spurgeon*, 3 vols. (London, 1892).

[78] E.T. McLaren, *Dr. McLaren of Manchester, A Sketch* (London, 1911), and D. Williamson, *Life of Dr. Alexander McLaren . . . With a Chapter by Rev. J. H. Shakespeare* (London, 1910); James Marchant, *Dr. John Clifford, C.H.: Life, Letters, and Reminiscenses* (London, 1924); D. Thompson, "John Clifford's Social Gospel," *Baptist Quarterly* 31 (1986), 199-217; W. R. Nicoll, *Princes of the Church* (London, 1921); J. H. Shakespeare, *Baptist and Congregational Pioneers* (London, 1906); D. W. Bebbington, "The Life of Baptist Noel: Its Setting and Significance," *Baptist Quarterly* 24 (1972), 389-411; F. W. Butt-Thompson, "William Vidler, Baptist and Universalist," *Transactions of the Baptist Historical Society* 1 (1908-9), 42-55.

[79] T. H. Darlow, *William Robertson Nicoll: Life and Letters* (London, 1925); G. W. Lawrence, "William Robertson Nicoll, 1851-1923, and Religious Journalism in the Nineteenth Century" (Ph.D.thesis, University of Edinburgh, 1954); Jane T. Stoddart, *William Robertson Nicoll, Ll.D., Editor and Preacher* (London, 1903); R. Buick Knox, "Dr. John Cuming and Crown Court Church, London," *Records of the Scottish Church History Society* 22 (1986), 57-84, and "James Hamilton and English Presbyterianism," *Journal of the United Reformed Church Historical Society* 9 (1982), 286-307.

type and a joy to read. A.W.W. Dale's marvellous study of his father, *Life of R. W. Dale of Birmingham* (London, 1898), is a case in point. Dale was arguably the most influential Congregationalist in the second half of the nineteenth century. The biography by his son is a minor classic. Most of the nineteenth- and early twentieth-century biographies are less impressive, but they are worth consulting, for they constitute a major part of the published record of Victorian Nonconformity.

A few good nineteenth-century novels re-create aspects of Nonconformity in ways that scholarship does not. Mark Rutherford (the pen name of William Hale White), *The Revolution in Tanner's Lane*,[80] is *the* classic Nonconformist novel. Hale White had once been a candidate for the Congregationalist ministry; he wrote about Nonconformity with the authority of an insider. Mrs. Margaret Oliphant's *Salem Chapel* (1863) is written by an outsider and reveals more about the snobbery towards Nonconformity than it does about Dissenting life itself. George Eliot's sympathetic portrait of the Dissenting minister Rufus Lyon in *Felix Holt* (1866) is probably the best treatment of a Nonconformist in mainstream literature.[81] In addition to the novels, W. Haslam Mills, *Grey Pastures* (London, 1924), a nostalgic memory of provincial Congregationalism in the 1880s, is well worth reading.

It was stated earlier that the reorganization of the Baptist Union and the formation of the Congregational Union in the early 1830s were responses to the Evangelical Revival as well as to the exigencies of contemporary politics. The creation of central denominational administrative structures was a result of the revival. Domestic and foreign missions, itinerancy, the distribution of Bibles and religious tracts, and other forms of the great drive to convert the world as soon as possible required planning and organization. This was the source of the initial impulse towards unions, first at the regional level and then at the national.[82]

However, there were two great obstacles to central organization, both doctrinal.

The Baptists and the Congregationalists were traditionally committed to an ecclesiastical polity of congregational independence. The independ-

---

[80] London, 1887, and much reprinted.

[81] Valentine Cunningham's well-informed and solidly conceived study, *Everywhere Spoken Against: Dissent in the Victorian Novel* (Oxford, 1975), is an important contribution to the meagre body of work on Nonconformist culture. See also Robert Lee Wolff, *Nineteenth-Century Fiction: A Bibliographical Catalogue Based on the Collection . . . Formed by Robert Lee Wolff* (New York, 1981), for a comprehensive general treatment of Victorian religious novels; and Donald Davie, *A Gathered Church: The Literature of the English Dissention Interest, 1700-1930* (London, 1978).

[82] See Albert Peel, *These Hundred Years*, and Ernest Payne, *Baptist Union*.

ence of each congregation was an organizational form that arose out of the tumultuous history of the church in the seventeenth century, and it was an arrangement for which Baptists and Congregationalists believed they had scriptural support. Even after the creation of central bureaucracies, Baptists and Congregationalists continued to lay heavy emphasis on the importance of congregational autonomy and freedom from any sort of central control. Within their scheme of church organization, sovereign authority lay with the meeting of all members of the congregation, not with the clergy and not with any organized body beyond the congregation. For much of the nineteenth century, indeed, that ideal of congregational independence was a much valued distinguishing feature of both denominations. The polity of congregational independence was an obvious impediment to creation of unions that could be viewed as wielding central denominational authority.

The other doctrinal objection to unions was also related to the ideals of independency. Traditionally, Congregationalists and Baptists were Calvinists. They accepted the doctrine of predestination, and they were committed to the idea that each independent congregation was made up of members gathered out of the world and predestined by God for salvation. During the second half of the eighteenth century and on into the nineteenth, there was powerful tension between those Calvinists who adhered to the idea of a predestined elite and the growing number of Evangelical activists who believed, democratically, that salvation came to all who would accept the good news in the Scriptures and embrace Christ crucified. Christ's substitutionary atonement for the sin of all mankind, so maintained the Evangelicals, made it possible for all humankind, at least all right-thinking believers, to be saved. This tension was itself an obstacle to unions. The coming of the unions signified, paradoxically, both the victory of the Evangelicals within the denominations and, to some extent, the victory of denominationalism over the pan-Evangelical ideals and organizations of the earlier nineteenth century.

Theological conflict was stronger among the Baptists than among the Congregationalists. More Baptist ministers and congregations clung to the old Calvinist formulae than was the case for the generally more progressive Congregationalists. The relative weakness of theological consensus explains why the Baptist Union, at its refoundation in 1833, did not attempt to set out a formal statement of denominational faith. With no central theological accord, Baptists throughout the rest of the century continued to do battle. Until the last twenty years of the century, combat tended to be between the Evangelicals, who advocated an expansionary churchmanship with the communion table open to all believers who considered themselves to have been saved, and the Calvinists, who applied more rigorous tests and closed their communion tables to all except that elite that they considered God's elect. Towards the end of the century, the battle shifted to the Evangelicals, now the old-fashioned cohort of resistance, versus the modernists. This new theological struggle will be discussed later.

The Congregationalists, shortly after the foundation of their union, were able to adopt the *Declaration of the Faith, Church, Order, and Discipline of the Congregational, or Independent Dissenters.* While the *Declaration* came in for criticism at the time and is dismissed by Tudur Jones as a "disappointing document that suggests a bureaucratic memorandum,"[83] it did represent a statement of generally agreed Congregational theology that helped to unify the denomination throughout the nineteenth century. The theology that was briefly outlined in the *Declaration* was called "moderate Calvinism" and took the compromising line that God's elect did not constitute a small elite, but, with sufficient effort on the part of men and women dedicated to making the Gospels broadly known, might include most, if not all, of humankind. The connection between the "moderate Calvinism" of the Congregational Union and the more rigorously intellectual theology of the seventeenth-century Independents might have been tenuous, consisting more in the preservation of some forms of words than in genuine continuity of ideas, but "moderate Calvinism" enabled Victorian Congregationalists to consider that they had not broken faith with their past. Until late in the century, moderate Calvinism defined an accepted Evangelical theological position that enabled the Congregationalists to avoid any cataclysmic internal theological warfare. Theological conflict within Congregationalism centered on the new biblical criticism, or "Germanism" as it was sometimes called. For a decade from the late 1840s to the late 1850s, the fiercely combative John Campbell, prominent London pastor and editor of the most popular Congregational periodicals and the widely circulated newspaper, the *British Banner*, acted as denominational watchdog, raising the alarm whenever he scented the intrusion of modern German thought.[84] Willis B. Glover provides an excellent treatment of Baptist and Congregationalist reactions to German scholarship and biblical criticism.[85] Glover argues that Congregationalists and many

---

[83] *Congregationalism in England*, 243.

[84] The two most prominent denominational theological controversies, fanned into crises of the moment by Campbell, centered on a book of religious poetry by the Congregationalist minister T. T. Lynch, *Hymns for Heart and Voice: The Rivulet*, published in 1855, and on the Higher Criticism of the Bible as it was taught by Samuel Davidson at Lancashire Independent College, a denominational school for training ministers. The best account of the *Rivulet* affair is in Peel, *These Hundred Years*, 142-58. The Davidson case is treated at length in Samuel Davidson's *Autobiography and Diary* (Edinburgh, 1899), still the best source for this important early challenge to scientific examination of the Bible.

[85] *Evangelical Nonconformists and Higher Criticism in the Nineteenth Century* (London, 1954).

Baptists in the decade of the 1860s came to terms with modern biblical criticism more easily and quickly than did the clergy of the Established Church. Glover's book, even though it is limited in focus, provides a good introduction to the general subject of nineteenth-century orthodox Nonconformist theology. More wide-ranging are Alan P. F. Sell's well-documented and thoughtful essays on Dissenting theology in the mid-Victorian period.[86] In spite of a great quantity of published sources, in the form of lectures, sermons, and sustained theological treatises, there has been no comprehensive modern study of the theology of orthodox Nonconformity in the nineteenth century.

In the main, Baptist and Congregational theology in the Victorian period was more practical than theoretical. Theological studies in the training colleges were aimed at producing preachers rather than scholars and at locating the limits of denominational orthodoxy rather than at advancing the cause of abstract truth. The best guide to the training colleges is the work of K. D. Brown. Brown takes a somewhat dispirited view of the Nonconformist ministry, partly the result of his statistical method, which concentrates attention on the many ill-paid and undereducated ministers of small and poor congregations, and partly a result of his sense of decline, a persistent theme in twentieth-century writing about Dissent.[87] As the fervor of the Evangelical Revival settled down, some of the training colleges, especially among the Congregationalists, became centers of serious academic theological activity in the second half of the century. This was markedly true of Mansfield College, which was settled in Oxford in 1886 with Alexander Fairbairn as the first Principal.[88]

During the generation following 1875 or 1880, massive changes transformed the character of orthodox Nonconformity.[89] By the early 1890s, even the name "Nonconformist" began to fall into disuse as the new term

---

[86] *Dissenting Thought and the Life of the Churches: Studies in an English Tradition* (San Francisco, 1990).

[87] K. D. Brown, *A Social History of the Nonconformist Ministry in England and Wales, 1800-1930* (Oxford, 1988); also his "College Principals—A Cause of Nonconformist Decay?" *JEH* 38 (1987), 236-53.

[88] For the early history of Mansfield College and for a provocative general discussion of the place of theological change in orthodox Nonconformity in the late nineteenth and early twentieth centuries, see Mark Johnson, *The Dissolution of Dissent, 1850-1918* (New York, 1987). For a stimulating critical examination of Johnson's argument, see Alan P. F. Sell, "English Evangelical Dissent: Dissoluble or Dissolute?" *Baptist Quarterly* 33 (1990), 243-46. The best study of Andrew Fairbairn remains W. B. Selbie, *The Life of Andrew Martin Fairbairn* (London, 1914).

[89] For general discussions of these changes, see R. J. Helmstadter, "The Nonconformist Conscience," *The Conscience of the Victorian State*, ed. by Peter

"Free Churchman" began to supplant it. The old theological formulae of moderate Calvinism were gradually abandoned, although not without considerable battle, especially among the Baptists.[90] The new theological drift was away from the Evangelical concentration on the central place of the Atonement and towards placing primacy on the Incarnation. This movement of ideas was by no means peculiar to the Nonconformists, and the fact that they shared the change with Anglicans helped to underscore the reality that in theology and increasingly in general culture there was little to distinguish Nonconformity from the Church of England. Even in politics, the distinctive position of Nonconformity began to fade. Almost all the barriers to full participation in national life on the same basis as Anglicans had been removed by the beginning of the 1880s, and with the closure of their traditional "grievances," Nonconformists lost their enthusiasm for the Liberation Society and its campaign to disestablish the Church of England. The sense of a solid Liberal identity among Nonconformists was violently disturbed by the Liberal split over Home Rule in 1885 and 1886. While few orthodox Nonconformists followed Joseph Chamberlain into Unionism, the old political imperatives that had forged powerful links between Liberalism and Nonconformity were subjected to review, and a new basis for Nonconformist political activity emerged.[91] For a time Nonconformists came to think of themselves as the conscience of the nation, not so much as a group of saints gathered out of the world, not as a people set apart and determined to defend their own heritage, but, rather, as defenders of civil rights generally and as spokesmen for the downtrodden. Even in the provincial towns, Nonconformists began to lose their social and political cohesion, their sense of belonging to a different world from that of their Anglican neighbors.[92] As Nonconformists lost the

Marsh (Syracuse, 1979); Bebbington, *Nonconformist Conscience*; and Munson, *Nonconformists*.

[90] There is an excellent and thoroughly documented discussion of the "Downgrade Controversy" in Kruppa, *Spurgeon*.

[91] For the new political role of Nonconformity, see Stephen Koss, *Nonconformity in Modern British Politics* (London, 1975).

[92] Stephen Yeo, *Churches and Voluntary Organizations in Crisis*, argues that provincial towns themselves lost distinctiveness as the nation's economy and culture grew more homogenized. Hugh McLeod, *Class and Religion in the Late Victorian City* (London, 1974), makes it clear that denominations in turn-of-the-century London still had identifiable places in the social pecking order, but social character was being attached increasingly to particular congregations and neighborhoods. Jeffrey Cox, *The English Churches in a Secular Society: Lambeth, 1870-1930* (Oxford, 1982), shows that in the years leading up to 1914, Anglican parishes and Nonconformist congregations organized for social action in similar ways.

sense that they were rooted in an alternative culture, as they grew more willing to abandon their tradition of separateness, they gradually lost their old identity and their reason for being. Their new name, "Free Church," itself signified a major break with the past and a new relationship with the Church of England and with the culture of the nation. After the First World War, Free Churchmen ceased to be as important a force in English society or as dynamic an element in English religion as they had been earlier.

4

Quakers and Unitarians

R. K. Webb

BRINGING QUAKERS AND Unitarians together in this chapter is a marriage of convenience, but a union dictated by editorial considerations is as likely as one arising from family strategy or social constraints to mask profound incompatibilities.[1] To be sure, a casual observer in the late twentieth century might well see the two denominations (particularly in the United States) as representing the essence of liberalism in religion, and, to judge from much that historians have written, it would be a pardonable conclusion that the same identity existed in the nineteenth century. But the impression can be seriously misleading.

Quakers and Unitarians tend to be seen as belonging to the same prosperous, educated, middle- and upper-middle-class segment of society—with some justice, though both extended farther down the social scale than is usually assumed, with the Unitarians perhaps having the broader range. More important is their sharply differing attitude to society. At the end of the eighteenth century and well into the nineteenth, Quakers, deeply conscious of their heritage as a "peculiar people," maintained barriers in dress, speech, and custom against a wider world and distrusted the growing involvement of some of their brethren in politics and social activism. The Unitarians, on the other hand, were liberals and reformers by instinct, interest, and theological compulsion. They prided themselves on their political involvement and influence—in the first reformed Parliament of 1833, all but one of the fifteen or so M.P.s representing Dissent were said to be Unitarians, and they were increasingly important in local government, particularly after it was reformed in 1835. If they were excluded

---

[1] I am indebted to Dr. G. M. Ditchfield and Professors Thomas C. Kennedy, Jean Soderlund, and Richard T. Vann for helping me to avoid sins of both omission and commission.

from the wider world, it was not from choice or principle, but because of orthodox refusal to have anything to do with them.

Although, by the end of the nineteenth century, the Quakers were moving rapidly to the liberal pole in theology, for most of the century they were dominated by Evangelicalism, which entailed a biblicist, rule-bound outlook, while the Unitarians never wavered in their religious liberalism and took the advances of scientists and biblical scholars at home and abroad in stride. At a deeper level, rationalism was at odds with mysticism: the Unitarian commitment to the objective and external authority of science and criticism could scarcely have differed more from Quaker reliance on the "inner light."

However great these differences, historiographical peculiarities may go some distance towards justifying the linkage of this chapter. Both denominations can point to general, transatlantic histories, monumental in scope and intention, that remain widely and justly influential. W. C. Braithwaite's *The Beginnings of Quakerism* (London, 1912; rev. ed. 1955) and *The Second Period of Quakerism* (London, 1919; rev. ed. 1961) deal mostly with the seventeenth century, while the American scholar Rufus M. Jones, in the two volumes of *The Later Periods of Quakerism* (London, 1921), takes up the eighteenth and (rather unsatisfactorily) the nineteenth centuries. Earl Morse Wilbur's *A History of Unitarianism* ranges even more widely: the first volume, subtitled *Socinianism and Its Antecedents* (Boston, 1945), deals with Michael Servetus, the sixteenth-century martyr, and follows the transmission of Unitarian ideas from Italy and Switzerland to Poland and Hungary and into Germany and the Low Countries; the second volume, *In Transylvania, England, and America* (Boston, 1952), also places great emphasis on the Hungarian church.

As these references suggest, historians of both denominations—as true of detailed as of general work—have been most interested in their early history, understandably enough, given pious or polemical quests for heroic ages. Indeed, in the Unitarian case, this fascination is with their pre-history, for the continuous denominational history of Unitarianism in England begins only in the third quarter of the eighteenth century, with the phenomenal literary and personal impact of Joseph Priestley and with the much publicized departure of Theophilus Lindsey from the Church of England in 1774, to found the first openly Unitarian chapel in the country, in Essex Street in London, a bold move since Unitarianism remained illegal in Britain until 1813.[2]

---

[2] Priestley (1733-1804), the discoverer of oxygen, is a major figure in the history of science and is also important for his contributions to political theory and controversy. Lindsey (1723-1808), son-in-law of the Anglican advocate of comprehension, Archdeacon Francis Blackburne (1705-1787), was vicar of Catterick, Yorkshire, before his emergence as a Unitarian.

Further, denominational traditions, reflected in much historical work, have tended to emphasize the famous names associated with the two bodies. We think almost instinctively of Cadburys, Peases, Rowntrees, and Gurneys, of John Bright and Joseph Sturge, of Elizabeth Fry and Seebohm Rowntree among the Quakers; of Strutts, Courtaulds, Kenricks, Rathbones, and Martineaus, of William Smith and Joseph Chamberlain, of Mary Carpenter and Octavia Hill among the Unitarians. Much remains to be done with these and other celebrated figures of Quaker and Unitarian background, but we need to be less dazzled by the great than perhaps we have been and generally to take a broader and less awed stance towards both histories.

Historians of nineteenth-century England are fortunate in having a magisterial single-volume study of Quakerism in that century by Elizabeth Isichei.[3] She sets out the structure of the denomination and maps its theological evolution and the growth of "conformity to the world." Then, using case studies of Manchester and Norwich, she analyzes the recruiting and losses of members and examines the social characteristics of Friends and their role in Victorian politics, philanthropy, and adult education. Placing both Quakers and Quakerism in broad contexts, Isichei's book is a model of denominational history.

What Isichei has to say about Quaker demography in the nineteenth century has been impressively supplemented by Richard T. Vann, an historian whose important early work on the first century of Quakerism rested on case studies in Buckinghamshire and Norfolk, and David Eversley, a distinguished demographer. They have constructed a national sample of 8,000 Quakers (taking in Ireland as well), covering the period from 1650 to 1900, evaluating the typicality of that sample against the country as a whole and speculating convincingly about the relevance of the Quakers to the "demographic transition" from the relatively small preindustrial family, to the much larger families of the turn of the eighteenth century, to the modern family whose small size is accounted for by deliberate choice.[4]

The work of these historians speaks to the remarkable state of surviving Quaker records, in the library at Friends House in London and in record offices about the country, which can be supplemented by available census records, parish registers, and, after 1837, the records of births, deaths, and marriages compiled in the office of the Registrar-General.[5] Most local

---

[3] *Victorian Quakers* (Oxford, 1970).

[4] *Friends in Life and Death: The British and Irish Quakers in the Demographic Transition, 1650-1900* (New York, 1991); Vann's earlier book is *The Social Development of English Quakerism, 1655-1755* (Cambridge, Mass., 1969).

[5] The Registrar-General's records for England and Wales are available at St. Catherine's House, Kingsway, London; the census enumerators' books can be found in the Public Record Office; and for wills after 1858, which are calendared,

studies of Quakerism tend, however, to draw on surviving records for the colorful and quaint and fall far short of professional standards, leaving context unexamined and important questions unexplored. These histories are generally aimed at Quakers themselves, either to note commemorative occasions or to reinforce a general denominational investment in their past. A few are valuable within their given limitations, and even the most scrappy and chatty can be consulted, with caution and some profit, by historians with a broader mission than local pride and sectarian piety.[6] Not many broadly based historians will devote themselves to the history of meetings or congregations, but Quaker materials are there to be drawn on in more widely conceived local studies. Isichei and Vann and Eversley provide the stimulus, interpretive criteria, and guides to methodology.

Quaker biography, though not without its own pious, conceptual, or generational shortcomings, has been rather more successful than local studies. Having no formal ministry—the dignity of minister is conferred on those with recognized capacity for speaking well and weightily in meetings and for carrying the message abroad—the society lacks those large, often multivolumed biographies that Victorians of other denominations devoted to the leading figures in their pulpit history. But the balance is more than redressed by the homage paid to the great Quaker dynasties. Inevitably, there are extensive genealogical information and ample provision, usually from within, of books on families and individuals, some of them excellent, though one must always watch out for roseate hues and discreet silences. Two samplings may serve.

the place is Somerset House, Strand, London. Most of these records can also be consulted on microfilm at the Family History Library of the Church of Jesus Christ of Latter-Day Saints in Salt Lake City, Utah.

[6] A good, brief local history is Joyce Godber, *Friends in Bedfordshire and West Hertfordshire* (Bedford, privately printed, 1975), the last chapters of which deal with the nineteenth century. Violet A. Rowe, "The Quaker Presence in Hertford in the Nineteenth Century," *Journal of the Friends Historical Society* 55 (1986), 80-111, is excellent. Leslie Stephens, *Cirencester Quakers, 1655-1973* (Cirencester, 1973), is on a level with the usual chapel histories of other denominations, as are Stephen Allott, *Friends in York: The Quaker Story in the Life of a Meeting* (York, 1978), and William Pearson Thistlethwaite, *Yorkshire Quarterly Meeting (of the Society of Friends), 1665-1966* (Harrogate, privately printed, 1979). It is unfortunate that the important Quaker center at Tottenham—distinguished as it was by the presence of the philanthropist William Forster (see below, n. 22)—can claim only an amateur essay by Mrs. M. A. Collie, *Quakers of Tottenham, 1775-1825* (Edmonton 100 Historical Society, Occasional Paper No. 37, 1978). H. William Cundy, *Hammersmith Quakers' Tercentenary, 1677-1977* (London, 1978), is open to similar strictures.

The most important figure in the doctrinal history of nineteenth-century Quakerism was certainly Joseph John Gurney (1788-1847), whose family had been Quakers from the beginnings of the sect. Established in the woollen business and later in banking in Norwich, the Gurneys at the end of the eighteenth century were living in splendor just outside the town, deeply involved in the wealthy and liberal intellectual society of Norwich, numbering Unitarians and Roman Catholics among their close friends and given to "marrying out." Joseph John Gurney turned his back on this cultivated and relaxed situation to become the leader of the Quaker Evangelicals, a new departure that owed much to the success of Evangelicals in other denominations.[7] A devoted scholar and a businessman actively involved in the bank, which was of the first importance in English economic life, Gurney, like his father-in-law, Thomas Fowell Buxton, was deeply engaged in the antislavery movement, a commitment that helped to extend his influence to the West Indies and the United States, where Earlham College in Indiana takes its name from the Gurney estate.[8]

Gurney himself is the subject of a straightforward modern biography by David E. Swift, but a two-volume evocation of the family written at the end of the last century by Augustus J. C. Hare remains valuable for its glimpses into the interplay of Quaker theory and practice.[9] Gurney's sister Elizabeth (1780-1845) married Joseph Fry, from another great Quaker clan, and became celebrated as one of the leading prison reformers of her time. She has inevitably been the subject of several brief, admiring biographies aimed at a popular audience, but a serious examination of her life,

[7] On the movement generally, D. W. Bebbington, *Evangelicalism in Modern Britain: A History from the 1730s to the 1980s* (London, 1989).

[8] There is a small ironic note in that the Gurneys did not own the estate but leased it for the entire period of their tenure. Gurney's best-known and most important religious work was *Observations on the Religious Peculiarities of the Society of Friends* (London, 1824), directed at confirming the faith of younger members of the society; in the seventh edition (1834), he changed the title, in response to objections, to *Distinguishing Views and Practices of the Society of Friends*. A recent republication is called simply *A Peculiar People* (Richmond, Ind., 1979). For the evolution of Earlham College from the Friends' Boarding School and the decision about its name, see Opal Thornburg, *Earlham: The Story of the College, 1847-1962* (Richmond, Ind., 1963).

[9] David E. Swift, *Joseph John Gurney, Banker, Reformer, and Quaker* (Middletown, Conn., 1962); Augustus J. C. Hare, *The Gurneys of Earlham* (London, 1895). Another account of a late phase of Earlham life is Percy Lubbock, *Earlham* (London, 1922; repr. Westport, Conn., 1974). Swift made extensive use of the Gurney Papers in the Library at Friends House; see Arthur J. Eddington, *et al.*, *List and Index of the Gurney Manuscripts at the Friends House Library, London*, List and Index Society, Special Series, 6 (London, 1973).

which could say much about a well-placed woman in the first half of the century as well as about the dynamics and contours of philanthropic reform, is still lacking.[10]

Although their fortune was acquired later than that of the Gurneys, the Rowntree family of York could claim similar distinction in the worlds of religion, business, and philanthropy. A family grocery business established in Scarborough was removed to York in 1822 and in 1862 took over the cocoa and chocolate business abandoned by another family of Quaker grocers and tea merchants, the Tukes. Although the new line of trade did not become a major enterprise until the end of the century, the Rowntrees were sufficiently well established to permit family members to play a major role in denominational and public life throughout the second half of the century.

In the twentieth century, the firm became celebrated for its imaginative industrial policy, ranging from housing to profit-sharing, and its members were active propagandists for the improvement of society in particular ar-

[10] The number of popular lives is legion, but mention might be made of John Kent, *Elizabeth Fry* (London, 1962), and June Rose, *Elizabeth Fry* (London, 1980). One is really thrown back on *Memoir of the Life of Elizabeth Fry, with Extracts from Her Journal and Letters*, edited by two of her daughters, 2 vols. (London, 1847; rev. ed., 1848). One of the daughters set down her own reminiscences of the household: *Katharine Fry's Book*, ed. by Jane Vansittart (London, 1966). The branch of the Frys into which Elizabeth Gurney married was based in London, where they ran a tea business, but the Bristol branch, which expanded a tea business into a major enterprise in cocoa and chocolate, made impressive contributions to English life in a number of fields. Agnes Fry, *A Memoir of the Rt. Hon. Sir Edward Fry* (London, 1921), is compiled from a manuscript autobiography of a distinguished judge (1827-1918) and ambassador to the second Hague Peace Conference in 1907. Of Sir Edward's children, several had significant careers. Anna Ruth remained a Friend and carried on extensive relief work, which she recalled in *A Quaker Adventure: The Story of Nine Years' Relief and Reconstruction* (London, 1926), and *Three Visits to Russia, 1922-25* (London, 1942); she was also an historian of Quakerism. Isabel turned to education: Beatrice Curtis Brown, *Isabel Fry, 1869-1958: Portrait of a Great Teacher* (London, 1960). Margery (1874-1958) entered academic life, first at the new University of Birmingham and then as principal of Somerville College, Oxford; she, too, had an important philanthropic career, but she resigned from the Society of Friends in 1935, having already distanced herself from the connection; see Enid Huws Jones, *Margery Fry, the Essential Amateur* (London and New York, 1966). A much earlier departure was made by their brother Roger (1866-1934), one of the most important artistic and aesthetic influences of the early twentieth century and a member of the Bloomsbury Group; see Virginia Woolf, *Roger Fry* (London, 1940).

eas of Quaker concern.[11] These interests grew out of a long-standing attachment to Quakerism. In 1859, while he was still a young man, John Stephenson Rowntree (1834-1907), the eldest son of Joseph, the founder of the York operation, won a prize for an essay on the subject of Quaker decline, in which, while giving full recognition to the importance of the original religious perceptions of the founders, he deplored the exclusive deductions drawn from them in the eighteenth century, especially after the introduction of birthright membership in 1737—the neglect of teaching, the failure to establish an effective ministry, the formulistic character of devotion, and, above all, the rigorous imposition of disownment on those who married out or strayed in any way from the orthodox path.[12]

John Wilhelm Rowntree (1868-1905), a nephew of John Stephenson, having surmounted a crisis of faith, began the summer religious schools in 1897 and inspired, after his early death, the establishment of a Quaker settlement and the publication of the seven volumes of Quaker history by W. C. Braithwaite and Rufus M. Jones. John Wilhelm's younger brother, Benjamin Seebohm Rowntree (1871-1954), while continuing in the family business, won fame as a social investigator with an important study of poverty in York at the beginning of the twentieth century, which was followed by two further studies before and after the Second World War.[13]

The examples of the Gurneys and the Rowntrees could be multiplied, in history and in writing about it, many times over. As industrial paternalists, the Cadburys of chocolate fame have been as celebrated as the Rowntrees.[14] Other well-to-do families have their biographies and rem-

[11] Anne Vernon, *A Quaker Business Man: The Life of Joseph Rowntree, 1836-1925* (London, 1958); Elfrida Vipont, *Arnold Rowntree, a Life* (London, 1955); William Wallace, *Prescription for Partnership: A Study of Industrial Relations* (London, 1959). See also Maurice L. Rowntree, *Co-operation or Chaos? A Handbook* (London, 1917), and *Mankind Set Free* (London, 1939).

[12] *Quakerism, Past and Present: being an Inquiry into the Causes of its Decline in Great Britain and Ireland* (London, 1859).

[13] Rufus M. Jones, *John Wilhelm Rowntree* (Philadelphia, 1942); Thomas C. Kennedy, "History and the Quaker Renaissance: The Vision of John Wilhelm Rowntree," *Journal of the Friends Historical Society* 55 (1985-86), 35-56. B. Seebohm Rowntree, *Poverty, a Study of Town Life* (London, 1901); *Poverty and Progress* (London, 1941); and *Poverty and the Welfare State* (London, 1951). There is an excellent biography by Asa Briggs, *Social Thought and Social Action: A Study of the Work of Seebohm Rowntree, 1871-1954* (London, 1961).

[14] John F. Crosfield, *A History of the Cadbury Family*, 2 vols. (Cambridge, 1985), is a very grand, extensively illustrated biographical dictionary, branch by branch; William A. Cadbury, *Richard Tapper Cadbury, 1768-1860* (Birmingham, privately printed, 1944), is a brief sketch of the man who established the family in the textile business in Birmingham; T. Insull, *John Cadbury, 1801-89* (Birm-

iniscences.[15] Mention should be made, too, of Barbara Strachey's delightful account of an American Quaker family who cut a wide swath in England.[16] But not all Quaker families were rich.[17]

Family as an organizing principle can be transcended to view Quakers involved in various fields of activity. The close ties of Friends to business—not foreclosed by either their own scruples or legislative and customary exclusion—have attracted considerable attention from historians.[18] Most of these historians note at the outset the ingrown character of

ingham, 1979), deals with the real founder of the family fortunes in the cocoa and chocolate business; Helen Cadbury Alexander, *Richard Cadbury of Birmingham* (London, 1906), is a life of John's eldest son (1835-1899); Richard's second son, George, played an important part in the Liberal Party and figured prominently in this century as proprietor of the *News Chronicle*: A. G. Gardiner, *Life of George Cadbury* (London and New York, 1923). Two Cadbury women have also been the subjects of biographies: Janet Whitney, *Geraldine S. Cadbury, 1865-1941, a Biography* (London, 1948), deals with the wife of Borrow Cadbury, Richard's eldest son; seeing herself as continuing the work of Elizabeth Fry, she devoted her career to the problem of juvenile delinquency. Richenda Scott, *Elizabeth Cadbury, 1858-1951* (London, 1955), is an account of the life of George Cadbury's wife, who was active in Birmingham philanthropy and particularly in the activities of the Bournville Village Trust, which centred on the model town of Bournville outside Birmingham.

[15] Agnes Yates, *Putting the Clock Back: Reminiscences of Childhood in a Quaker Country House, during the Latter Middle Years of Last Century* (London, 1939), is a charming portrait of family life. For the Tuke family, see William K. and E. Margaret Sessions, *The Tukes of York in the Seventeenth, Eighteenth, and Nineteenth Centuries* (London, 1971); *Samuel Tuke; His Life, Work, and Thoughts*, ed. by Charles Tylor (London, 1900); and Sir Edward Fry, *James Hack Tuke, a Memoir* (London, 1899).

[16] *Remarkable Relations: The Story of the Pearsall Smith Family* (London, 1980).

[17] Trudi Abel, "The Diary of a Poor Quaker Seamstress: Needles and Penury in Nineteenth-Century London," *Quaker History* 75 (1986), 102-14, based on a journal kept in 1833 and now in the Haverford College Library.

[18] Paul H. Emden, *Quakers in Commerce: A Record of Business Achievement* (London, 1939), is a breathless, glowing account; most of the sketches are only a few pages long, but the book has its uses as a catalogue. David Burns Windsor, *The Quaker Enterprise: Friends in Business* (London, 1980), is a thoughtful overview, without scholarly apparatus, of the most famous firms; in addition to Rowntrees and Cadburys, it deals with the Birmingham banking family of the Lloyds, the ironmasters the Darbys, the soapmaking Crosfields, the Huntley and Palmer biscuit business, and the pharmaceutical firm of Allen and Hanbury. Peter Mathias, *The Brewing Industry in England, 1700-1830* (Cambridge, 1959), nec-

the Quaker economic community and the ties of blood that reinforced economic bonds. What is generally missing, however, is any serious consideration, often any consideration at all, of how Quaker religious and organizational presuppositions helped to shape the thought and actions of businessmen.

That same criticism is applicable, though not quite so uniformly, to studies of Quaker activities in other fields. John Bright[19] and Joseph Sturge[20] were the two Quakers who figured most prominently on the Victorian political scene and who helped, by their example and urging, to

essarily pays extensive attention to Quaker firms. Arthur Raistrick, *Quakers in Science and Industry, being an Account of the Quaker Contributions to Science and Industry during the 17th and 18th Centuries* (London, 1950; repr. New York, 1968), is a valuable scholarly survey that, despite its subtitle, does come into the nineteenth century; it can be supplemented by Raistrick's *Dynasty of Ironfounders: The Darbys and Coalbrookdale* (London, 1953), and *Two Centuries of Industrial Welfare: The London (Quaker) Lead Company, 1601-1905* (Buxton, 1977). Further accounts of Quaker firms without much stress on the Quakerism beyond the connectional aspect are T.A.B. Corley, *Quaker Enterprise in Biscuits: Huntley and Palmers of Reading, 1822-1972* (London, 1972); Audrey M. Taylor, *Gilletts, Bankers at Banbury and Oxford: A Study in Local Economic History* (Oxford, 1964); and R. S. Sayers, *Gilletts in the London Money Market, 1867-1967* (Oxford, 1968)—the billbroking firm that grew out of the bank. Iolo A. Williams, *The Firm of Cadbury, 1831-1931* (London, 1931), is a good house centennial history. The most important of the Quaker banks are dealt with in (for the Gurneys) W. H. Bidwell, *Annals of an East Anglian Bank* (Norwich, 1900), and *History of Barclays Bank Limited, Including the Many Private and Joint Stock Banks Amalgamated and Affiliated with It*, ed. by P. W. Matthews and A. W. Tuke (London, 1926), which gives sketches of the twenty constituent banks including the various Gurney banks. The most recent foray into the field is by David H. Pratt, *English Quakers and the First Industrial Revolution: A Study of the Quaker Community in Four Industrial Counties—Lancashire, York, Warwick, and Gloucester, 1750-1830* (New York and London, 1985); Pratt is concerned to test the hypotheses of Max Weber and Ernst Troeltsch, but the overall effect is naive and, at times, misleading.

[19] Bright (1811-1889) came to prominence in the Anti-Corn Law agitation in the 1840s. Defeated in a celebrated Manchester election in 1857, when his pacifist criticism of Palmerstonian foreign policy encountered strong popular resistance, he came back to prominence in the agitation for parliamentary reform in the early 1860s and served in the second Gladstone cabinet of 1880, resigning in 1882 over British involvement in Egypt.

[20] Sturge (1793-1859) was primarily important for his work in the causes of peace and antislavery and in his championing of middle-class and working-class cooperation in the Complete Suffrage Movement of the early 1840s.

break down the insulation of the Quakers from public life.[21] Bright, as a major political figure in his own right, has been the subject of much attention, but one large work has been devoted exclusively to his relationship to the Quakers; a recent study of Sturge, whilst on a smaller scale, also pays significant attention to his Quakerism.[22]

Historians of science have shown much interest in the greatest Quaker scientific luminary, John Dalton, who formulated the atomic hypothesis, but without the close scrutiny of his Quakerism that has, for example, been given to the influence of Michael Faraday's Sandemanianism or of Joseph Priestley's theological views on their science.[23]

One of the most important areas of Quaker philanthropy, education, is understudied as a general phenomenon apart from commemorative histories of individual schools.[24] In some respects, the most important figure

[21] Although concerned mostly with American Quakerism, Frederick B. Tolles, *Quakers and the Atlantic Culture* (New York, 1960), deals with the general question of Quaker involvement in politics in the third chapter, which has some discussion of the English situation.

[22] The most accessible biography of Bright is now Keith Robbins, *John Bright* (London and Boston, 1979), but it has little to say about Quakerism. By contrast, see J. Travis Mills, *John Bright and the Quakers*, 2 vols. (London, 1935), and Alex Tyrell, *Joseph Sturge and the Moral Radical Party in Early Victorian Britain* (London, 1987). W. E. Forster (1818-1886) was another major politician, the son of the Tottenham philanthropist William Forster (1784-1854), on whom see Benjamin Seebohm, *Memoirs of William Forster*, 2 vols. (London, 1865). The younger Forster is best known for his sponsorship of the much-contested Education Act, 1870, often called by his name, which generalized state-supported primary education in the country; he served as chief secretary for Ireland in the second Gladstone cabinet formed in 1880, but resigned two years later in protest over the so-called Kilmainham Treaty, which the government negotiated with the Irish nationalist leader Charles Stewart Parnell. T. Wemyss Reid, *Life of the Rt. Hon. William Edward Forster*, 2 vols. (London, 1888; repr. New York, 1970).

[23] Dalton (1755-1844) spent his scientific career at the Manchester Literary and Philosophical Society; by a curious irony, he taught science for a time at the new Unitarian Manchester Academy in the 1790s. The best way into the extensive Dalton literature is Arnold Thackray, *John Dalton: Critical Assessments of His Life and Science* (Cambridge, Mass., 1972); the second and fourth chapters deal with contextual matters, but while the latter has something to say about Quakerism, it is not very searching. Compare Geoffrey Cantor, *Michael Faraday, Sandemanian and Scientist: A Study of Science and Religion in the Nineteenth Century* (London, 1991); on Priestley, see below.

[24] Howard H. Brinton, *Quaker Education in Theory and Practice* (Wallingford, Penna., n.d.), is primarily concerned with the United States, but has some English material. W. A. Campbell Stewart, *Quakers and Education, as seen in their*

in educational history associated with the Quakers was Joseph Lancaster, who devised his "monitorial system," in which older children taught the younger, early in the century. Lancaster—a Dissenter of distant Quaker background who became a Quaker by convincement and was then disowned for his financial irresponsibility—was the educational motor of the British and Foreign School Society, founded in 1814, which sponsored elementary education under Dissenting auspices and in stern competition with the National Society, the larger Anglican body that drew its educational inspiration from the similar method put forward by the Rev. Andrew Bell. Lancaster has not been the subject of a major modern book, nor has his collaborator, the great Quaker philanthropist William Allen.[25]

Schools in England (London, 1953; repr. Port Washington, N.Y., 1971), is a useful overview that deals with the impulse to educational involvement and with the schools, their history, costs, curriculum, staffing, and administration—more from the point of view of an educationalist than an historian. Most of the schools have useful, though often slight, histories: *Friends' School, Wigton, Cumberland, 1815-1953*, ed. by David W. Reed (Carlisle, 1954); David W. Bolam, *Unbroken Community: The Story of the Friends' School, Saffron Walden, 1702-1952* (Cambridge, 1952), a school that goes back to earlier incarnations in Clerkenwell, Islington, and Croydon; Elfrida Vipont, *Ackworth School, from its Foundation in 1779 to the Introduction of Co-education in 1946* (London, 1959), and, for a headmaster of that school from 1877 to 1920, Isaac Henry Wallis, *Frederick Andrews of Ackworth* (London, 1924); *Bootham School, 1823-1923* (London, 1926), and, on its headmaster (when it was York Friends' School) from 1828 to 1857, *Memorials of John Ford*, ed. by Silvanus Thompson (London, 1877), and L. John Stroud, "John Ford (1801-1875): The Life, Work, and Influence of a Quaker Schoolmaster" (Ph.D. thesis, University of London, 1947); Francis A. Knight, *A History of Sidcot School: A Hundred Years of West Country Quaker Education, 1808-1908* (London, 1908), which can be supplemented by George W. Hutchinson, *Bevan and Mabel Lean of Sidcot: A Record of Life and Progress at Sidcot School, 1902-1930* (Winscombe, 1981); H. Winifred Sturge and Theodora Clark, *The Mount School, York, 1784 to 1814, 1831 to 1931* (London and Toronto, 1931); *History of Great Ayton School* (Middlesbrough, 1891), begun as the North of England Agricultural School; S. W. Brown, *Leighton Park: A History of the School* (Leighton Park, 1952); R.H.S. Randles, *History of the Friends' School, Lancaster* [now the George Fox School] (Lancaster, 1982).

[25] Lancaster and Allen are dealt with in Henry Dunn, *Sketches*, Part 1, *Joseph Lancaster and His Contemporaries*, Part 2, *William Allen, his Life and Labours* (London, 1848). See also Edward C. Wall, "Joseph Lancaster and the Origins of the British and Foreign School Society" (Ph.D. thesis, Columbia University, 1966), and *Joseph Lancaster and the Monitorial School Movement: A Documentary History*, ed. by Carl F. Kaestle (New York, 1973). For Allen, *Life of William Allen, with Selections from his Correspondence*, 3 vols. (London, 1846). The only

The most famous areas of Quaker philanthropy are their work against the slave trade and slavery and for peace. There is no book on the Quaker antislavery campaign in itself, nor has Thomas Fowell Buxton, perhaps its leading nineteenth-century agitator, received a modern biographical study. But the many general works on abolition pay much and gratifying attention to the Quakers.[26] Like antislavery, the peace movement has received generous attention.[27] Of equal interest, though perhaps less well known, has been Quaker activity in relief work around the world, which flowed naturally from their concerns with peace and antislavery and also from

recent life is a brief popular sketch, Helena Hall, *William Allen, 1770-1843, Member of the Society of Friends* (London, 1953). L. Hugh Doncaster, *Friends of Humanity, with Special Reference to the Quaker William Allen, 1770-1843*, Friends of Dr. Williams's Library, Nineteenth Lecture (London, 1965), is a brief overview of the remarkable range of Allen's philanthropy.

[26] David Brion Davis, *The Problem of Slavery in Western Culture* (Ithaca, 1966), has a discussion of Quakers, 291-333, which, though mostly American in emphasis, includes the British. There is fuller attention in Davis's *The Problem of Slavery in the Age of Revolution, 1770-1823* (Ithaca, 1975). See also Roger Anstey, *The Atlantic Slave Trade and British Abolition, 1760-1810* (London, 1975), especially ch. 9. Fowell Buxton worked in the later agitation, after the abolition of the British slave trade in 1807 and of slavery in 1833. His influential pamphlet, *The African Slave Trade and Its Remedy* (London, 1839), was reprinted in New York in 1967; and *Memoirs of Sir Thomas Fowell Buxton*, edited by his son Charles and published in London in 1848, has often been reprinted.

[27] The newly standard account is Peter Brock, *The Quaker Peace Testimony, 1660 to 1914* (York, 1990), though it does not entirely replace Margaret E. Hirst, *The Quakers in Peace and War: An Account of their Peace Principles and Practice* (London, 1923). See also Stephen Frick, "Joseph Sturge and the Crimean War: I. The Search for a Cause" and "II. The Founding of the *Morning Star*," *Journal of the Friends Historical Society* 53 (1974-75), 236-55, 335-58; Richard A. Rempel, "British Quakers and the South African War," *Quaker History* 64 (1975), 75-95; Hope Hay Hewinson, *Hedge of Wild Almonds: South Africa, the Pro-Boers, and the Quaker Conscience* (London, 1989); Thomas C. Kennedy, "The Quaker Renaissance and the Origins of the Modern British Peace Movement, 1895-1920," *Albion* 16 (1984), 243-72, and *The Hound of Conscience: A History of the No-Conscription Fellowship, 1914-1919* (Fayetteville, Ark., 1981); and Brian David Phillips, "Friendly Patriotism: British Quakerism and the Imperial Nation, 1890-1910" (Ph.D. thesis, Cambridge University, 1989). For the period after the First World War, see Peter Brock, *Pacifism in Britain, 1914-1945: The Defining of a Faith* (Oxford, 1980). For a biography of a major Quaker figure in the early twentieth-century movement, see James Dudley, *The Life of Edward Grubb, 1854-1939: A Spiritual Pilgrimage* (London, 1946).

their missionary activity.[28] In the 1870s and 1880s, Quaker Evangelicals found a new enthusiasm in the setting up of home missions with a view to conversion. The missionaries were generally of humble origin and not well educated and seemed to other Quakers to be the opening wedge for a paid ministry. Without strong support, the movement gradually withered away.[29]

Turning to the denomination's internal history, all the general studies of the Society of Friends deal with the important and complex question of its organization, but the structural evolution is dealt with helpfully by L. Hugh Doncaster, who also discusses the roles of Quaker ministers and overseers and changes in Quaker discipline.[30] One especially interesting and distinctive aspect of Quaker organization was the existence of separate women's meetings. From the beginning of the sect, George Fox insisted on the spiritual equality of women, which resulted in the establishment of

[28] John Ormerod Greenwood, *Friends and Relief: A Study of Two Centuries of Quaker Activity in the Relief of Suffering Caused by War or Natural Calamity* (York, 1975). Scattered and partial accounts of the Quakers' important role in the Irish Famine of the 1840s have now been supplanted by Helen Hatton, *The Largest Amount of Good: Quaker Relief in Ireland, 1654-1921* (Montreal and Kingston, Ont., 1993). See also the fascinating story in Richenda C. Scott, *Quakers in Russia* (London, 1964), which recounts Friends' involvement with Tsar Alexander I—reflecting the Quaker penchant, despite their mistrust of politics, for going directly to the great of this world—and, more extensively, Quaker relief activity there. Missionary work is discussed generally in Henry T. Hodgkin, *Friends beyond the Seas* (London, 1916), and in the serious narrative account by Marjorie Sykes, *Quakers in India: A Forgotten Century* (London, 1980). See also John V. Crangle, "Joseph Whitwell Pease and the Quaker Role in the Campaign to Suppress the Opium Trade," *Quaker History* 68 (1979), 63-74; J. W. Pease (1800-1900), the principal spokesman for the Anglo-Indian Society for the Suppression of the Opium Trade, succeeded his brother Edward, who founded the society in 1874. Special mention should be made of a commendable little history of a Quaker mental hospital, Mary R. Glover, *The Retreat, York: An Early Quaker Experiment in the Treatment of Mental Illness* (York, 1984), which also figures pleasingly in the more general work of Kathleen Jones, *Lunacy, Law, and Conscience, 1744-1845: The Social History of the Care of the Insane* (London, 1955), 57-65. Elizabeth Isichei points out (168) that Quakers generally admitted to a high incidence of insanity, explaining it on grounds of extensive inbreeding.

[29] See Isichei, *Victorian Quakers*, 99-101; and below for the contrasting Unitarian domestic mission movement.

[30] L. Hugh Doncaster, *Quaker Organisation and Business Meetings* (London, 1958). See also Richard E. Stagg, "Friends' Queries and General Advices, 1860-1928," *Journal of the Friends Historical Society* 49 (1961), 249-69, useful for changes in discipline and perceptions of Quaker society.

parallel meetings, but, in fact, real power lay only with the men's meetings, and even after a woman was chosen to preside over the London Yearly Meeting in 1918, it was a long time before women established themselves firmly in the leadership.[31]

On the theological side, Isichei describes the successive schisms that troubled a declining denomination during the nineteenth century. At the end of the eighteenth century and early in the nineteenth, liberal theological challenges came from across the Atlantic, first in the person of Hannah Barnard and then in the movement sparked by the American Elias Hicks, who badly split American Quakerism; the heterodox tendencies in both Barnard and Hicks appalled the Evangelicals dominant in America and newly emerging in Britain.[32]

The Evangelicals' reliance on the Bible and their tendency to think in terms of laying down the essentials of the faith—to which they added hymn-singing and in time even professional preaching—were deeply distressing to those who valued the individualism implicit in the doctrines of the seventeenth-century founders, whilst Evangelical activism alienated those loyal to old "peculiar" ways. There was firm, quietist resistance throughout the first half of the century to the Evangelical hegemony, but only in the little Derbyshire village of Fritchley, with offshoots in Birmingham and Canada, did this kind of protest come to schism, which persisted (in the tiniest numbers) to 1968.[33] But the Evangelicals were also attacked by those who thought they did not go far enough, notably, Isaac Crewdson, a manufacturer from Manchester, who in 1835 published *A Beacon to the Society of Friends*, in which he turned an attack on the Hicksites into an attack on some Quaker fundamentals like the "inner

[31] The new clerk in 1918 was Mary Jane Godlee, who contributed a chapter on "The Women's Yearly Meeting" to *London Yearly Meeting During 250 Years* (London, 1919); but although there was much contemporary discussion of women's role in nineteenth-century Quaker periodicals, there has been little historical attention to the subject. This lacuna has been partially filled by Thomas C. Kennedy, "The Real Work of Friends: Quakerism and Feminism, 1860-1920," a paper given at the Western Conference on British Studies in 1990, to be published in the near future.

[32] David W. Maxey, "New Light on Hannah Barnard, a Quaker 'Heretic,'" *Quaker History* 78 (1989), 61-86. On the Hicksites on their home ground, H. Larry Ingle, *Quakers in Conflict: The Hicksite Reformation* (Knoxville, 1986), and on the English response, Edwin B. Bronner, *"The Other Branch": London Yearly Meeting and the Hicksites, 1827-1912* (London, 1975).

[33] The Fritchley schism has been examined in great detail in a commendable amateur work, Walter Lowndes, *The Quakers of Fritchley, 1863-1980* (Fritchley, 1981; repub. 1987). Compare Thomas D. Hamm, *The Transformation of American Quakerism: Orthodox Friends, 1800-1907* (Bloomington, 1988).

light," which left the Evangelicals little recourse but to condemn their more enthusiastic brother, whose followers withdrew into the Beaconite schism.[34]

The liberal and Unitarian tendencies that the Hicksites embodied were not rooted out, and the enthusiastic enforcement of disownment for marrying non-Quakers often redounded to the advantage of the Unitarians, most notably in the case of the great Liverpool merchant family, the Rathbones. The Unitarians were also the primary beneficiaries of another small disruption that occurred in Manchester in the 1860s, where the Evangelical majority in the Monthly Meeting disowned a convert, David Duncan, for Unitarian tendencies revealed in a lecture on the controversial Anglican exposition of critical findings, *Essays and Reviews*, and then in his interest in the renegade Anglican clergyman Charles Voysey. Despite Duncan's sudden death and the abandonment of Quakerism by many of his admirers, the liberal leaven continued to work, the lead often taken by sons of Evangelical fathers, most dramatically by William Charles Braithwaite, the future historian of Quakerism and a son of William Bevan Braithwaite, Sr., who had succeeded Joseph John Gurney as the most prominent Evangelical leader. The anonymous publication of *A Reasonable Faith* in 1884 was followed seven years later by the conversion of the *British Friend*, founded earlier in the century by Quietists to oppose the Evangelicals, into the organ of the liberals. Finally, in 1895, a conference at Manchester gave public voice to liberal insistence that Quaker theology be fruitfully related to nineteenth-century developments in science and criticism and evoked a striking response within the denomination. The transformation, sudden and complete, did much to help the recovery of the denomination. By midcentury the number of Friends is said to have shrunk to a quarter of the estimated 60,000 Friends in George Fox's time, but the late-Victorian "Quaker Renaissance" reversed that trend.[35]

[34] The Beaconite controversy is examined in Roger C. Wilson, *Manchester, Manchester and Manchester Again: From "Sound Doctrine" to "A Free Ministry"—The Theological Travail of London Yearly Meeting throughout the Nineteenth Century*, Friends Historical Society, Occasional Series No. 1 (London, 1990); and Jean E. Mortimer, "Leeds Friends and the Beaconite Controversy," *Journal of the Friends Historical Society* 54 (1977), 52-66; for an American view of it, Donald G. Good, "Elisha Bates and the Beaconite Controversy," *Quaker History* 73 (1984), 34-47.

[35] The fullest discussion of Duncan and his consequences is Thomas C. Kennedy, "Heresy-Hunting among Victorian Quakers: The Manchester Difficulty, 1861-1873," *Victorian Studies* 30 (1990-91), 227-53. The controversy is also touched on in Wilson, *Manchester*, which moves on to the end-of-century conference. See also Edwin B. Bronner, "Moderates in the London Yearly Meeting, 1857-1873: Precursors of the Quaker Liberals," *CH* 59 (1990), 356-71; and Roger

The serious study of Quaker social history and of Friends' beliefs and their consequences has taken impressive steps, but much remains to be done to advance our understanding of the Society of Friends in its intellectual, devotional, and social aspects. The resources are magnificent.[36]

The Quakers have had an excellent press from contemporaries and from historians, both impressed by Friends' piety and philanthropy and by their firm stand on moral principles in matters like slavery and peace. The Unitarians were in no way laggard in philanthropy or in taking principled stands. Moreover, like the Quakers, they had an influence, locally and nationally, out of all proportion to their numbers: as one Unitarian journalist put it, "they weighed more than they measured."[37] Unitarians played a much larger part in political life, however, and they were everywhere in Victorian literary culture.[38] It is understandable that some orthodox Victorians were so horrified by the most obvious distinguishing doctrine of the Unitarians—the rejection of belief in the Trinity for a purely

C. Wilson, "The Road to Manchester, 1895," *Seeking the Light*, ed. by J. William Frost and John M. Moore (Wallingford, Penna., 1986), 145-62. On the elder Braithwaite, Ann Lloyd Thomas, *J. Bevan Braithwaite, a Friend of the Nineteenth Century* (London, 1907). Kennedy is preparing a major study of the Quaker Renaissance.

[36] To the library at Friends House, London, may be added the Friends Historical Library at Swarthmore College and the Quaker Collection at Haverford College, both just outside Philadelphia. Here monographic and manuscript materials exist in abundance, and, of course, the transatlantic ties so important in the denomination make American resources important for the study of English Quakerism. There is a typescript dictionary of Quaker biography in Friends House, London, and the *Annual Monitor* provides obituaries for Friends from 1813. The two principal Quaker periodicals for the nineteenth century, *The Friend* (Evangelical in tendency) and the *British Friend* (traditionalist), were monthlies, both founded in 1843, and in 1913 the former (by then a weekly) absorbed the latter. On these, as on all denominations, Josef L. Altholz, *The Religious Press in Britain, 1760-1900* (New York, 1989). The *Journal of the Friends Historical Society* was founded in England in 1903 and continues as an annual; *Quaker History* was founded as the *Bulletin of the Friends Historical Association of Philadelphia* in 1906 and took its present title in 1962. More general publications in church history also carry occasional articles about the Society of Friends.

[37] Henry Parris in *Inquirer*, 19 Dec. 1903.

[38] On their remarkable role in journalism, R. K. Webb, "Flying Missionaries: Unitarian Journalists in Victorian England," *The Political Culture of Modern Britain: Studies in Memory of Stephen Koss*, ed. by J.M.W. Bean (London and New York, 1987), 11-31. Stephen Koss' two volumes on *The Rise and Fall of the Political Press in Britain* (London and Chapel Hill, 1981 and 1984) provide more detail on individual journalists and papers.

human Christ—that they could not bring themselves to give the slightest nod of recognition, or that some later Anglicans found it uncomfortable to acknowledge the Unitarianism of their forebears. But, though many historians are aware of the wide ramifications of Unitarianism through most of the century, it is surprising when some overlook a Unitarian connection that is as plain as a pikestaff and depressing when others slip into careless, or even deliberate, language of denigration.[39]

Some of the explanation for oversight or misunderstanding must rest with the Unitarians themselves, for some of their history writing has been narrowly defensive or extravagantly partisan. It is significant that no other work of Unitarian history has been so frequently cited by general historians as Raymond V. Holt's alarmingly titled *The Unitarian Contribution to Social Progress in England* (London, 1938; rev. ed., 1952), surely the worst

[39] Unitarians and their forerunners are denounced to a comical degree in that early nineteenth-century classic of Dissenting polemic masquerading as history, David Bogue and James Bennett, *The History of the Dissenters from the Revolution to the Year 1808*, 4 vols. (London, 1813). For later instances of refusal to acknowledge any role for Unitarianism when it was in fact central, see Mrs. C. L. Lewes, *Dr. Southwood Smith, A Retrospect* (Edinburgh, 1897), and Julia Wedgwood, *The Personal Life of Josiah Wedgwood the Potter* (London, 1915), the latter the more remarkable in that the book was revised and edited by C. H. Herford, Professor of English Literature at the University of Manchester, whose family produced a succession of distinguished Unitarian ministers. Nor does Anthony Burton, in *Josiah Wedgwood, a Biography* (London, 1976), give overt acknowledgment of Unitarianism, referring to Joseph Priestley only as a Dissenter whose "definition of 'Christian' was somewhat limited" (15). The most egregious recent instance of hostility of which I am aware is Donald Davie, *A Gathered Church: The Literature of the Dissenting Interest* (London, 1978), though note should also be taken of the prejudice in the otherwise indispensable book by the Congregationalist Bernard Law Manning, *The Protestant Dissenting Deputies* (Cambridge, 1952), edited by the Quaker scholar Ormerod Greenwood. J.C.D. Clark, in *English Society, 1688-1832* (Cambridge, 1985), sees Dissent as the essential threat to, and an ultimate dissolvent of, the confessional state he finds in the "long eighteenth century," so perhaps one should expect his almost automatic resort to language implying decline and corruption to Arians and Unitarians, but other historians do it, too, e.g., A. D. Gilbert, *Religion and Society in Industrial England: Church, Chapel, and Social Change, 1740-1914* (London, 1976), 36-7 and 40-41; thereafter, he simply ignores them. Owen Chadwick is fully alive to the importance of Unitarians and to the part they played, as challenge and influence, in Victorian religion; he summarizes their public and legislative circumstances brilliantly, but is misleading and mystifying when it comes to the doctrinal topography of the denomination: *The Victorian Church*, Part 1, 3rd ed. (London, 1971), 391-98.

book cited anywhere in this chapter; the italics Holt uses to identify Unitarians are conferred on many people who simply associated with or admired Unitarians, while they are denied to those who forsook the denomination without forsaking its influence. Far better is Herbert McLachlan's *The Unitarian Movement in the Religious Life of England: Its Contribution to Thought and Learning, 1700-1900* (London, 1934), though it is now more useful as a guide to the range of Unitarian activity than as an interpretation of it.

So far, the only Unitarian analogue to Elizabeth Isichei's study of Victorian Quakers is a brilliant sketch by H. L. Short, in a collaborative history of English Presbyterianism.[40] Short's coverage of the last 200 years occupies less than a quarter of the book, the preceding 200 claiming the rest. Despite his Procrustean mandate, Short managed to include every development of importance in his chapter, with interpretive sureness and a splendid sense of proportion. A book-length history of English Unitarianism since Priestley is in prospect from R. K. Webb, to which two additional studies, mentioned later, will be prefatory; his general interpretive approach is indicated in the opening chapter of a volume of essays published to commemorate the bicentennary of Manchester College.[41]

If J.C.D. Clark posits a long eighteenth century, Unitarian historians must posit a long nineteenth century, because Unitarianism in that century cannot be understood without taking account of Joseph Priestley, who, raised as an orthodox Calvinist, turned Arian at Daventry Academy in the 1750s and found his way to Unitarianism in the late 1760s.[42] Priestley celebrated his newfound faith with a series of remarkable treatises and polemics that spoke convincingly to many ministers and laymen and in the 1780s produced a rash of conversions among young men in orthodox Dissenting academies. Happily, the last twenty years have seen an explosion of splendid work on Priestley, mostly by historians of science who have at last understood that his science cannot be divorced from his religion; and the exploration of Priestley's thought and its consequences has been greatly forwarded by that admirable journal *Enlightenment and Dis-*

[40] "Presbyterians under a New Name," *The English Presbyterians: From Elizabethan Puritanism to Modern Unitarianism*, ed. by C. G. Bolam et al. (London, 1968), 219-86.

[41] "The Unitarian Background," *Truth, Liberty, Religion: Essays Celebrating Two Hundred Years of Manchester College*, ed. by Barbara Smith (Oxford, 1986), 1-30.

[42] Arians, who accepted a subordinate divinity for Jesus, and Socinians, who insisted on his humanity, shared the label of Anti-Trinitarians. Unitarianism displaces Socinianism, which had become a term of derogation, in the 1770s.

sent.[43] Close attention has also been given to Richard Price, Priestley's friend and theological adversary—Price remained an Arian, though the two were as one on political questions.[44]

Political questions posed a terrible threat to Unitarians at the end of the eighteenth century. As the most vocal and advanced segment of Dissent and still its acknowledged leaders, they were severely threatened by the national reaction to the French Revolution and to fears that it might be replicated in Britain. The cry of "Church and King" put them in peculiar danger, dramatically realized in the Birmingham Riots of 1791, when, amid much other damage to the property of those thought dangerous to the state, Priestley's house and laboratory were burned, an outrage that led three years later to his emigration to the United States, where he was joined by a significant number of his coreligionists.[45] In the dark days of the 1790s, the fledgling Unitarians lost strength and numbers, but by the

[43] For an older perspective, F. W. Gibbs, *Joseph Priestley: Adventurer in Science and Champion of Truth* (Edinburgh, 1965). The eagerly awaited first volume of a two-volume life by Robert E. Schofield is near publication. Schofield is one of the contributors to an impressive collection of historical studies of Priestley in a most unlikely place: Royal Society of Chemistry, *Oxygen and the Conversion of Future Feedstocks*, Third BOC Priestley Conference (London, 1984). Some of the contributions to that symposium have been republished, along with other essays, in *Motion toward Perfection: The Achievement of Joseph Priestley*, ed. by A. T. Schwartz and J. G. McEvoy (Boston, 1990). The key essay in modern Priestley studies is J. G. McEvoy and J. E. McGuire, "God and Nature: Priestley's Way of Rational Dissent," *Historical Studies in the Physical Sciences* 6 (1975), 325-404. *Enlightenment and Dissent* is the successor of the *Price-Priestley Newsletter*.

[44] Price (1723-1791) was of much less importance in the development of English Unitarianism, but he is of great interest for his contributions to philosophy and many other fields. See D. O. Thomas, *The Honest Mind: The Thought and Work of Richard Price* (Oxford, 1977).

[45] The long-standard account by R. B. Rose, "The Priestley Riots of 1791," *Past and Present*, No. 18 (1960), 68-88, has been profoundly qualified by G. M. Ditchfield, "The Priestley Riots in Historical Perspective," and David L. Wykes, "'The Spirit of Persecutors Exemplified': The Priestley Riots and the Victims of the Church and King Mobs," *Transactions of the Unitarian Historical Society* 20 (1991), 3-16, 17-39. The other émigrés offer a wonderful subject for a book, an opportunity not at all qualified by Richard J. Twomey, *Jacobins and Jeffersonians: Anglo-American Radicalism in the United States, 1790-1820* (New York, 1989), which is depressingly weak on nearly every aspect of English radicalism. A promising preliminary enquiry is Willard C. Frank, Jr., "Harry Toulmin and William Christie in Virginia, 1793-1801," *Transactions of the Unitarian Historical Society* 19 (1987), 24-37.

second decade of the new century, they were recovering confidence and even predicting victory in their religious as in their political program.

The legacy of Priestley and his contemporaries to early nineteenth-century Unitarians both affected, and was affected by, many other currents in Dissenting society; and Unitarians made vital contributions to the emerging amalgam of liberalism that was to play so large a part in the nineteenth century. That growing liberal consensus, helped on by the political skill of William Smith, M.P., the Unitarian leader of the Dissenting Deputies, redounded to the benefit of the Unitarians in legalizing their worship in 1813.[46] But once we are well into the new century, recent scholarship has left significant gaps.

Unitarian leadership of Dissent, which was inherited from the Presbyterians, began to be contested early in the new century by newly confident and rapidly growing orthodox churches. The rift was precipitated by two lawsuits, over possession of a chapel in Wolverhampton after 1816 and over a charity in York in 1830, in which the plaintiffs argued that the intentions of orthodox donors had been betrayed by the Unitarians. In 1842, the House of Lords (as the ultimate court of appeal) found for the orthodox side, but that merely threw the question to Parliament, where, helped by the Unitarians' political clout, the Dissenters' Chapels Act was passed in 1844, confirming, in the absence of any explicit statement of doctrinal intent, the rights of any foundation that could demonstrate possession over twenty-five years prior to the date of the commencement of an action. During these same years the Unitarians withdrew from their association with the Protestant Dissenting Deputies, the body that, in its quiet but effective way, had represented Dissent to government and Parliament and protected its civil liberties.[47]

While Unitarians could count important members of Parliament throughout the nineteenth century, the dominance they claimed in 1832

[46] These various initiatives have been the particular province of Dr. G. M. Ditchfield. See "Some Aspects of Unitarianism and Radicalism, 1760-1810" (Ph.D. thesis, Cambridge University, 1968), and "The Parliamentary Struggle over the Repeal of the Test and Corporation Acts, 1787-1790," *EHR* 89 (1974), 551-57, one of a number of articles Dr. Ditchfield has devoted to aspects of that engagement. See also R. W. Davis, *Dissent in Politics, 1780-1830: The Political Life of William Smith, M.P.* (London, 1971).

[47] Arthur J. Long, *The Lady Hewley Dispute, 1830-42* (York, 1988), is a brief account, but the broader controversy and its resolution in 1844 cry out for a major study. The origins of the Dissenting Deputies in the early eighteenth century have been authoritatively traced in N. C. Hunt, *Two Early Political Associations: The Quakers and the Dissenting Deputies in the Age of Sir Robert Walpole* (Oxford, 1961), and their whole history can be found in Manning, *Protestant Dissenting Deputies*, which is, however, marred by anti-Unitarian animus.

was quickly eroded by the growth in numbers of M.P.s from orthodox Dissenting backgrounds, and in the twentieth century Unitarian numbers in Parliament dwindled to insignificance. (They remained of the first significance in local government throughout the century.)[48] For thirty years after 1874, however, Joseph Chamberlain, a practicing Unitarian for much of his life, was one of the major political players, while his son Neville, as prime minister from 1937 to 1940, brought the Unitarians their highest, if now sadly clouded, political honor.[49]

Unitarianism was, so to speak, a coalition of religious groups that felt the impress of rationalism. Although the largest element in its makeup was Presbyterianism, it was not always easy to disentangle Presbyterians from the ill-differentiated Dissent of the mid-eighteenth century. But the rapid spread of Evangelicalism in the latter part of the century crystallized differences that had only been implicit in many places, leading to congregational splits and struggles between competing points of view. The rationalistic minorities came together in Unitarianism, among them the so-called Old Connexion of the General Baptists, particularly strong in the rural areas and small towns of the southeast of England, and the Methodist Unitarians in northern Lancashire.[50] There was a steady stream of ministerial recruits from Anglicanism and an approximately equal stream of

[48] Stephen Koss, *Nonconformity in Modern British Politics* (London, 1975), deals primarily with the twentieth-century decline. Some historians of local government have given full recognition to the role played by Unitarians, e.g., A. Temple Patterson, *Radical Leicester* (Leicester, 1954), and E. P. Hennock, *Fit and Proper Persons: Ideal and Reality in Nineteenth-Century Urban Government* (Cambridge, 1973), which is based on Birmingham and Leeds.

[49] The first volume of J. L. Garvin's *Life of Joseph Chamberlain* (London, 1935), is very perceptive on Unitarianism—not surprisingly since Garvin, a famous newspaper editor in the early decades of this century, knew them at first hand. Denis Judd, *Radical Joe: A Life of Joseph Chamberlain* (London, 1977) also takes effective, if brief, note of it, but Richard Jay, *Joseph Chamberlain, a Political Study* (Oxford, 1981), virtually overlooks a Unitarianism that had some real effect on Chamberlain's political position. Neither the older biography of Neville Chamberlain by Keith Feiling (London, 1946; repr. Hamden, Conn., 1970) nor the immense first volume of David Dilks, *Neville Chamberlain* (Cambridge, 1984) has anything useful to say on the subject, a little surprising since the rabidly Conservative Anglican M.P., Lord Hugh Cecil, feared for the future of the Church with the prime minister's appointive powers in the hands of a Unitarian.

[50] Russell E. Richey, "Did the English Presbyterians Become Unitarian?" *CH* 37 (1968), 389-403, argues that Unitarianism is better understood as emerging from generalized Dissent. See also Ian Sellars, "The Old General Baptists, 1811-1915," *Baptist Quarterly* 24 (1971-72), 31-41, 73-88; and Herbert McLachlan, *The Methodist Unitarian Movement* (Manchester, 1919).

defectors to the Church, which, among laymen, became a flood after the middle of the nineteenth century.

Scholars working on Joseph Priestley have begun to take a proper measure of his philosophical position, known as "necessarianism," a psychological determinism based on the teachings of the midcentury physician and theologian David Hartley—with, in Priestley's own case, the addition of materialism. To its enemies, necessarianism seemed rank fatalism, but its adherents found that it both explained the evils about them and offered a sovereign remedy (generally through one or another variety of education) to resolve them and to bring mankind to perfection. The working out of this philosophical position was done following Priestley's death by a number of Unitarian ministers, the most important of whom were Thomas Belsham[51] and Southwood Smith, the latter also a physician of distinction who became one of the most important figures in the sanitary movement.[52]

Well past the middle of the century, necessarianism retained an impressive number of adherents, but it began to be challenged seriously from the 1830s in response to a number of currents—Romanticism, the importation of German critical ideas, the impact of the American Unitarian

[51] Thomas Belsham (1750-1829), the Congregationalist principal of Daventry Academy, created a sensation when, in 1789, as a result of his biblical studies, he converted to Unitarianism. A prize catch, he became principal of the new Hackney College until its closure in 1796. In 1794, he succeeded Priestley as minister at the Gravel Pit Chapel in Hackney and in 1805 became minister of the premier Unitarian congregation in Essex Street, London. An important theologian, Belsham is without modern studies, so recourse must still be had to the life by John Williams, *Memoirs of the Late Rev. Thomas Belsham* (London, 1833).

[52] Thomas Southwood Smith, a strict Baptist from Bristol, was converted to Unitarianism in 1808, studied medicine at Edinburgh, practiced as minister and physician at Yeovil, and in London after 1820 combined a successful medical practice with membership in the intimate circle around Jeremy Bentham. Smith held several government posts after 1833, falling with his colleague Edwin Chadwick in the reaction against centralism in 1854. As a theological writer, Smith drew his philosophical positions from Hartley and Belsham, who had far more profound influence on his ministerial, medical, and governmental career than did Bentham. He has interested historians of medicine and of administration, but his Unitarian significance has been dealt with in R. K. Webb, "Southwood Smith: The Intellectual Sources of Public Service," *Doctors, Politics, and Society: Historical Essays*, ed. by Roy and Dorothy Porter (Amsterdam, 1993), 46-80, and works cited therein. For another "Benthamite," see R. K. Webb, "John Bowring and Unitarianism," *Utilitas* 4 (1992), 43-79; and *Sir John Bowring: Aspects of His Life and Career*, ed. by Joyce Youings (Plymouth, 1993); Bowring was a reformer, poet, M.P., and governor of Hong Kong.

preacher William Ellery Channing, even generational rebellion—and the struggle between the "Old School" and the "New School" dominated the theological history of Unitarianism for the middle two quarters of the century. Here the figure of James Martineau is of surpassing importance. As minister in Dublin and Liverpool, then as professor and later principal at Manchester College, a philosopher of considerable importance in his own time, a writer and reviewer of great brilliance, and a combatant of amazing skill and startling deviousness, he dominated Unitarianism from the 1830s and, by the end of his life in 1900, was as close to canonization as Unitarians could safely come. He was the subject of two excellent biographies shortly after his death, but has been little studied since, a serious lacuna not only in Unitarian studies but in Victorian intellectual history generally.[53] The fragmentation of Unitarian thought that began while Martineau was still active was, in part, a response to the challenge laid down by the antisupernaturalism of the American Theodore Parker, but much remains to be done to elucidate its sources and its consequences.[54]

[53] James Drummond and C. B. Upton, *The Life and Letters of James Martineau*, 2 vols. (London, 1902); J. Estlin Carpenter, *James Martineau, Theologian and Teacher* (London, 1905); Ralph Waller, "James Martineau: The Development of his Thought," *Truth, Liberty, Religion*, 225-64. On Martineau's colleagues in the "New School," John James Tayler (1797-1869) and John Hamilton Thom (1808-1894), see Howard M. Wach, "A 'Still, Small Voice' from the Pulpit: Religion and the Creation of Social Morality in Manchester, 1820-1850," *JMH* 63 (1991), 425-45; and R. K. Webb, "John Hamilton Thom: Intellect and Conscience in Liverpool," *The View from the Pulpit: Victorian Ministers and Society*, ed. by P. T. Phillips (Toronto, 1978), 210-43. Webb's promised book, *A Christian Necessity*, will consider the history of necessarianism largely through a series of case studies, some of them drawn from articles cited elsewhere in this chapter. Webb has also traced a perhaps surprising strain persisting from eighteenth-century Rational Dissent into nineteenth-century Unitarianism in "Rational Piety," *Enlightenment and Religion: Rational Dissent in Eighteenth-Century Britain*, ed. by Knud Haakonssen (Cambridge, forthcoming 1996).

[54] Joseph Estlin Carpenter (1844-1927) was a major figure in the study of non-Christian religions: Arthur J. Long, "The Life and Work of J. Estlin Carpenter," *Truth, Liberty, Religion*, 265-89. In "Rationality, Economic Man and Altruism," ibid., 291-311, Ian Steedman considers one aspect of the polymathic career of the Rev. Philip Henry Wicksteed, a figure who deserves a broad-scale study. See also Bruce Findlow, "The Free Catholic Movement," *Transactions of the Unitarian Historical Society* 11 (1958), 147-62. Note should be taken of the persistence of a liturgical tradition in a large minority of Unitarian congregations: Alexander Elliott Peaston writes authoritatively on the origins of that tradition in *The Prayer Book Reform Movement in the XVIIIth Century* (Oxford, 1940); however, his *The Prayer Book Tradition in the Free Churches* (Edinburgh, 1964)

There is a wide range, in age, size, and quality, of histories of individual congregations, and particular mention should be made of a valuable recent survey of the chapels themselves that makes an important contribution to architectural history.[55] Very little has been done, however, with the organizational history of the denomination apart from H. L. Short's essay on the founding in 1825 of the British and Foreign Unitarian Association (BUFA), a consolidation of several Unitarian propaganda bodies that served as the only central body of the Unitarians until the creation of the General Assembly more than a century later.[56] The BFUA was also the target of much of James Martineau's hostility to the name Unitarian, which he saw as representing a transient doctrine defining a sect rather than the church he hoped for; but Martineau's various strategems to replace or supplement it—the launching of the Free Christian movement of the 1860s, the setting up of the triennial National Conference in the 1880s, and his scheme for restructuring the denomination in 1887—remain to be examined in any detail.

One vital departure in Unitarian history began with the founding of a domestic mission in London in 1833, followed by similar missions in large towns elsewhere in the kingdom. Here was an enterprise in which the two increasingly hostile wings of the denomination could co-operate, directed as it was at reclaiming what one minister called "the moral waste" of the great cities. Modelled on the work of the American minister Joseph Tuckerman, a close associate in Boston of William Ellery Channing, the

neglects the Unitarians except for those in the Free Catholic movement; but see his listing of Unitarian liturgies in "The Unitarian Liturgical Tradition," *Transactions of the Unitarian Historical Society* 16 (1976), 63-81.

[55] Instances of the best of the chapel histories would include William Blazeby, *Rotherham Old Meeting House, & Its Ministers* (Rotherham, 1906); E. D. Priestley Evans, *A History of the New Meeting House, Kidderminster, 1782-1900* (Kidderminster, 1900); H. D. Roberts, *Hope Street Church, Liverpool, and Allied Nonconformity* (Liverpool, 1909); and Anne Holt, *Walking Together: A Study in Liverpool Nonconformity, 1688-1938* (London, 1938), on the famous congregation at Benn's Garden/Renshaw Street/Ullet Road, Liverpool. Basil Short's delightful history, *A Respectable Society: Bridport, 1593-1835* (Bradford-on-Avon, 1976), has much to say about the Unitarian New Meeting, whose members dominated the government of the town even before the repeal of the Test and Corporation Acts. The splendidly organized and illustrated account of chapel buildings is Graham Hague et al., *The Unitarian Heritage: An Architectural Survey of Chapels and Churches in the Unitarian Tradition in the British Isles* (Sheffield, 1986). Anthony J. Pass, *Thomas Worthington: Victorian Architecture and Social Purpose* (Manchester, 1988), deals with the premier Unitarian architect.

[56] H. L. Short, "The Founding of the British and Foreign Unitarian Association," *Transactions of the Unitarian Historical Society* 16 (1975), supplement.

movement recruited domestic missionaries—often from among Methodist converts who were thought able to communicate to the poor more effectively than old-line Unitarians could—to visit the poor and to provide religious services and schools, though, in general, they were not dedicated to proselytizing. Some of the missions became full-fledged congregations; in other places, they continued as missions well past the Second World War. The London and Liverpool missions have received very good centennial celebrations, and the latter has figured in other works as well.[57] The English Unitarians were not, however, much interested in foreign missions. This lack of interest may have been owing, in part, to their certainty that Unitarianism was so convincing to the unprejudiced mind that it was only a matter of time; certainly, they drew great comfort from the close association that developed with the Hindu religious leader Rajah Rammohun Roy in the 1820s, and they thought that they had a special advantage in appealing to other monotheistic religions like Islam.[58]

Unitarians were among the earliest recruits to antislavery, at least from Priestley's sermon on the slave trade of 1780, and their involvement both before and after the abolition of slavery in 1833 has been carefully traced.[59] In other areas of social reform, Unitarians were sometimes more divided, in part, by self-interest, in part, by commitment to the principles of political economy. Factory reform is a good illustration: it was the area in which Southwood Smith made his debut as a government official and in which the great Todmorden textile manufacturer John Fielden (from a

[57] V. D. Davis, *The London Domestic Mission Society: Record of a Hundred Years, 1835-1935* (London, 1935); Anne Holt, *A Ministry to the Poor, being the History of the Liverpool Domestic Mission Society, 1836-1936* (Liverpool, 1936); the latter appears prominently in Margaret B. Simey, *Charitable Effort in Liverpool in the Nineteenth Century* (Liverpool, 1951), and in R. K. Webb, "J. H. Thom." See also Daniel T. McColgan, *Joseph Tuckerman, Pioneer in American Social Work* (Washington, 1940).

[58] Spencer Lavan, *Unitarians and India: A Study in Encounter and Response* (Boston, 1977), is concerned mostly with American Unitarian efforts. There is a vast, mostly Indian, literature on Rammohun Roy, but there is room for a study of the English involvement with him.

[59] G. M. Ditchfield, "Repeal, Abolition and Reform: A Study in the Interaction of Reforming Movements in the Parliament of 1790-1796," *Anti-Slavery, Religion and Reform: Essays in Memory of Roger Anstey*, ed. by Christine Bolt and Seymour Drescher (Folkestone and Hamden, Conn., 1980), 101-18, and "Manchester College and Anti-Slavery," *Truth, Liberty, Religion*, 185-224. I agree with Ditchfield that Douglas Charles Stange, *British Unitarians against American Slavery, 1833-65* (Rutherford, N.J., 1984), puts too much weight on an alleged "evangelical Unitarianism."

Quaker background) was a major player,[60] but the celebrated writer Harriet Martineau—the daughter of a textile manufacturer and famous for her tales to illustrate political economy—argued that the difficulties were town problems, not factory problems, and most Unitarian businessmen would have agreed with her.[61]

The area of reform with which Unitarians were especially closely associated is education, central to a religion that essentially equated sin with ignorance and believed in the ultimate perfection of the human race. Subject to exclusion as they were, Unitarians were forced to educate their own, and in the first half of the century most ministers supplemented their pastoral incomes by schoolkeeping. The Unitarians were also heirs to the liberal remnant of the great eighteenth-century tradition of the Dissenting academies, as embodied in Manchester College, successively located in Manchester, York, Manchester again, London, and Oxford; the domestic mission movement, as well as a certain tension between North and South, led in 1854 to the founding of a training college that eventually became a second full-fledged theological school in Manchester. Unitarians were also active founders of Sunday schools and day schools associated with chapels and domestic missions. The new London University (later University College), opened in 1828, drew heavily on Unitarian students excluded from the old universities and numbered many Unitarians amongst its staff, governors, and benefactors; and the founding of provincial universities was indelibly associated with them. The one notable division about education came over Sir James Graham's Factory Bill of 1843, which granted Anglicans oversight of state-funded schools; some Unitarians recognized the political reality that underlay that provision, but others stood with the mass of Dissenters to bring about the bill's defeat.[62]

---

[60] Stewart Angas Weaver, *John Fielden and the Politics of Popular Radicalism, 1832-1847* (Oxford, 1987), follows Fielden from Quakerism to his Methodist Unitarian commitment, but Weaver's interpretation is generally weak on Unitarianism.

[61] The writer, journalist, and traveller Harriet Martineau (1802-1876) has received much attention. The older, admiring biographies can now be dismissed, though her *Autobiography* (London, 1877) remains a revealing and important work. R. K. Webb, *Harriet Martineau, a Radical Victorian* (London and New York, 1960), makes Unitarianism—although she abandoned it for atheism—a key to understanding her remarkable career, and this can be supplemented by *Harriet Martineau's Letters to Fanny Wedgwood*, ed. by Elisabeth Sanders Arbuckle (Stanford, 1983), and *Harriet Martineau—Selected Letters*, ed. by Valerie Sanders (Oxford, 1990).

[62] There has been no overall study and not much in the way of detailed work. On one congregation's effort, see Lester Burney, *Cross Street Chapel Schools, Manchester, 1734-1942* (Manchester, privately printed, 1977). The Unitarian in-

Local cultural institutions were a source of informal education in the nineteenth century, and here Unitarian leadership was important.[63] One notable area of Unitarian, or Unitarian-descended, philanthropy was the creation of major art collections and museums, of which the most famous are the Tate and the Courtauld Galleries. Quaker prejudices would have been a strong influence against involvement in the arts.[64]

Unitarians in business provided as many household names as the Quakers and may, indeed, have included in their ranks a larger number of leaders of major firms, but the histories of firms and industries in which they played a key role suffer, for the most part, from the same foreshortening we have seen with the Quakers—a noting of the connection (with perhaps less understanding of its content) and neglect of the influence of religion. A notable exception to these strictures is D. C. Coleman's history

volvement in universities must be disentangled from separate histories. On schools for Unitarians, John Seed, "Unitarian Ministers as Schoolmasters, 1780-1850: Some Notes," *Transactions of the Unitarian Historical Society* 17 (1982), 170-76; but the famous schools like Lant Carpenter's in Exeter and then in Bristol, Dr. Morell's in Brighton, those of the Misses Lawrence (their school was a forerunner of Roedean) and of the two Swiss émigrés John Brunner and Carl Voelker outside Liverpool await their chroniclers. There is a privately printed history of the one effort at creating a Unitarian public school, *Willaston School, 1900-1937*, ed. by G. E. Walker (Willaston, 1973). A useful guide to the Dissenting academies of all orientations is Herbert McLachlan, *English Education under the Test Acts, Being the History of the Nonconformist Academies, 1662-1820* (Manchester, 1931), but see the important corrective to persisting myths in D. L. Wykes, "Dissenting Academies and the Emergence of Rational Dissent," *Enlightenment and Religion*, ed. by Haakonssen. There is a good older history of Manchester College, V. D. Davis, *A History of Manchester College, from Its Foundation in Manchester to Its Establishment in Oxford* (London, 1932), and the essays in *Truth, Liberty, Religion* are indispensable. The Unitarian Home Missionary Board, later Unitarian College, Manchester, and Carmarthen College in Wales, which while enrolling all kinds of Dissenters was a nursery of Unitarians, still await careful study. On a vital force in supporting Unitarian education and scholarship, see Alan R. Ruston, *The Hibbert Trust, A History* (London, 1984).

[63] Arnold Thackray, "Natural Knowledge in Cultural Context: The Manchester Model," *AHR* 79 (1974), 673-709; and Derek Orange, "Rational Dissent and Provincial Science: William Turner and the Newcastle Literary and Philosophical Society," *Metropolis and Province: Science in British Culture, 1780-1850*, ed. by Ian Inkster and Jack Morrell (London, 1983), 205-30.

[64] On the provincial background, C. P. Darcy, *The Encouragement of the Fine Arts in Lancashire, 1760-1860*, Chetham Society, Remains Historical and Literary, 3rd ser. 24 (Manchester, 1976), is studded with Unitarian names, though the author makes nothing of the connection.

of the great textile firm of Courtaulds, which is exemplary in its recognition
of the importance of Unitarianism in the Courtauld family and in the work
of the real founder of the firm, Samuel Courtauld.[65]

Although Unitarians in the early nineteenth century were a remarkably
cohesive and intermarrying group, they are not perceived as having the
same distinctive identity as the Quakers, which may account for the lack
of historical work on Unitarians qua Unitarians in different fields of activity. Nor has there been the same awareness of Unitarian dynasties,
though they, too, were an historical reality. But Unitarians prominent in
public and intellectual life in the Victorian era have been far better served
by their biographers than have their analogues in the Society of Friends,
whatever the field in which distinction was earned.[66]

[65] See the first volume of D. C. Coleman, *Courtaulds: An Economic and Social
history* (Oxford, 1969). The Unitarian family background is well sketched in
Francis E. Hyde and J. R. Harris, *Blue Funnel: A History of Alfred Holt and
Company of Liverpool from 1865 to 1914* (Liverpool, 1956), but the importance
of Unitarianism is more implicit than explicit in R. S. Fitton and A. P. Wadsworth, *The Strutts and the Arkwrights, 1758-1830* (Manchester, 1958; repr. New
York, 1968), which deals primarily with the former, Unitarian members of the
partnership, and in W. G. Rimmer, *Marshall's of Leeds, Flax-Spinners,
1788-1886* (Cambridge, 1960). Sheila Marriner, *Rathbones of Liverpool, 1845-73*
(Liverpool, 1961), is a useful business history that touches not at all on the extensive Unitarian concerns in the Rathbone Papers; a similar comment applies to
Mary B. Rose, *The Gregs of Quarry Bank Mill: The Rise and Decline of a Family
Firm, 1750-1914* (Cambridge, 1986). Philippe Chalmin, *The Making of a Sugar
Giant: Tate and Lyle, 1859-1959* (Chur, Switzerland, 1990), is a French doctoral
thesis that concentrates solely on the commercial and technical history of that
spectacular enterprise; Sir Henry Tate, one of the great Victorian philanthropists
and a life-long Unitarian, does not emerge as a person, nor has he had any serious
biographical attention. W. J. Reader, *Imperial Chemical Industries: A History*,
1, *The Forerunners, 1870-1926* (London, 1970), does not concern itself with the
Unitarianism of Sir John Brunner, one of the two founders of the combine, but
the gap is filled by Stephen E. Koss, *Sir John Brunner, Radical Plutocrat, 1842-
1919* (Cambridge, 1970).

[66] Jo Manton, *Mary Carpenter and the Children of the Streets* (London, 1976),
deals perceptively with a great Victorian crusader, the daughter of the eminent
Unitarian minister Lant Carpenter, for the cause of neglected and delinquent
children. T. S. Simey and M. B. Simey, *Charles Booth, Social Scientist* (London,
1960), is an exemplary life of the social investigator who produced the monumental *Life and Labour of the People of London* (1889-1903); Booth's family
were, and remained, staunch Unitarians, but Booth himself severed his connection. Sheila R. Herstein, *A Mid-Victorian Feminist, Barbara Leigh Smith
Bodichon* (New Haven, 1985), is a study of one of the founders (1827-1891) of

Again because of their easier definition, the Quakers have had the historiographical edge when it comes to social history. The kind of demographic work that Isichei and Vann and Eversley have done for the Quakers has not even begun for Unitarians. It would have to proceed by way of reconstructing congregations, which is a manageable task for some chapels, but sampling the Unitarian population as a whole is probably impossible, given the state of the   records.[67] There are instances of more limited approaches. David Wykes has carefully analyzed laymen associated, as supporters or students, with Manchester College. R. K. Webb has used fragile evidence from contemporary surveys to estimate Unitarian numbers in the early nineteenth and early twentieth centuries and is com-

Girton College, Cambridge. Other recent lives, with differing emphases, include Valerie Kossew Pichanick, *Harriet Martineau: The Woman and her Work, 1802-76* (Ann Arbor, 1980), and Gillian Thomas, *Harriet Martineau* (Boston, 1985). The Spanish émigré intellectual Joseph Blanco White, who ended his astonishing odyssey among the Liverpool Unitarians, is the subject of Martin Murphy, *Blanco White, Self-Banished Spaniard* (New Haven and London, 1989), though the Unitarian discussion is largely derivative. Another startling Victorian, Francis Newman, the brother of Cardinal Newman, was closely associated for a time with Unitarians and still awaits a serious study, though there is a brief and perceptive book by William Robbins, *The Newman Brothers: An Essay in Comparative Intellectual Biography* (London, 1966). There are many other eminent Victorians who were Unitarians or who ceased to be so, and others who had important Unitarian associations—Samuel Taylor Coleridge, Charles Darwin, George Eliot, Florence Nightingale, and Beatrice Webb are among the first-rank figures who still await careful explication of the connection. But see John P. Frazee, "Dickens and Unitarianism," *Dickens Studies Annual* 18 (1989), 119-43; R. K. Webb, "The Gaskells as Unitarians," *Dickens and Other Victorians: Essays in Honour of Philip Collins*, ed. by Joanne Shattock (London, 1988), 144-71, which reviews the extensive literature that has dealt with Elizabeth Gaskell's (1809-1862) religion and suggests Unitarian influences in her novels; and Richard J. Helmstadter, "W. R. Greg: A Manchester Creed," *Victorian Faith in Crisis: Essays on Continuity and Change in Nineteenth-Century Religious Belief*, ed. by Richard J. Helmstadter and Bernard Lightman (London and Stanford, 1990), 187-222. On the most important theologian to abandon his ancestral Unitarianism, see David Young, *F. D. Maurice and Unitarianism* (Oxford, 1993).

[67] The Unitarian Historical Society began a survey of the whereabouts of congregational records in the early 1970s and has encouraged their placement in proper repositories. The results can be found in Andrew M. Hill, "Unitarian Congregations in Great Britain: A Location List of their Records," *Transactions of the Unitarian Historical Society* 17 (1981-82), 111-24, 155-69, with subsequent deposits noted in subsequent issues. Some of the surviving records are immensely rich sources; others have suffered badly from carelessness and neglect.

pleting a study of the Unitarian ministry from 1780 to 1980, which, drawing on a database of something over 2,000 ministers, will examine patterns in their social and religious origins, education, and careers.[68]

John Seed takes a different approach to social history—from a sociological perspective—in his thesis on Unitarianism, which has spun off some valuable interpretive articles; what Seed has written about Manchester culture will be supplemented in a fascinating way by a comparative study of Manchester and Boston, Massachusetts, now being made by Howard M. Wach.[69]

Although the Unitarians lack the centralized system that has helped the survival of Quaker records, the resources for other aspects of their history are immensely rich and still largely untouched.[70] This chapter can end,

[68] David Wykes, "Sons and Subscribers: Lay Support and the College, 1786-1840," *Truth, Liberty, Religion*, 31-77; R. K. Webb, "Views of Unitarianism from Halley's Comet," *Transactions of the Unitarian Historical Society* 18 (1986), 180-95. When Webb's work on the ministry is published, it can be used for comparisons with the analyses of the Congregationalist, Baptist, and Methodist ministries in Kenneth D. Brown, *A Social History of the Nonconformist Ministry in England and Wales, 1800-1930* (Oxford, 1988).

[69] John Seed, "The Role of Unitarianism in the Formation of Liberal Culture, 1775-1851" (Ph.D. thesis, University of Hull, 1981); "Theologies of Power: Unitarianism and the Social Relations of Religious Discourse, 1800-1850," *Class, Power, and Social Structure in British Nineteenth Century Towns*, ed. by R. J. Morris (Leicester, 1986), 108-56, a stimulating study of religion and class formation in Newcastle, Leeds, Wakefield, and Hull; "Unitarians, Political Economy and the Antinomies of Liberal Culture in Manchester, 1830-50," *Social History* 7 (1982), 1-26.

[70] The principal libraries, with vast holdings in printed books, journals, and manuscripts, are Dr. Williams's Library in London, Manchester College, Oxford, and the collections of Unitarian College, Manchester, now deposited in the John Rylands University Library of Manchester. On the last-named, see Clive D. Field, "Sources for the Study of Protestant Nonconformity in the John Rylands University Library of Manchester," *Bulletin of the John Rylands University Library of Manchester* 71 (1989), 103-39. Correspondence and diaries of major Unitarians (and some obscure ones) can be found not only there but in other libraries and record offices, e.g., the extensive and much quarried diary of Henry Crabb Robinson in Dr. Williams's Library, the very large diaries of the Rev. Timothy Davis in the National Library of Wales, and the diary of George Holt in the Liverpool Record Office. The Unitarians have an advantage over the Quakers in the existence of three weekly newspapers, the *Inquirer*, from 1842 to the present, the *Unitarian Herald*, from 1861 to 1889, and *Christian Life*, from 1876 to 1929, as well as some excellent journals and magazines. The most famous of the latter has been the subject of a fine book by Francis E. Mineka, *The Dissidence of*

therefore, with invoking another element of commonality between its two ill-matched subjects. No claim is, or can be, made that either Quakerism or Unitarianism is central to an understanding of the nineteenth century. But as the centrality of Victorian religion becomes more and more apparent, there is need to press forward with a proper valuation of these two tiny minorities whose beliefs and activities made so great, if not always so favourable, an impression on their contemporaries and who played a disproportionate role in nearly every aspect of their society. That need cannot be satisfied by merely noting connections or by vaguely invoking formulistic and inherited characterizations. It requires careful assessment of fluctuating numbers, of the detailed working of organizations, and of the evolution of theology, worship, and devotion. But, above all, it demands an understanding that men and women were deeply moved and powerfully motivated by religious imperatives not embraced in the orthodoxies of the bigger battalions.

Dissent: The "Monthly Repository," 1806-1838 (Chapel Hill, 1944). The *Christian Reformer* also had an impressive run from 1815 to 1861. On other Unitarian periodicals, see J. L. Altholz, *Victorian Religious Periodicals*, and volume 3 of the *Wellesley Index to Victorian Periodicals*, which contains splendid introductions. The *Transactions of the Unitarian Historical Society* is an annual begun in 1915. The linkage between the United States and Britain that we have observed with the Quakers is not so close for the Unitarians, but there were contacts to be followed up in, e.g., the letter-books of the American Unitarian Association held at Harvard University. There are two major American Unitarian libraries—in the Harvard Divinity School in Cambridge, Mass., and the Meadville/Lombard Theological School in Chicago—which hold all the major English material and have significant, though not always complete, runs of the periodicals.

5

Methodism

David Hempton

THE PUBLICATION OF volume four of *A History of the Methodist Church in Great Britain* (1988), a project begun over a quarter of a century before, seems an appropriate point to attempt a retrospect and prospect of Methodism in English society between the death of John Wesley and the outbreak of the First World War.[1] Its massive bibliography, extending to some fifty pages for this period alone and including many of the most influential historians of modern Britain, is both a tribute to the strange power that Methodism has exercised over generations of research students and a revealing guide to the main turning points of Methodist historiography.

Most obviously, there have been a marked decline in the number of words devoted to Methodist theology, spirituality, and biography and a corresponding increase in studies of the personal, social, and political impact of Methodism on English localities. Such a trend was accelerated by the attention brought to the subject by the socialist historians Christopher Hill, Eric Hobsbawm, and Edward Thompson,[2] whose pioneering, if sometimes crude, work stimulated a remarkably rich literature culminating in the History Workshop volume *Disciplines of Faith*.[3] The high quality of many of its contributions and the fact that it was dedicated to John

---

[1] *A History of the Methodist Church in Great Britain*, ed. by Rupert Davies, A. R. George, and Gordon Rupp, 4 vols. (London, 1965-88).

[2] E. J. Hobsbawm, "Methodism and the Threat of Revolution in Britain," *History Today* 7 (1957), 115-24, and *Labouring Men: Studies in the History of Labour* (London, 1968), 23-33; E. P. Thompson, *The Making of the English Working Class* (London, 1963).

[3] *Disciplines of Faith: Studies in Religion, Politics, and Patriarchy*, ed. by Jim Obelkevich, Lyndal Roper, and Raphael Samuel (London, 1987).

Walsh, show that reductionist interpretations of popular religion are almost dead and that the previously wide gulf between ecclesiastical historians and social historians of religion is now less impassable.[4] More recently, much of the creative work on Methodist history has concentrated on the religious experiences of ordinary people, men, women, and children and the ways that social change, family structure, gender, and emotion shaped those experiences. Much of this work is, of necessity, grounded in intensive local studies, which have drawn attention to the sheer variety and complexity of nineteenth-century Methodism, despite the occasional misplaced attempt to find the holy grail of Methodism's national essence.[5] But if the telephoto lens has brought clearer definition to the Methodism of the English regions, the wide angle has shown that regional particularity must be viewed against the backdrop of an international religious revival from the Urals in the East to the American frontier in the West.[6]

Most of the contested areas of Methodist historiography ultimately go back to rival explanations of its growth and decline; much else depends on positions taken on that fundamental issue. The facts themselves are not much in dispute, thanks to the convenience of class membership figures as a reasonable guide to Methodist strength, if not Methodist influence. The various Methodist connexions grew faster than the population as a whole before 1840, held their own until the middle of the 1880s, and then declined relative to the total adult population until 1906 before declining in absolute terms thereafter.[7] Both the rapidity and the chronological and

[4] For views on the writing of religious history, see Christopher Brooke et al., "What Is Religious History?," *History Today* 35 (1985), 43-52; and *What Is History Today?*, ed. by Juliet Gardiner (London, 1988).

[5] Many excellent local studies remain unpublished, but can be traced through the bibliography in *History of the Methodist Church*, 4. Among published works, the following are the most useful: Robert Moore, *Pit-Men, Preachers, and Politics: The Effects of Methodism in a Durham Mining Community* (London, 1974); James Obelkevich, *Religion and Rural Society: South Lindsey, 1825-1875* (Oxford, 1975); John Rule, "Methodism, Popular Beliefs, and Village Culture in Cornwall, 1800-50," *Popular Culture and Custom in Nineteenth-Century England*, ed. by R. D. Storch (London, 1982), 48-70; and Stephen Yeo, *Religion and Voluntary Religious Organisations in Crisis* (London, 1976).

[6] W. R. Ward, "The Relations of Enlightenment and Religious Revival in Central Europe and in the English-Speaking World," *SCH*, subsidia 2 (1979), 281-305; and "Power and Piety: The Origins of Religious Revival in the Early Eighteenth Century," *Bulletin of the John Rylands University Library of Manchester* 63 (1980), 231-52.

[7] Robert Currie, Alan Gilbert, and Lee Horsley, *Churches and Churchgoers: Patterns of Church Growth in the British Isles since 1700* (Oxford, 1977); A. D. Gilbert, *Religion and Society in Industrial England: Church, Chapel and Social*

geographical unevenness of Methodist growth were clearly linked to wider changes in the English economy and society, but attempts to relate spurts of Methodist growth to economic depression on the one hand, and the growth of political radicalism on the other, have not proved very fruitful.[8] There are examples of Methodist growth in periods of economic depression including Yorkshire in the 1790s[9] and Lancashire during the great cotton depression of the 1860s, but, more generally, the data are ambiguous, and R. B. Walker is right to conclude that "no clear pattern of relationship between religious revivals and economic change emerges" in Victorian Methodism.[10] What does seem to be the case is that whereas short, sharp bursts of economic hardship or epidemics of contagious diseases could temporarily stimulate religious enthusiasm, long-term economic decline was a disaster for religious connexions dependent on voluntary subscriptions.[11] Similarly, the relationship between the growth of Methodism and political radicalism is more complicated than either Thompson's oscillation theory or Hobsbawm's concurrent expansion ideas would permit.[12] It is hard to resist the conclusion that religious attraction or repulsion is neither a straightforwardly economic nor political transaction.

A more constructive approach to understanding the expansion of Methodism, without in any way diminishing its distinctive theology, or-

---

Change, 1740-1914 (London, 1976); and Robert Currie, "A Micro-Theory of Methodist Growth," *Proceedings of the Wesley Historical Society* 36 (1967-68), 65-73.

[8] I briefly survey this historiography in *Methodism and Politics in British Society, 1750-1850* (London, 1984), 74-80. See also E. P. Stigant, "Wesleyan Methodism and Working-Class Radicalism in the North, 1792-1821," *Northern History* 6 (1971), 98-116; and A. D. Gilbert, "Methodism, Dissent, and Political Stability in Early Industrial England," *Journal of Religious History* 10 (1978-79), 381-99.

[9] John Baxter, "The Great Yorkshire Revival, 1792-6: A Study of Mass Revival among the Methodists," *A Sociological Yearbook of Religion in Britain* 7 (1974), 46-76.

[10] R. B. Walker, "The Growth of Wesleyan Methodism in Victorian England and Wales," *JEH* 34 (1973), 267-84.

[11] For interesting regional comparisons of this theme, see C. B. Turner, "Revivalism and Welsh Society in the Nineteenth Century," *Disciplines of Faith*, 311-23; and David Hempton, "Methodism in Irish Society, 1770-1830," *TRHS*, 5th ser. 36 (1986), 117-42. More extensive treatments of revivalism are to be found in Richard Carwardine, *Trans-Atlantic Revivalism: Popular Evangelicalism in Britain and America, 1790-1865* (Westport, Conn., 1978); and J.H.S. Kent, *Holding the Fort: Studies in Victorian Revivalism* (London, 1978).

[12] E. S. Itzkin, "The Halévy Thesis—A Working Hypothesis?" *CH* 44 (1975), 47-56.

ganization, and evangelical zeal, is to see it as part of much wider structural changes in English society in the generation after the French Revolution. In this period, a complex of social tensions caused by population growth, subsistence crises, and the commercialization of agriculture, and further exacerbated by prolonged warfare, sharpened class conflict and undermined the old denominational order.[13] W. R. Ward has shown, for example, how many Anglican parsons benefited from enclosure and tithe commutation at the expense of their influence among small freeholders and laborers.[14] The rising social status of the clergy and their unprecedented representation on the bench of magistrates cemented the squire and parson alliance at the very time that establishment ideals were most under attack. In such circumstances, the Church of England was in no position to resist a dramatic upsurge in undenominational itinerant preaching and cottage-based religion, which even the various Methodist connexions struggled to keep under control.[15]

Methodism thus made its fastest gains in areas least amenable to paternalistic influence, including freehold parishes, industrial villages, mining communities, market towns, canal and sea ports, and other centers of migratory populations.[16] Obelkevich's classic local study of South Lindsey is a vivid illustration of how the Church of England's attempt to reinforce an older paternalistic, hierarchic, and integrated society was vigorously challenged by more emotionally vibrant and populist forms of religion such as that offered by the Primitive Methodists.[17] The result was a mix-

[13] W. R. Ward, *Religion and Society in England, 1790-1850* (London, 1972), and "The Religion of the People and the Problem of Control, 1790-1830," *SCH* 8 (1972), 237-57.

[14] W. R. Ward, "Church and Society in the First Half of the Nineteenth Century," *History of the Methodist Church*, 2, 11-96; and "The Tithe Question in England in the Early Nineteenth Century," *JEH* 16 (1965), 67-81. See also E. J. Evans, "Some Reasons for the Growth of English Rural Anti-Clericalism, c. 1750-c. 1830," *Past and Present* No. 66 (1975), 84-109.

[15] Deborah M. Valenze, *Prophetic Sons and Daughters: Female Preaching and Popular Religion in Industrial England* (Princeton, 1985).

[16] Alan Everitt, *The Pattern of Rural Dissent: The Nineteenth Century* (Leicester, 1972); and John D. Gay, *The Geography of Religion in England* (London, 1971).

[17] Obelkevich, *Religion in Rural Society*, 183-258. Since Primitive Methodism has not been well served in the new four-volume *History of the Methodist Church in Great Britain*, H. B. Kendall's *The Origin and History of the Primitive Methodist Church*, 2 vols. (London, 1906), remains the standard work. But the first decade of Primitive Methodist expansion has been carefully etched in by Julia Stuart Werner, *The Primitive Methodist Connexion: Its Background and Its Early History* (Madison, Wisc., 1984). See also R. W. Ambler, "From Ranters to Chapel

ture of class and cultural conflict that reflected the economic and social structure of the area and led to the growth of an agricultural trade union-ism almost entirely under Methodist leadership.[18]

If the explanation for the rapidity of Methodist growth in the period 1790-1840 is still contested territory among historians, so, too, is its con-tinued growth at a slower pace in the Victorian period. John Kent, for example, regards the institutional development of nineteenth-century Wesleyanism, and ultimately of the other connexions also, as a relative success, given what might have happened if self-opinionated zealots had gained control.[19] Thus, Jabez Bunting[20] and his supporters, far from de-basing virginal Methodism, performed the unpleasant but necessary task of giving a structure and sense of coherence to Wesleyanism as a national connexion. The many problems and bitter controversies that he encount-ered were not so much the result of heavy-handed ecclesiastical manage-ment as the inevitable consequence of coping with the inner contradictions of Methodism, which he inherited but did not create. In Kent's view, the continued growth of Methodism throughout the nineteenth century was therefore a vindication of Bunting's strategy. Those who criticized him most, then as now, were guilty of holding a romanticized view of early Methodism's impact on the poor and consequently developed an unreal-istic assessment of its potential among the industrial proletariat of Victo-rian England, who remained beyond the pale of any form of organized Christianity. Recent surveys of the social constituency of eighteenth-cen-tury Methodism seem to confirm that it drew most of its members from the upper echelons of the lower orders and lower income groups within the

Builders: Primitive Methodism in the South Lincolnshire Fenland, c. 1820-1875," *SCH* 23 (1986), 319-31.

[18] N.A.D. Scotland, *Methodism and the Revolt of the Field: A Study of the Methodist Contribution to Agricultural Trade Unionism in East Anglia, 1872-96* (Gloucester, 1981); and Pamela Horn, *The Rural World, 1780-1850: Social Change in the English Countryside* (London, 1980).

[19] John Kent, "The Wesleyan Methodists to 1849," *History of the Methodist Church*, 2, 213-75, and *The Age of Disunity* (London, 1966).

[20] Jabez Bunting (1779-1858) was Wesleyan Methodism's leading ecclesiastical statesman from 1820, when he became President of Conference for the first time, until 1850 when the Wesleyan Reform secessions began. See T. P. Bunting, *The Life of Jabez Bunting*, 2 vols. (London, 1859-87); W. R. Ward, *The Early Cor-respondence of Jabez Bunting, 1820-1829*, Camden 4th ser., 11 (London, 1972); W. R. Ward, *Early Victorian Methodism: The Correspondence of Jabez Bunting, 1830-1858* (Oxford, 1976); and J.H.S. Kent, *Jabez Bunting, the Last Wesleyan: A Study in the Methodist Ministry after the Death of John Wesley* (London, 1955), and *Age of Disunity*, 103-26.

middle ranks, rather than from the lowest and most desperate.[21] But neither can there be any denying the upward social mobility of mainstream
Methodism in the Victorian period, as "piety, profit and paternalism"
made a formidable contribution to the commercial life of the North of
England and built a culture of stubborn respectability, described by David
Martin as a "brand of individualism, decency, self-improvement, homes-
pun piety and service."[22]

An alternative picture of nineteenth-century Methodist development is
presented by W. R. Ward, who takes a less sympathetic view of the growth
of Wesleyan connexional management than does John Kent. He suggests
that the Wesleyan leadership, when confronted by rapid expansion in the
years of high social tension between Wesley's death and Peterloo, tried to
retain control by clamping down on religious revivalism, political radicalism, undenominational Sunday schools, and other popular causes.[23] In the
process, Methodism became more centralized, more bureaucratic, more
clerical, and more respectable. While not suggesting that Methodism
would ever have taken control of the urban proletariat in nineteenth-century England, Ward convincingly shows that by 1820 the Wesleyan connexion at least had changed in important respects and had consequently
become less attractive to urban workers. Bunting was not, of course, the
architect of all these developments. Rather, he grew up during their implementation and became committed through personal experience to the
idea that Methodist growth had been too indisciplined and too polluted
with other causes for the religious connexion's long-term health. But
equally convincing is Ward's argument that in the period of Bunting's hegemony between 1820 and 1850, when Methodism was convlused by major secessions from which it never fully recovered, the divisive issues were
not simply thrown up by problems of connexional government, as Kent
suggests, but had their roots in a more general hardening of denominational boundaries that made sectarian conflict, with class overtones, the
most characteristic feature of English politics in the early Victorian
period.[24]

[21] C. D. Field, "The Social Structure of English Methodism: Eighteenth-
Twentieth Centuries," *British Journal of Sociology* 28 (1977), 199-225; John Q.
Smith, "Occupational Groups among the Early Methodists of the Keighley Cir-
cuit," *CH* 57 (1988), 187-96.

[22] David Martin, "Faith, Flour and Jam," *Times Literary Supplement*, 1 April
1983, 329-30.

[23] Ward, "Religion of the People," 237-57.

[24] Ward, *Religion and Society*, 177-278. See also D. A. Gowland, *Methodist
Secessions: The Origins of Free Methodism in Three Lancashire Towns: Manchester, Rochdale, Liverpool*, Chetham Society, *Remains, Historical and Literary
connected with the Palatine Counties of Lancashire and Cheshire*, 3rd ser., 26

Moving on from general interpretations of Methodist growth and decline in the nineteenth century to the formidable literature now available on regional revivalism, from Cornwall to Ulster and from the Trent valley to the South Wales coalfield, a number of consistent themes have emerged.[25] Generally speaking, revivalism flourished either in very cohesive communities such as mining settlements or among rural migrants to industrial villages. Although there is some evidence to link revivalism to economic dislocation and political repression, there is a general acknowledgement that religious revivals had internal social and psychological dynamics regardless of external circumstances. While epidemic diseases and hazardous occupations could add a cutting edge of urgency to religious enthusiasm, the most consistent factor was a desire for revival and sense of expectancy within Methodist communities themselves. The existence of a population with at least a smattering of biblical knowledge and familiarity with basic Christian concepts of salvation and damnation was also important. In some regions, therefore, religious revivalism became a local tradition in its own right, manifesting itself in recurring generational pulses. But by 1830, this kind of folk revivalism had become confined to the Celtic fringes of British society, and Victorian flirtation with the American "new measures" version proved to be a less powerful, if more socially acceptable, alternative. Technique revivalism, whatever its claimed successes in specific urban crusades may have been, was no remedy for the complex forces that were at work in the slowing down of Methodist expansion from the middle of the century.[26]

Population movements from country to town and from city centers to suburbia posed new structural problems at a time when Methodist morale had taken a pounding from the reform controversies and secessions of the 1840s and 1850s.[27] From then on, the various Methodist connexions, including the Primitives, which had always recruited rapidly at the bottom and lost members less rapidly at the top, made less and less impression on

(Manchester, 1979); and G.I.T. Machin, *Politics and the Churches in Great Britain, 1832 to 1868* (Oxford, 1977).

[25] For a brief survey, see my *Methodism and Politics*, 92-8. Also, David Luker, "Revivalism in Theory and Practice: The Case of Cornish Methodism," *JEH* 37 (1986), 603-19; J. M. Turner, *Conflict and Reconciliation: Studies in Methodism and Ecumenism in England, 1740-1982* (London, 1985), 82-8; and *Disciplines of Faith*, Obelkevich, 309-34.

[26] Kent, *Holding the Fort*, 356-68.

[27] H. D. Rack, "Wesleyan Methodism, 1849-1902," *History of the Methodist Church*, 3, 119-66; D. M. Thompson, "Church Extension in Town and Countryside in Later Nineteenth-Century Leicester," *SCH* 16 (1979), 427-40; and J.H.S. Kent, "The Role of Religion in the Cultural Structure of the Later Victorian City," *TRHS*, 5th ser., 23 (1973), 153-73.

the unchurched English population. Such growth as still took place was largely due either to denominational migration or to the natural increase of the Methodist community itself. Far from offering any long-term prospect of Methodist revitalization, both were essentially negative developments, for they further emphasized Methodism's, especially the Wesleyan Connexion's, creeping withdrawal into a respectable religious cocoon within which institutional concerns took precedence over more vital matters.[28] Institutional order, then institutional unity, were paths guaranteed to lead to national integration and popular indifference.

The changes within Methodism over the course of the nineteenth century have been more precisely documented in impressive recent studies of the Methodist ministry, lay spirituality, popular education, and the relationship between Methodist communities and their surrounding culture. The contrast, for example, between Deborah Valenze's analysis of the male and female itinerants who serviced an extensive cottage-based religion in the first half of the nineteenth century and K. D. Brown's statistical survey of Nonconformist ministers in the second half is particularly striking, even allowing for the fact that Valenze's preachers are an unrepresentative sample of Methodist preachers as a whole.[29] Indeed, it has been shown that a high doctrine of the pastoral office, as opposed to itinerant flexibility and enthusiasm, was already well established in the Wesleyan Connexion within a quarter of a century of Wesley's death.[30] But as the connexional leadership presented an increasingly respectable and authoritarian model of ministerial behavior, the more unruly preaching of revivalists and women opened up a more intimate relationship with lower-class life. Women made up a significant proportion of preachers within Primitive Methodism, the Bible Christian movement and other Methodist minorities, at least until the 1840s, when they disappear from the circuit plans.[31] The peak of their influence coincided with the high point of cottage religion within popular Evangelicalism, when "unprofessional

[28] H. D. Rack, "Wesleyanism and 'the World' in the Later Nineteenth Century," *Proceedings of the Wesley Historical Society* 42 (1979-80), 34-54.

[29] Valenze, *Prophetic Sons and Daughters*; K. D. Brown, *A Social History of the Nonconformist Ministry in England and Wales, 1800-1930* (Oxford, 1988).

[30] J. C. Bowmer, *Pastor and People: A Study of Church and Ministry in Wesleyan Methodism from the Death of John Wesley (1791) to the Death of Jabez Bunting (1858)* (London, 1975); W. R. Ward, "The Legacy of John Wesley: The Pastoral Office in Britain and America," *Statesmen, Scholars and Merchants: Essays in Eighteenth-Century History Presented to Dame Lucy Sutherland*, ed. by Anne Whiteman, J. S. Bromley, and P.G.M. Dickson (Oxford, 1973), 323-50.

[31] W. F. Swift, "The Women Itinerant Preachers of Early Methodism," *Proceedings of the Wesley Historical Society* 28 (1951-52), 89-94, and 29 (1953-54), 76-83.

This can be attributed to the black churches.

preaching in noninstitutional surroundings encompassed the immediate, tangible, and private aspects of life."[32] The temporary emergence of female preaching on a scale not seen since the Civil War period was but one consequence of a much wider outburst of itinerant preaching between 1780 and 1830, when the Established Church's hold on the English population was substantially undermined. As Lovegrove has recently shown, itinerant preaching was not confined to the various Methodist connexions, but made an important contribution to the metamorphosis of English Calvinistic Dissent from an exclusive emphasis on the spiritual well-being of church members to a renewed concern for outsiders in hitherto untouched communities.[33]

A diluted itinerancy, along with a high ratio of lay to regular preachers, survived in the main Methodist connexions throughout the nineteenth century, but there were important changes in the recruitment, training, and duties of the preachers. By 1900, for example, 58 percent of all active Methodist preachers had been to theological college, where the training they received was inadequate, both in educational terms and as a preparation for chapel ministry. Most recruits were from families poised uncomfortably between the middle and lower classes, with teachers, white-collar workers, clerks, small craftsmen, and sons of the manse all figuring prominently. There were, moreover, disproportionately more preachers from rural areas and the Celtic fringes than from English towns and cities, where the demographic pressures were most acute. Although supply and demand were in rough equilibrium, the Methodist ministry not only attracted fewer popular enthusiasts as the century went on—a fact not related to the steady decline of an evangelical conversion as a catalyst for a preaching vocation—but also was too unappealing a career to attract men of talent from higher social groups. That a career as a Nonconformist preacher was scarcely a bed of roses in Victorian England is confirmed by the high percentage of withdrawals, particularly from Primitive Methodism, within four years of the commencement of ministry. The inconveniences of itinerancy, friction with the laity, financial pressures, moral frailty, and inadequate training all played their part in creating an unsettled and often ineffective ministry, far removed from the conventional stereotype of Nonconformist giants preaching to thousands from metropolitan pulpits.[34]

[32] Valenze, *Prophetic Sons and Daughters*, 24.

[33] D. W. Lovegrove, *Established Church, Sectarian People: Itinerancy and the Transformation of English Dissent, 1780-1830* (Cambridge, 1988).

[34] K. D. Brown, "An Unsettled Ministry? Some Aspects of Nineteenth-Century British Nonconformity," *CH* 56 (1987), 204-23; and Brown, *Social History of the Nonconformist Ministry*.

A similar spiritual retrenchment into denominational consolidation is also detectable within the Methodist laity in the second half of the nineteenth century. The class meeting, for example, which had always been the chief means of promoting holiness both within individuals and the Wesleyan community, became the focus of an unprecedented number of attacks and defenses.[35] As Wesley's writings make clear, the class had never been a uniformly successful institution within Methodism, but while religious experiences were fresh and vital, its spiritual utility was above question. The problem in the later nineteenth century was that, for many, the classes had become dull, repetitious, ritualistic, and irrelevant to their daily lives. As is the way with religious denominations, much organizational tinkering was advocated and much ink was spilt over the relationship, if any, between class membership and church membership, but the nub of the matter was that the decline of the class meeting was a symptom of much more fundamental changes within both the nature of Methodism itself and its social setting. According to Henry Rack, "the Wesleyans of the later nineteenth century seemed to have lost a great deal of the confidence of their fathers, not only in the capacity of religious exercises to hold people in the church, but also in the capacity of Wesleyans to enter the world without succumbing to it and ceasing to be Wesleyans."[36] Increasing numbers of respectable but unenthusiastic attenders, and the counterattractions of a more secular society, left the class meeting without the intensity of religious commitment that alone could guarantee its success.

It would, of course, be a mistake to portray late nineteenth-century Methodism as spiritually moribund by comparison with its pristine eighteenth-century predecessor. Much energy was expended, for example, on home missions targeted at the urban poor, but even here it was soon apparent that the profound gap between the churched and the unchurched was as much a matter of social class as of religious preference and was consequently unbridgeable by the relatively unimaginative methods employed. In truth, more effort was made to "reach" the working classes than to accommodate them in meaningful cultural forms, with the result that the Methodist urban missions did more to retain the support of the faithful than to make inroads into the heartland of infidelity.[37]

[35] H. D. Rack, "The Decline of the Class-Meeting and the Problem of Church-Membership in Nineteenth-Century Wesleyanism," *Proceedings of the Wesley Historical Society* 39 (1973-74), 12-21; W. W. Dean, "The Methodist Class Meeting: The Significance of its Decline," *ibid.* 43 (1981-82), 41-48.

[36] Rack, "Wesleyanism and 'the World,'" 53-54.

[37] For recent surveys of the relationship between religion and the working class, see Hugh McLeod, *Religion and the Working Class in Nineteenth-Century Britain* (London, 1984); and my "'Popular Religion', 1800-1986," *The British: Their Religious Beliefs and Practices, 1800-1986,* ed. by Terence Thomas (London and

One religious innovation that did attract considerable working-class support throughout the nineteenth century was Sunday school education, approximately one-third of which was under the control of the various Methodist connexions by 1851.[38] The dramatic expansion of Sunday schools began in the late eighteenth century as a result of interdenominational cooperation and private philanthropy, but they soon fell victim to sectarian rivalry and political conflict.[39] By the mid-nineteenth century, they were firmly in the control of the religious denominations, which understandably tried to exploit their potential for recruiting new church and chapel members.[40] Within Methodism, the conflicts over the control of Sunday schools reflected many of the tensions in early nineteenth-century society, including class conflict, anticlericalism, anticentralization, and denominational competition. The Wesleyans, disturbed by reports of radical and heterodox penetration and by the apparent absence of tangible connexional benefits from the Sunday schools, pushed hard for clerical control and took a stand against teaching children how to write on the sabbath.

The Wesleyan leadership, well marshalled by Bunting,[41] was successful on both counts, but the victory was costly in terms of connexional harmony and working-class allegiance, and, more significantly, it never achieved its prime objective of turning the Sunday schools into chapel nurseries. According to Laqueur's figures, Sunday schools attracted a remarkably high percentage of working-class children, but delivered a remarkably low percentage of them into committed chapel membership. Parental pressure and the prize of literacy were clearly more effective inducements than church services and class meetings. But if Sunday schools never quite fulfilled denominational expectations, they made an important contribution to mass literacy and to Victorian chapel culture through anniversary celebrations, street parades, Whitsun outings, prize distributions,

New York, 1988), 181-210. See also Brian Harrison, "Religion and Recreation in Nineteenth-Century England," *Past and Present*, No. 38 (1967), 98-125.

[38] T. W. Laqueur, *Religion and Respectability: Sunday Schools and Working-Class Culture, 1780-1850* (New Haven, 1976).

[39] A. P. Wadsworth, "The First Manchester Sunday Schools," *Bulletin of the John Rylands Library* 33 (1951), 299-326.

[40] There is still considerable debate about whether Sunday schools were tools of middle-class paternalism or were genuine expressions of a respectable working-class culture. The various positions are set out in Laqueur, *Religion and Respectability;* Malcolm Dick, "The Myth of the Working-Class Sunday School," *History of Education* 9 (1980), 27-41; Gail Malmgreen, "Economy and Culture in an Industrializing Town: Macclesfield, Cheshire, 1750-1835" (Ph.D. thesis, Indiana University, 1981), 313-19; and Hempton, *Methodism and Politics*, 86-92.

[41] Ward, *Early Correspondence of Jabez Bunting*, 148-49, 150-52, 165-72, 228.

and the weekly rhythms of prayer, preparation, and planning. They also offered women, both young and old, a socially acceptable form of religious teaching without threatening the patriarchal conventions of chapel life.

The various changes within nineteenth-century Methodism, as it left behind its societary origins and acquired more formal denominational characteristics, were vigorously contested and resulted in manifold secessions and some spontaneous new creations. Although each revivalistic offshoot and formal secession had a unique context, many of the same themes reappear. At issue each time, from the formation of the Methodist New Connexion in 1797 to the withdrawal of the Christian Lay Churches from Primitive Methodism in the 1870s, were fundamental disagreements about the essence of the "authentic" Wesleyan tradition, which was, of course, sufficiently eclectic to support a range of interpretations. So much has now been written about Methodism's "age of disunity" in this avowedly ecumenical generation that it seems pointless to rehearse the familiar explanations of how it became one of the most fissiparous religious movements in English history.[42] Nevertheless, a few broad lines of interpretation remain to be etched in.

In the first place, the old dichotomy between those who interpreted Methodist secessions as the sad but inevitable consequence of stresses within the religious community itself and those political and social historians who saw them as mere symptoms of external pressures affecting the whole of British and European society has been an unfortunate barrier to proper historical understanding. The manifold local studies of Methodist secessions have shown conclusively that superimposed on "religious" disagreements about the nature of the ministry, connexional management, and spiritual priorities, there were undoubtedly class and cultural differences, conflicting political allegiances, and social tensions that also affected the wider society.[43] The precise balance of forces varied, of course, from secession to secession and even from town to town, but they cannot be uncovered by either denominational or social reductionism. Thus, what is striking about Methodism in the first half of the nineteenth century is the way in which its internal cleavages and structures of power acted as lightning conductors for the endemic political and social tensions of the age. Tensions declined after midcentury, but so, too, did the importance of what was at stake within the Methodist community. Secession is, after all,

[42] Robert Currie, *Methodism Divided: A Study in the Sociology of Ecumenicalism* (London, 1968); Benjamin Gregory, *Side Lights on the Conflicts of Methodism during the Second Quarter of the Nineteenth Century, 1827-1852* (London, 1898); Kent, *Age of Disunity*; and Turner, *Conflict and Reconciliation.*

[43] J. T. Wilkinson, "The Rise of Other Methodist Traditions," *History of the Methodist Church*, 2, 276-329; Gowland, *Methodist Secessions*; and Hempton, *Methodism and Politics*, 67-73, 92-98, 197-202.

as much a product of intense commitment as unity is of comfortable acquiescence.

A second point worth emphasizing is that although Methodism's internal crises reached their peak during Bunting's period of personal ascendancy, his contribution to the shaping of Methodism, though substantial, should not be exaggerated. Consider, for example, this letter to the *Sunderland Daily Echo*: "All confidence is at an end ... this division has been effected by a Conference clique ... infatuated by a love of power ... characteristic of the whole priestly hierarchy; they seek not the chief good but little circuits and large salaries."[44] This letter might have been written by a string of Methodist radicals from Alexander Kilham[45] to the author of the *Fly Sheets*,[46] but it was, in fact, an attack on the Primitive Methodist preachers of the Northeast of England in 1877. The point is that once Methodism became established in an area over several generations and benefited from the upward mobility of its social constituency, there were inexorable structural pressures within the connexional system towards a more "centralized and disciplined church structure, towards the growing authority of Conference over local affairs, towards a more refined and less evangelical ministry exercising its duties in smaller circuits, and towards more dignity in chapel-design and worship."[47] Those who swam with the tide, including Bunting, thought—mistakenly as it turned out—that it was possible to construct a Methodism that was both evangelistic and ecclesiastical, popular and cultivated, disciplined and flexible, professional and spontaneous, lively and restrained. But as with all strong positions, their ideology served their own interests and legitimized their power within the connexion, which is why their opponents were often motivated as much by a sense of exclusion as by a desire to return to primitive simplicity. Secession was the final proof that this was a genuine contest and that there was something vital at stake in the result.

[44] Geoffrey Milburn, "Tensions in Primitive Methodism in the Eighteen-Seventies," *Proceedings of the Wesley Historical Society* 40 (1976), 93-101, 135-43.

[45] (1762-1798), expelled by Conference in 1796 and founder of the Methodist New Connexion in 1797. He wrote a number of controversial pamphlets between 1795 and 1797, including *The Progress of Liberty amongst the People called Methodists. To which is added the Out-Lines of a Constitution* (Alnwick, 1795), and *An Account of the Trial of Alexander Kilham, Methodist Preacher, before the General Conference in London* (Nottingham, 1796).

[46] James Everett (1784-1872) was widely suspected of being the author of the anti-Buntingite Fly Sheets (1845-48) and was expelled from the Connexion in 1849 for refusing to deny his guilt. He was at the forefront of the Wesleyan Reform agitations and became the first President of the United Methodist Free Churches in 1857.

[47] Milburn, "Tensions in Primitive Methodism," 142.

Finally, some of the problems encountered by Methodist connexions in the nineteenth century were specific neither to themselves nor to the century, but were deeply embedded within the historical traditions of English religion and society, dating back at least as far as the Reformation. Anticlericalism, especially when clerical wealth, status, and legal powers were in evidence, anti-centralization, and opposition to an urbane liturgical uniformity were—and still are—consistent characteristics of English popular Protestantism that frustrated Laud as much as Bunting.

Perhaps the chief reason for the fragmentation of Evangelical Nonconformity in the first half of the nineteenth century, however, was the way in which social tensions and class consciousness undermined the old denominational order and then posed insuperable problems of control for the leaders of new religious movements.[48] In this area, of trying to assess the significance of Methodism in the wider social history of England in the period of the Industrial Revolution, most disagreement has occurred among historians. The most fertile conceptual frameworks, from Halévy to Thompson and from Hobsbawm to Semmel,[49] though containing inspired insights, have not succeeded in doing justice to the complexity of relationships between religion and politics and belief and practice in English regions over the course of a century of bewildering change. The main reason for this is that, despite their ideological claims to the contrary, many of the most influential "theses" about Methodism in English society have been imposed, sometimes on the basis of disconcertingly thin evidence, from above and without. More impressive for their intellectual coherence than for their capacity to explain the data, they have only recently had to come into contact with more sophisticated statistical approaches and with a cluster of impressively researched local and regional studies. Since there already exist a considerable number of historiographical surveys of the Halévy Thesis and its subsequent refinements, the aim here is not to rehearse familiar arguments but to offer some reflections on more recent work.[50]

[48] W. R. Ward, "Revival and Class Conflict in Early Nineteenth-Century Britain," *Erweckung am Beginn des 19. Jahrhunderts*, ed. by Ulrich Gäbler and Peter Schram (Amsterdam, 1986), 87-104.

[49] Elie Halévy, *A History of the English People in the Nineteenth Century*, 4 vols. (London, 1949-51), and *The Birth of Methodism in England*, trans. and ed. by Bernard Semmel (Chicago, 1971); Thompson, *Making of the English Working Class*; Hobsbawm, "Methodism and the Threat of Revolution"; and Bernard Semmel, *The Methodist Revolution* (New York, 1973).

[50] J.H.S. Kent, "Methodism and Revolution," *Methodist History* 12 (1974), 136-44; Gilbert, "Methodism, Dissent and Political Stability"; and D. N. Hempton, "Evangelical Revival and Society: A Historiographical Review of Methodism and British Society, c. 1750-1850," *Themelios* 8 (1983), 19-25.

There is now widespread agreement that the remarkable growth of Evangelical Nonconformity in the period 1790-1830 substantially undermined the Established Church, religious deference, and traditional systems of dependency, which had been at the heart of the old order in church and state. Even Jonathan Clarke, who is certainly no exponent of social and political determinism, has shown how English society had moved beyond the pale of the Anglican parochial system and that the sheer scale of the opposition to Sidmouth's Bill against itinerant preaching in 1811 meant that there had been a profound shift of allegiance in the country as a whole.[51] Parallel pressures from a more radical Irish Roman Catholicism, the old antiexclusionist wing of Protestant Dissent, urban popular radicalism, and new commercial interests did not make a constitutional revolution inevitable, but they did lay the foundations for alternative forms of politics in which religion was just as central as it had been in the ideological defenses of the eighteenth-century constitution. Methodism could not, of course, avoid the social and political tensions that accompanied its own growth. In the quarter-century after the French Revolution, its leadership, both clerical and lay, struggled hard to maintain the connexion's legal privileges,[52] while at the same time recruiting from sections of the population less interested in the chauvinistic traditions of the freeborn Englishman than in the political and economic causes of their appalling conditions. Ironically, the secretive Committee of Privileges that the Methodists had set up to guard their legal rights soon became an inquisitorial instrument in the expulsion of disaffected radicals in the years leading up to Peterloo.[53] This task was accomplished with such vigor, in the North of England especially, that when the next great upsurge in urban popular radicalism occurred in the late 1830s, the Wesleyans were relatively untroubled and were able to devote most of their energy to the defense of their denominational corner against Roman Catholics, Tractarians, and radical Nonconformists. In this way, class control and denominational discipline were mutually reinforced, and class tensions were to some extent redirected into sectarian conflict.

In the first thirty years after Wesley's death, therefore, Methodist growth most alarmed established interests, from bishops and parsons to landed and industrial magnates.[54] At the same time, Methodism's capacity to develop qualities of self-discipline, personal responsibility, and sobriety

[51] J.C.D. Clarke, *English Society, 1688-1832* (Cambridge, 1985), 365.

[52] D. N. Hempton, "Thomas Allan and Methodist Politics, 1790-1840," *History* 67 (1982), 13-31.

[53] Methodist Church Archives, John Rylands University Library of Manchester, MS. Minutes of the Committee of Privileges, 1803-22. I survey some of this material in *Methodism and Politics*, 104-10.

[54] See, e.g., the *Gentleman's Magazine* 70, Pt. 1 (1800), 241, and Pt. 2, 1077.

was appreciated by those who were able to set aside their prejudices against religious enthusiasm and who recognized that the Established Church was in no position to reclaim the unchurched. This paradox, which has generated much heat but little illumination among historians, was there from the start and often depended on local circumstances for its resolution. In Belper, for example, which had grown from an insignificant village to the second largest town in Derbyshire, largely as a result of the entrepreneurial talents of the Strutt family, both Wesleyan and Primitive Methodism grew extraordinarily fast between 1790 and 1825. The Unitarian Strutts recognized the beneficial effects of Methodism among their workforce with restrained paternalistic generosity, but they also saw fit to launch a fund for a hugely expensive Anglican church, which architecturally dwarfed its Dissenting rivals and was opened in 1824 amid much pomp and circumstance by the Duke of Devonshire, the county's greatest landowner. Here was no exercise in crude employer coercion; the Strutts merely paid symbolic tribute to a set of social arrangements that they had come to believe were instrumental in maintaining order and stability and that had consequently facilitated their own social advance. With so much at stake, a declaration of faith in a stable past offered more reassurance than a future clouded by unrestrained ranterism or political radicalism. The imposing Anglican monument that the Strutts helped pay for was thus not meant to eliminate religious deviance, but to show the limits within which it must be seen to operate.[55]

After 1820, the Wesleyans were not entirely immune from problems caused by urban radicals within their midst, as the celebrated case of Joseph Rayner Stephens[56] showed, but, increasingly, the Primitive and secession Methodists were most closely bound up with radical causes in both town and country. Recent studies of Chartism in English localities, for example, have drawn attention to the importance of Methodist organizational models, the crusading zeal of local preachers, and perhaps most important, the ideological fusion of biblical warnings against social injustice with Chartist denunciations of the rich and the powerful.[57] All over the

[55] Valenze, *Prophetic Sons and Daughters*, 159-83; Eric Hopkins, "Religious Dissent in Black Country Industrial Villages in the First Half of the Nineteenth Century," *JEH* 34 (1983), 411-24.

[56] (1805-1879); Wesleyan preacher in the Ashton-under-Lyne Circuit (1833-34). He resigned under pressure for his commitment to the Church Separation Society, led a small connexion in the Ashton area, and achieved national fame as an activist in the Ten-Hours, Anti-Poor Law, and Chartist movements. See Dale A. Johnson, "Between Evangelicalism and a Social Gospel: The Case of Joseph Rayner Stephens," *CH* 42 (1973), 229-42.

[57] James Epstein, "Some Organisational and Cultural Aspects of the Chartist Movement in Nottingham," *The Chartist Experience*, ed. by James Epstein and

North of England in the 1830s, as the Anti-Poor Law, Ten Hours, and Anti-State Church movements shaded off into Chartism, there was a sizeable minority of non-Wesleyan Methodists, conspicuous for their leadership ability, who combined a radical critique of clericalism and the religious hypocrisy of the rich with a more general humanitarian mission to reform social and political abuses. Some were willing to make chapels available for Chartist meetings, and some chapels even severed their Methodist connexions altogether.

But there were also unresolved tensions between the two. As Chartists tried to create a mass movement of class solidarity, Methodist communities had alternative loyalties that caused them to repudiate Chartist bawdiness, tavern conviviality, and sabbath-breaking. Although many Chartist leaders were aware of the potential of religion to offer ideological legitimation and crusading zeal to their movement, it soon became clear to Christian Chartists like the Rev. William Hill, the editor of the *Northern Star*, that "in almost all the churches and chapels, appertaining to whatever sect, the principles of social benevolence and justice, of civil equality and of political right, though recognised by the Bible, are denounced by the priesthood."[58] Even the more radical Methodist sects, though closer in spirit to Chartist ideals than either Anglicanism or Wesleyanism, were sufficiently peripheral to mass Chartism to make large-scale theories about the relationship between Methodism and urban radicalism in these years seem rather forced.

The same cannot be said, however, of those mining and agricultural communities of England where Methodism, especially the Primitive Connexion, became the dominant feature of both the religious and political landscape. Indeed, Methodism's contribution to rural radicalism and agricultural trade unionism, so long ignored in the debates surrounding the Halévy Thesis, has only recently attracted the attention it deserves. In his study of East Anglia in the second half of the nineteenth century, Nigel Scotland has shown how Primitive Methodism, emerging initially as a form of religious protest, became also the basis of a social protest against both the harsher realities of laboring life and "the oligarchical troika of

Dorothy Thompson (London, 1982), 221-68; T. M. Kemnitz and F. Jacques, "J. R. Stephens and the Chartist Movement," *International Review of Social History* 19 (1974), 211-17; Eileen Yeo, "Christianity in Chartist Struggle, 1838-42," *Past and Present*, No. 91 (1981), 109-39. Older, but still useful, accounts of the relationship between Chartism and Methodism include H. U. Faulkner, *Chartism and the Churches: A Study in Democracy* (New York, 1916); R. F. Wearmouth, *Methodism and the Working-Class Movements of England, 1800-1850* (London, 1937), and *Some Working-Class Movements of the Nineteenth Century* (London, 1948).

    58 Yeo, "Christianity in Chartist Struggle," 139.

parson, squire and farmer." With a mixture of biblical idealism, millennial optimism, and disciplined protest, both Wesleyan and Primitive Methodist local preachers brought their chapel-honed skills of public speaking and effective organization to an agricultural trade unionism that developed a quasi-religious atmosphere of its own.[59]

A similar combination of community solidarity built around religious forms and experiences is evident in the pit-village Methodism of the Northeast of England, though here the lines of class and religious conflict are, if anything, less clear-cut.[60] Once again the disciplines and opportunities of chapel life threw up a high proportion of Methodist political leaders who made their mark in trade unionism, the cooperative movement, and other forms of local politics. But theirs was a trade unionism infused with moral energy to achieve fair play and just treatment from their largely Nonconformist employers, rather than an instrument for pursuing narrowly class interests as such. Hence, the impact of Methodism on the mining communities of the Northeast was partly responsible for the region's reluctance to exchange Liberal for Labour politics at the beginning of the twentieth century. This provincial Liberalism was based on the acceptance of a market economy, opposition to Anglican educational privileges, dislike of the Tory brewing interest, and an emphasis on mutual obligations between employers and employees, and was thus regarded as a more appropriate political vehicle than that offered by class conflict and the emerging labor movement. The essential difference, therefore, between Methodism's relationship with Chartism and its contribution to agricultural and mining trade unionism is that within Chartism, Methodism was only one strand among many influences, some of which were antithetical to Methodist piety or peripheral to Methodist interests, whereas, in the other cases, Methodist involvement in politics grew naturally out of its social setting and was widely approved as a legitimate expression of an essentially religious morality.

Whatever may be said about the relationship between Methodism and popular radicalism, or religion and social class, the fact is that most nineteenth-century Methodists encountered the world of politics either as voters[61] or as participants in the great extraparliamentary pressure crusades

[59] Scotland, *Methodism and the Revolt of the Field*, 175.

[60] Robert Colls, *The Collier's Rant* (London, 1977); and Moore, *Pit-Men, Preachers and Politics.*

[61] Research on Methodist electoral behavior is still at an early stage, but see J. R. Vincent, *Pollbooks: How Victorians Voted* (Cambridge, 1967); T. J. Nossiter, *Influence, Opinion and Political Idioms in Reformed England: Case Studies from the North-East, 1832-74* (Brighton, 1975); Henry Pelling, *Social Geography of British Elections, 1885-1910* (London, 1977); J.P.D. Dunbabin, "British Elections in the Nineteenth and Twentieth Centuries: A Regional Approach," *EHR* 95

from Sidmouth's Bill at the beginning of the century to the preoccupations of the Nonconformist Conscience at the end.[62] No sense can be made of such politics through social and economic categories alone. Rather, they show the profoundly religious basis, however narrow and sectarian, of much Nonconformist political behavior. At the heart of Methodist commitment to extraparliamentary pressure campaigns, despite the old Wesleyan no-politics rule, was a religious worldview that sought to defend denominational interests against governmental and secularist encroachments, to wage war on the moral evils of slavery, sexual licence, and intemperance, and to oppose the "heretical" advances of Roman Catholicism, Tractarianism, and Unitarianism.

The peculiar twists and turns of such campaigns, their party political significance, and their intersection with the apparently inexhaustible Church and Chapel conflicts have attracted much attention, most recently from myself on the first half of the century and from D. W. Bebbington on the second half. We agree that from the Great Reform Act to the end of the century, the Liberal Party was the main beneficiary of Methodist political loyalties, particularly those of the non-Wesleyan connexions, whose willingness to attack the vested interests of the Established Church went beyond that of most Wesleyans. The political allegiances of the latter were, of course, more complicated. In general, their social, occupational, and religious status led them to vote for the Liberal Party unless religious issues dictated otherwise. Then their Evangelicalism, their distant loyalty to the Church of England, and their deference to preachers and wealthy laymen within their own connexion influenced them against pro-Catholic, Unitarian, or radical disestablishment candidates. Anti-Catholicism, in particular, was a major element in the Wesleyan Toryism of the 1830s and 1840s,[63] and surfaced again in a remarkable way over Home Rule half a century later, when a substantial minority of Wesleyans were committed unionists.[64]

As with voting, so with extraparliamentary protest. Although the Wesleyans were of common purpose with the rest of Nonconformity in the great moral crusades against slavery and the Contagious Diseases Acts, the

(1980), 241-67; J. P. Parry, "The State of Victorian Political History," *HJ* 26 (1983), 469-84; and D. W. Bebbington, "Nonconformity and Electoral Sociology, 1867-1918," *HJ* 27 (1984), 633-56.

[62] D. W. Bebbington, *The Nonconformist Conscience* (London, 1982); D. A. Hamer, *The Politics of Electoral Pressure: A Study in the History of Victorian Reform Agitations* (Hassocks, 1977); and B. S. Turner and M. Hill, "Methodism and the Pietist Definition of Politics: Historical Development and Contemporary Evidence," *A Sociological Yearbook of Religion in Britain* 8 (1975), 159-80.

[63] Hempton, *Methodism and Politics*, 179-97.

[64] Bebbington, "Nonconformity and Electoral Sociology," 633-56.

connexion as a whole did not support the Liberation Society, nor did it approve of the disestablishment sentiments of the Free Church councils. When it came to specific matters like the removal of Nonconformist grievances over marriages and burials, the Wesleyans preferred to act through their own Committee of Privileges rather than join wholeheartedly with other Nonconformists. Thus, Methodist liberalism as proclaimed by Hugh Price Hughes,[65] from the mid-1880s was of a distinctive hue in which anti-Catholicism, imperialism, and denominational particularism were never far from the surface.[66] In saying this, one is not denying the degree of homogeneity that existed in Nonconformist culture nor casting doubt on the fact that the distinctive Nonconformist values of sobriety, self-help, hard work, and the free market fitted snugly into Victorian liberalism;[67] for Nonconformity offered "an alternative establishment whose attitudes it articulated."[68] But the Wesleyan Connexion, in particular, with its historic roots in Wesley's Churchmanship and its long-standing commitment to Protestant Ireland[69] and world mission,[70] could never be as committed to a free market in religion as it was in economics. Protectionism may have been commercially undesireable, but some form of it was deemed essential to maintain religious truth and eliminate heresy at home and overseas.

The Victorian Nonconformist world of men, chapels, and politics, so long dominant in Methodist historiography and cemented forever in the new official history, has given way in recent times to imaginative attempts to rediscover the human (including the female) face of Methodism in its

[65] *H.P.Hughes* (1847-1902); founded the influential West London Mission, edited the *Methodist Times*, and played an active part in public affairs in late Victorian England. See J.H.S. Kent, "Hugh Price Hughes and the Nonconformist Conscience," *Essays in Modern English Church History in Memory of Norman Sykes*, ed. by G. V. Bennett and J. D. Walsh (London, 1966), 181-205; and W. M. King, "Hugh Price Hughes and the British 'Social Gospel'," *Journal of Religious History* 13 (1984-85), 66-82. *Oldstone –Moore .*

[66] Stephen Koss, *Nonconformity in Modern British Politics* (London, 1975), and "Wesleyanism and Empire," *HJ* 18 (1975), 105-18; Ian Sellers, *Nineteenth-Century Nonconformity* (London, 1977), 65-91; *Nonconformity in the Nineteenth Century*, ed. by D. M. Thompson (London, 1972); and Bebbington, *Nonconformist Conscience*.

[67] J. R. Vincent, *The Formation of the British Liberal Party, 1857-1868* (Hassocks, 1976).

[68] Clyde Binfield, *So Down to Prayers: Studies in English Nonconformity, 1780-1920* (London, 1977), 132.

[69] D. N. Hempton, "The Methodist Crusade in Ireland," *Irish Historical Studies* 22 (1980), 33-48.

[70] N. A. Birtwhistle, "Methodist Missions," *History of the Methodist Church*, 3, 1-116.

many different cultural settings. Penetrating to the essence of Methodism's impact on ordinary people and their communities has brought forth fresh work using fresh materials and reaching fresh conclusions, which has done much to supersede the old models of repression and release made popular by E. P. Thompson and others.[71] The problem with Methodism, or perhaps more optimistically its greatest strength, is the way in which its hard disciplines and tender mercies could be adapted to a wide variety of social circumstances, not only in the British Isles but throughout the world. This may be dispiriting for those committed to either the Halévy Thesis or some convenient and crimping alternative, but it suggests that theoretical sophistication is no substitute for imaginative sympathy and cultural sensitivity in re-creating the history of popular religious movements.[72]

Space permits only two brief examples of these qualities, both from the Northeast of England, but from different social ranks. Robert Colls has sought to explain the strength of Primitive Methodism in the pit villages of the region by drawing attention to the "reactive exchanges" between popular Evangelicalism and mining culture in which the boundary lines between the secular and the sacred were almost obliterated. Such exchanges were promoted by vernacular preaching, the appropriation of popular tunes, and the emotional resonances of Methodism with its combination of passion and piety, zeal and order, faith and works, thrift and charity, puritanism and decency, individualism and community, and verve and vulgarity. But exchange also took place

> at the deepest meanings of life and death: in the zeal for a righteous death from a community whose traditional funeral rites were meticulous; in the capacity for mutuality of a class who had little else to offer each other; in the taste for a sudden salvation from a people whose lives were always a lottery and the translation from nothing to enough, illness to health, life to death was often arbitrary.[73]

[71] See, for example, Hugh McLeod, "New Perspectives on Victorian Working Class Religion: The Oral Evidence," *Oral History* 14 (1986), 31-49; Obelkevich, *Religion and Rural Society*; Valenze, *Prophetic Sons and Daughters*; and D. N. Hempton, "Popular Religion and Irreligion in Victorian Fiction," *The Writer as Witness: Literature as Historical Evidence*, ed. by Tom Dunne, *Historical Studies* 16 (1987), 177-96.

[72] See David Clark, *Between Pulpit and Pew: Folk Religion in a North Yorkshire Fishing Village* (Cambridge, 1982). Although this book is based on participant observation of present-day village religion, its insights are of much wider application.

[73] Colls, *Collier's Rant*, and "Primitive Methodists in the Northern Coalfields."

Such a faith was unselfconsciously all-embracing: it set standards for domestic economy and cleanliness; it educated the young and offered eternal bliss to the old; its festivals and choral entertainments were at the center of village life; its values informed public debate and wage negotiations; it even altered the language and the oral traditions at the very heart of the community. Not surprisingly, this culture withstood everything the nineteenth century could throw at it, but the twentieth-century combination of economic and ecclesiastical rationalization has inexorably undermined its social foundations.

A more familiar kind of cultural exchange between Methodism and society, going on in the same region at the same time, has been illuminated by the work of Geoffrey Milburn. His formidable list of Methodist entrepreneurs bound together by intermarriage and business interests is itself a testimony to the commercial utility of Evangelical Nonconformist values. Most of these Methodist entrepreneurial families had their origins among the skilled artisans, small tradesmen, farmers, and white-collar workers of the Northeast, with only a few from lower working-class backgrounds. With no apparent incompatibility between gold and the gospel, wealth was carefully husbanded over several generations of hard work, prudential marriages, and self-discipline. The wealth earned was solidly and respectably enjoyed and not conspicuously consumed. Although some abandoned religious morality in the pursuit of gain, most gained without indecent pursuit and were thus able to give some of what they received with clear paternalistic consciences. They were men who knew that "religion, self-discipline, temperance and hard work had been good for them, and they sought to employ whatever means they could, in their homes, Sunday schools, chapels, businesses and communities, to persuade, exhort and even oblige others to live by the same lights."[74] Here was a culture of "piety, profit and paternalism" that dominated great tracts of provincial England in the Victorian period, and that produced immense fortunes for Methodists like Joseph Rank (flour-milling) and Sir William Hartley (jam-making). With pardonable poetic exaggeration, David Martin has stated that Victorian and Edwardian Methodism was "not about Acts and Insurrections but about groceries. The Methodist grocer, like the Nonconformist Conscience, is, or was, a byword. Methodism is rooted and grounded not only in 'faith alone' but in flour and jam."[75] There was, however, a sufficient residue of Wesleyan teaching on stewardship to ensure that wealth and power were softened by public duty and religious

[74] G. E. Milburn, "Piety, Profit and Paternalism: Methodists in Business in the North-East of England, c. 1760-1920," *Proceedings of the Wesley Historical Society* 44 (1983), 45-92.

[75] Martin, "Faith, Flour and Jam," 329.

philanthropy, except in a few notorious cases where Nonconformist grit got the better of Christian generosity.

Explorations of the diverse ways in which Methodism both created and remade religious cultures are sure to continue, and will be all the more rewarding for the international comparative dimension, without which the Evangelical Revival is too easily portrayed as a mere epiphenomenon.[76]

As national boundaries have become less of an impediment in the reconstruction of popular religion, so, too, have gender barriers. Mention has already been made of Deborah Valenze's pioneering work on the tough minority of female itinerant preachers in early industrial England, but the less unconventional Methodist wives, mothers, and daughters are as silent in the connexional histories as they are in nineteenth-century ecclesiastical records, despite the fact that they were almost certainly a numerical majority.[77] In early Methodism, women made important contributions as class and prayer group leaders and by visiting the sick and offering hospitality to itinerants. Later in the century, they became the organizational and financial backbone of the ubiquitous Evangelical societies and managed chapel tea-meetings, bazaars, and special events.[78] But women had their most strategic influence in the home, as angels of frugality, temperance, and fidelity in the cult of domesticity promoted by

[76] Helpful examples from an earlier period include Susan O'Brien, "A Transatlantic Community of Saints: The Great Awakening and the First Evangelical Network, 1735-1755," *AHR* 91 (1986), 811-32; M. J. Crawford, "Origins of the Eighteenth-Century Evangelical Revival: England and New England Compared," *JBS* 26 (1987), 361-97; M. J. Westerkamp, *Triumph of the Laity: Scots-Irish Piety and the Great Awakening, 1625-1760* (New York, 1988). See also *Erweckung am Beginn des 19. Jahrhunderts*, ed. by Gäbler and Schram; and Hugh McLeod, "Religion in the British and German Labour Movements, c. 1890-1914: A Comparison," *Bulletin of the Society for the Study of Labour History* 51 (1986), 25-35. More work is forthcoming in this field from W. R. Ward and others and will no doubt benefit from the growing number of transatlantic conferences on popular religion.

[77] For pioneering work on women in Methodism, see E. K. Brown, "Women of the Word: Selected Leadership Roles of Women in Mr. Wesley's Methodism," *Women in New Worlds*, ed. by H. F. Thomas and R. S. Keller (Nashville, 1981), 69-87; E. K. Brown, *Women of Mr Wesley's Methodism* (New York, 1983); P. W. Chilcote, "John Wesley and the Women Preachers of Early Methodism" (Ph.D. thesis, Duke University, 1984); and Gail Malmgreen, "Domestic Discords: Women and the Family in East Cheshire Methodism, 1750-1830," *Disciplines of Faith*, 55-70. Malmgreen's article contains a short bibliography.

[78] Frank Prochaska, *Women and Philanthropy in Nineteenth-Century England* (Oxford, 1980).

Victorian Evangelicals. Women were the daily guardians of values, instructors of children, and supporters of husbands in the pursuit of family piety. Women's "essential nature," so it was held, was especially receptive to spiritual qualities of submissiveness, gentleness, and purity, while it fell to the lot of men to take the lead in resolution, energy, and firmness. In the chapels, men made policy and women followed, men preached and women listened, men were the trustees of buildings and women cleaned them, men ran the Sunday schools and women taught in them, men constructed their own social theology and women obeyed as unto God.

With research on this whole area set to increase, it is worth striking three obvious but cautionary notes. First, it is too easy to represent women as sacrificial victims in the male-dominated world of nineteenth-century popular Protestantism, when in fact most were willing participants in a campaign of moral reformation that offered tangible benefits to them as well as to their families. Second, women are no more a cohesive social group than men; therefore a shared gender does not in itself produce a common experience. The social filters of class, age, and personal circumstances are not gender-specific. Third, in the historical task of reconstructing the lives of women in nineteenth-century religion, modern concepts of gender differentiation and equality may present as substantial a barrier as contemporary male propaganda. The past's vulgarity is, after all, an essential part of the past.

The future agenda of nineteenth-century Methodist studies looks set to be dominated by the trends already mentioned, along with ever more sophisticated attempts to explore the religious meanings and experiences of ordinary people at work, at home, and at leisure as well as in church or chapel.[79] Oral and literary evidence, together with music and hymnody, England's "common religion," testify to the emotional resonances at the core of much popular religious behavior without which religious institutions are as dry as husks.[80]

But the most fruitful opportunities probably lie in the international spread of popular Protestantism in the eighteenth and nineteenth centuries and its impact on different kinds of societies, from Central Europe to America's expanding frontier. The intensive local studies of English

[79] Mark Smith, *Religion in Industrial Society: Oldham and Saddleworth, 1740-1865* (Oxford, 1994); Albion M. Urdank, *Religion and Society in a Cotsworth Vale: Nailsworth, Gloucestershire, 1780-1865* (Berkeley, 1990); and Theodore Koditschek, *Class Formation and Urban Industrial Society: Bradford, 1750-1850* (Cambridge, 1990). For an important point of comparison, see David Hempton and Myrtle Hill, *Evangelical Protestantism in Ulster Society, 1740-1890* (London, 1992).

[80] Jim Obelkevich, "Music and Religion in the Nineteenth Century," *Disciplines of Faith*, 550-65.

Methodism in the past twenty years may only achieve their full significance as part of a much larger picture.

After completing this survey in 1989, I had some further thoughts on some of the most perplexing of the unresolved issues of Methodist historiography, namely the nature of religious motivation, the complexity of Methodist growth patterns, and the international spread of Methodism across the North Atlantic world in the late eighteenth and early nineteenth centuries. I published some tentative suggestions, together with some guidance for further reading, in my 1994 Wesley Historical Society lecture, "Motives, Methods, and Margins in Methodism's Age of Expansion," *Proceedings of the Wesley Historical Society* 99 (1994), 189-207.

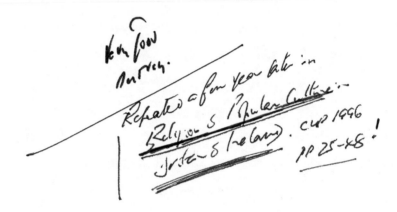

6

The Protestant "Sects"

Peter J. Lineham

PROTESTANT SECTARIANISM IS an area of nineteenth-century religion rather difficult to define. The intention of this chapter is to interpret the significance of all those groups outside traditional Dissent and the Methodists that are not part of organized unbelief. It is not a simple task. There have been major debates about the meaning of individual sects. The role of the sectarian wing of English religion cannot easily be dissected, and we can hope to offer only some general lines to possible interpretations.

For many years, interest in the history of these smaller sects was confined to their own members. Some sects were the subject of careful, if committed, studies, but in many other cases the writers were not willing to look at the real experience of the sect, but only to present an account of their religion's beliefs and a defense that they were right and blessed in all that they did. Such works were rarely written for outsiders, and nonbelievers found such works very obscure.

The nineteenth century was an age tolerant of, and fascinated by, the odd and unusual, and for this reason outsiders often braved a hostile reception to find out about such sects. Thus right through the nineteenth and twentieth centuries, accounts of "peculiar people" were published in books, journals, and newspapers. The Mormons and later the Spiritualists were the subject of intense interest. Some of the accounts were far from sympathetic, and few thought of entering into the internal world of the sect and sect members, but the information gathered is invaluable for contemporary researchers.[1] However, over the past forty years there has been a

[1] John Timbs, *English Eccentrics and Eccentricities* (London, 1875); *A Dictionary of Sects, Heresies, Ecclesiastical Parties and Schools of Religious Thought*, ed. by John Henry Blunt (London, 1874); and the works of Charles Maurice Davies: *Unorthodox London: or Phases in the Religious Life in the Ca-*

growing interest in these groups by outsiders. These outsiders tended to be influenced by two interests. Historians of labor and the working class have been fascinated by the less respectable side of English history and, following the lead of Eric Hobsbawm have recognized that strange textures have influenced the leaders of the working class. E. P. Thompson delineated the intention of his project as "to rescue ... even the deluded follower of Joanna Southcott, from the enormous condescension of posterity."[2] Although this comment seems somewhat condescending, Thompson's great book demonstrated how seeming "byways" in history did touch the social themes rediscovered by the new social history. J.F.C. Harrison's fascinating study of millennarians, *The Second Coming*,[3] is the high point of such research, and reflects how far historians have come in appreciating the sectarian aspects of English life.

But valuable as this research has been, it suffers certain problems from its own perspective. It is highly selective in its interests. Millennial and radical working-class sects were by no means the only English Protestant sects, and historical research continues to neglect the range of ultra-Protestant and Calvinist sects supported by middle-class people and to neglect the theological subtleties that were so central to their self-justification. To some extent, the same weakness is evident among the other researchers of sectarianism, the religious sociologists. The sociologists put sectarianism on the map, although sociologists like Worsley and Martin worked closely with Hobsbawm and other historians in the 1950s.[4] The traditional but dull denominations offered little to interest sociologists of the Weberian school, but they were fascinated by the dynamic force and commitment evident in many smaller religious groups. The focus of this research was defined by Weber's disciple Ernst Troeltsch, in his epochal study of Christian social thinking, for he noted the contrast in the later Middle Ages between the Church Universal and its patterns of social thought and the groups that he called "sects," which developed a very different approach to issues, in part, due to their inherent structure, which he saw as absolutist, radical, lower-class, and totally committed.[5] Subsequent sociologists

pital (London 1874), and ser. 2, 2nd ed. (London 1875); *Heterodox London: or Phases of Freethought in the Metropolis*, 2 vols. (London, 1874); and *Mystic London* (London, 1875).

[2] E. P. Thompson, *The Making of the English Working Class* (Harmondsworth, rev. Penguin ed., 1968), 13.

[3] J.F.C. Harrison, *The Second Coming: Popular Millenarianism, 1780-1850* (London, 1979).

[4] See *Millennial Dreams in Action: Essays in Comparative Study*, ed. by S. Thrupp (The Hague, 1962).

[5] Ernst Troeltsch, *Social Teaching of the Christian Churches* (London and New York, 1931), 328-69.

modified many aspects of Troeltsch's model; H. Richard Niebuhr argued that between sect and church today lay a middle ground, which he called the denomination, and he argued that sects slowly lost both the social and the attitudinal characteristics of sectarianism and became denominations, while denominations sought to become churches, with a close link with the state.[6] David Martin subsequently defended denominations as a category in their own right.[7]

Sociologists certainly found sects much more interesting, and attempts to categorize their "social function" were a favorite subject of religious sociologists in the 1950s and 1960s. In England much of this research was undertaken or supervised by the Oxford sociologist Bryan R. Wilson. Wilson's work partly clarified the analysis of Troeltsch, particularly in his analysis of the defining characteristics of sects (which he defined as voluntariness, exclusivity, merit, selection of members, self-identification, elite status, systems of expulsion, conscientious commitment, and legitimation). Other aspects of his work rejected Troeltsch's narrow model of the world-denying sect, realizing that sects formed and attracted members for a variety of reasons. His classification of sects focused on their different attitudes to the world. In his later work, his divisions are conversionist, revolutionist (transformatory), introversionist, manipulationist, thaumaturgical, reformist or utopian.[8]

By the 1970s, the perceived rise in the activity of religious sects and in particular of those groups that Wilson called reformist sects (although others called them cults) led most religious sociologists to turn their attention to contemporary, rather than historical, sectarianism. It became a field hotly debated. Some argued that there was a clear relationship between the growing secular mood of society, the decline of the mainline churches, and the rise of more "human potential" oriented cults. Others, including Roderick Stark and William Bainbridge, rejected any implicit contrast between sect and cult,[9] and recently the terminology of sect and cult is increasingly rejected and replaced by the term "new religious

[6] H. Richard Niebuhr, *The Social Sources of Denominationalism* (New York, 1929), 54-76.

[7] David Martin, "The Denomination," *British Journal of Sociology* 13 (1962), 1-14.

[8] *Patterns of Sectarianism: Organization and Ideology in Social and Religious Movements* ed. by B. R. Wilson (London, 1967); B. R. Wilson, *Sects and Society* (London 1961); B. R. Wilson, *Religion in Secular Society* (London, 1966); B. R. Wilson, *Religious Sects* (New York, 1970).

[9] Rodney Stark and William S. Bainbridge: "Of Churches, Sects and Cults," *Journal for the Scientific Study of Religion* 18 (1979), 117-31; "Sectarian Tension," *Review of Religious Research* 22 (1980), 105-24; *The Future of Religion: Secularisation, Revival and Cult Formation* (Berkeley, 1985).

movement." It is a helpful distinction, although some "new" religious movements in the nineteenth century were far from new, including the Quakers and the Muggletonians.[10]

The debate over contemporary new religious movements may have some significance for historians of the nineteenth century. Historians have become very cautious about functionalist interpretations of sectarianism, but contemporary discussions about the interrelationships of sect and cult may have more to say to the nineteenth century than might be thought. There is quite a range of what may be called cults in the nineteenth century. Moreover the variety of potential types of new religious movements in the nineteenth century needs to be evaluated. The assumption that groups begin as sects and drift into denominationalism has meant that groups of dropouts from the denominations—the Gospel Standard Baptists, the Free Church of England, and the Independent Methodists, for example—have been ignored. "Established" sects like the Quakers, which failed to find a comfortable place among the denominations, are problematic for the typology.[11] So some significant general questions that are being asked about sects and cults in contemporary society need to be asked about the nineteenth century, too.

For example, historical studies of sects need to consider their attitude and response to the world, the kinds of membership and the demands upon them, and the style of leadership in the movements. The reconstruction of the role of sectarianism in nineteenth-century religious life should not be neglected. Historians and sociologists need to return to the field. In the process, they need to pay more attention to the historical context that enabled sects to form and the ways in which sectarianism was legitimated. They also need to overcome their obsession with the formalized millennial sects. The preoccupation with sectarian organization in the past has meant that the informal groups of revivalists, small revivalist chapels, and independent preachers, so common throughout the century, have been overlooked. This omission would be avoided if we were less preoccupied with classifying sects into types. Some very significant research is now looking at a wider range of sects and looking at them in a more general way. It is helpful to ponder how various of the narrower

[10] See J. A. Beckford, *Cult Controversies: The Societal Response to the New Religious Movements* (London, 1985), esp. 78; and for a recent survey, Thomas Robbins, "Cults, Converts and Charisma: The Sociology of New Religious Movements," *Current Sociology* 36 (1988). For a summary of these questions, see Philip E. Hammond (ed.), *The Sacred in a Secular Age: Towards Revision in the Scientific Study of Religion* (Berkeley, 1985).

[11] See Michael Mullet, "From Sect to Denomination? Social Developments in Eighteenth Century English Quakerism," *Journal of Religious History* 13 (1984-85), 35-45.

parts of the Protestant community, and also the whole body of Protestant sectarianism, functioned in that society.

Any attempt to list the new religious movements that existed in nine-teenth-century England has problems. Perhaps the best approach is prag-matically to list all religious groups in the community and then to exclude the main English denominations. It is difficult to establish a complete list. My own list runs to some seventy-nine groups, and it is certainly far from complete and ignores some schisms within sects. Stephen Yeo, in a close study of Reading, could identify only forty of the eighty-five churches, chapels and mission halls in the town.[12] These groups are varied and re-quire some kind of classification. One approach is to classify all sects and denominations together, without excluding the "denominations." Thus, the student of contemporary American sects, J. Gordon Melton, classifies some 1,200 religious movements from the Roman Catholic and Anglican Churches to eastern mystical groups in twenty-two clusters, or "families."[13] His classification is interesting. Some of his families are twentieth-century ones, but we can find members of the Liturgical Family (Western) (the Church of England and the Roman Catholic Church, but also the sects of the Free Church of England and the Reformed Episcopal Church) and so on, although his recourse to "the Liberal Family" and "Independent Fundamentalist Family" alongside the families of Metho-dism, Presbyterian-Reformed, Baptist, and Adventist suggests that his ca-tegories are not historically derived.

Another approach would be to use Bryan Wilson's classifications, which have been gradually modified over the past thirty years. Yet, the more we know about the evolution of sects, the more limited these cate-gories seem. No doubt there is quite a sharp gap between the "Reforma-tory-Utopian" sects (i.e., cults) and other sects, but some of his other cat-egories appear clumsy. Conversionist sects would presumably include the Salvation Army and other various missions—but what about the Open Brethren and the Churches of Christ? Revolutionist (transformatory) groups would include the various Southcottians, but would it include the Catholic Apostolic Church? Introversionist groups presumably include the Gospel Standard Baptists and the Exclusive Brethren, but the Brethren also emphasize that God must bring about a total revolution in conditions. Manipulationist groups would include the healing sects, thaumaturgical would include the Catholic Apostolic Church (again), while the reformist and utopian groups should presumably include the labor sects. Indeed, with the latter, which most sociologists of religion call cults, because they

[12] Stephen Yeo, *Religion and Voluntary Organisations in Crisis* (London 1976), 68 ff.

[13] J. Gordon Melton, *The Encyclopedia of American Religion* (Wilmington, N.C., 1978).

are more open and world-affirming, and which include many of the liberal groups in our list, there is a confusing combination of millennial themes as well. The solution appears to be to try to determine the sorts of issues that marked sectarians out as minorities in their society and see how much these factors overlap. But it is first necessary to gauge the level of impact made by the sects.

One may ask whether the term "sect" has sufficient coherence as an historical experience (rather than just a sociological pigeonhole) to justify treating nineteenth-century sectarianism as one phenomenon. We should concede that few new religious movements feel any closer kinship to other sects than they do to the general world. Yet, sectarianism did function in a similar way, and many people moved around between sects. Sectarianism served as a meaningful tendency in nineteenth-century English society. Part of the decision involved in joining a sect was being willing to forsake the Established Church or a Nonconformist denomination.

The overall impact of the new religious movements in this period is not easy to establish. Many of these groups are so obscure that the census enumerators of 1851 missed them, and possibly the *British Weekly* survey of 1886 and the *London Daily News* survey of 1903 also overlooked some groups. Accepting their figures in the absence of others, it seems that some 1-2 percent of the English population attended Protestant sectarian groups in the period. There are severe problems in using the figures, but for the 1851 census 256,695 attendances of sectarian churches in England and Wales were recorded—according to Mann, representing some 174,817 persons, or 1 percent of the population of the time.[14] In London County in 1903-4 about 13.5 percent of all church attenders were found at the various independent and sectarian groups or (on another basis of calculation) 72,358 Londoners in a population of 4,536,541 (1.7 percent).[15] Including with this figure mission halls and non-aligned congregations, John Kent notes that "fringe Protestant" services attracted 167,000 persons by 1903, a figure well above any denomination other than the Church of England.[16]

Compared to contemporary American figures for sectarian church attendance or the scale of sectarian activity in the seventeenth-century Eng-

[14] "Census of Great Britain, 1851: Religious Worship, England and Wales," *Parliamentary Papers*, 1852-53, 89 (89), clxxviii-clxxx; W.S.F. Pickering, "The 1851 Census—A Useless Experiment?," *British Journal of Sociology* 18 (1967), 392; John Gay, *The Geography of Religion in England* (London, 1971) 168-201.

[15] *The Religious Life of London*, ed. by Richard Mudie-Smith (London, 1904), 271, 447.

[16] John Kent, *Holding the Fort: Studies in Victorian Revivalism* (London, 1979), 300-301. For another analysis of the figures see Hugh McLeod, *Class and Religion in the Late Victorian City* (London, 1974).

lish Commonwealth, this level of sectarianism is not, in fact, particularly impressive. In many ways Victorians overestimated the importance of religious sectarianism. For while good orthodox Christians disapproved of the sects, and while both Nonconformists and Anglicans were intolerant of them (thus H. W. Clark's comment: "Of the true Nonconformist ideal they had caught no glimpse; from the true Nonconformist spirit their waters did not flow"[17]), nevertheless they were very conscious of them. The new freedoms accorded to Dissenters and the more public presence of the sectarians during the century exaggerated the popular consciousness of what was, in fact, a period of not particularly dramatic sectarian growth. Moreover, the struggles of the Church of England, and, by the end of the century, the relative decline in the Nonconformists, confirmed the idea that the sects were successfully competing with the churches.[18] This approach assumes that sects find their primary opportunity in the failure of the denominations and that the extent of sectarianism in England is relative to the schisms in nineteenth-century Protestantism. While there is some truth in this assertion, the major sectarian ingatherings were on the basis of distinctive truths proclaimed by the sects, not the failure of the churches. The following sections give some indications of these "truths." The issues that particular sects emphasized were often reiterated in a slightly different form by others. Thus, the new religious movements of the nineteenth century are a study in the issues that caused the most tension in nineteenth-century society.

"Sectarianism" is the wrong term to use to classify the range of ultra-Protestantism found in Victorian society. Not all the groups of that age were exclusive in membership and ideology. Southcottians were very respectful of the Church of England, and members of some other sects often longed to return (if certain conditions were fulfilled) to the denominations they had left (e.g., members of the Free Church of England). Among the new religious movements we shall examine, there was great variation in the extent to which they were open or closed to the world, and how they percieved other religious groups. Victorian society encompassed a world of polemical religion, of religious debates in working-class communities, of violent swings in attitudes, and of strongly held personal opinions, particularly if the local people were self-employed and independent. Protestantism often gave rise to large-scale campaigns lacking denominational recognition, and to evangelistic activity through a staggering variety of charities and independent mission preachers, including Henry Varley,

[17] H. W. Clark, *History of English Nonconformity from Wiclif to the Close of the Nineteenth Century*, 2 vols. (London, 1913), II, 273.

[18] See R. Currie, A. D. Gilbert, and L. Horsley, *Churches and Churchgoers: Patterns of Church Growth in the British Isles since 1700* (London, 1977), 35-37, 155-60.

Gordon Forlong, and a great cluster of Spurgeon imitations. In Weberian terms, nineteenth-century society allowed a great deal of scope for the "prophet" or "shaman" or, in Marxist terms, the individual religious entrepreneur. Sectarianism by no means captured all of this energy. The little New Jerusalem Church of the Swedenborgians was typical, for it often furnished pulpits to such preachers, embarrassed by its shortage of clergy. Its leaders were eager to gain a public reputation as hospitable to progressive trends. The inevitable consequence was that the raison d'être of the sect and the "order" that seemed the concomitant of the possession of truth, were both upset. The London conference of the New Church lamented this lack of order, "since it is from order alone, that the church can obtain a permanent establishment amongst us."[19] Sectarianism was therefore one possibility for those who were independent of the Church of England and rejected Nonconformity, but it was by no means a final option. Yet, in this generation many sects were effective at perpetuating themselves.

Many smaller Protestant sects traced their roots to the eighteenth-century Evangelical Revival, although they were not necessarily orthodox growths from it. Research has shown just how much that revival was fluid in its theology, in its structures, and in its leadership. The theological diversity of early Evangelicalism is significant. The revival was convulsed in its early years by tensions between Arminian and Calvinist Methodists, and it also had a very significant Moravian third wing. Wesleyan Methodism soon developed institutional and ideological stability and insulated itself from the wider world. In contrast, the Calvinist wing was theologically troubled by antinomianism and was structurally chaotic.[20] Heterodox movements like Swedenborgianism gained strength in the aftermath of the revival in the North, attracting people who had experienced the new birth but had moved beyond Evangelical theology. Antinomianism attracted followers because it arose from an extreme interpretation of justification by faith. Only this can explain why most of the members of the independent Methodist Inghamite connexion in the Northwest fell under the influence of the Scottish Glassite antinomian Robert Sandeman (1718-1777). The same issue caused schisms in the West and London in

[19] New Jerusalem Church, *London Conference No. 2* (London, 1815), 13. See P. J. Lineham, "The English Swedenborgians, 1770-1840: The Social Dimensions of Religious Sectarianism" (D.Phil. thesis, University of Sussex, 1978), 341-44, 350-55, 361, 373.

[20] *Two Calvinist Methodist Chapels, 1743-1811: The London Tabernacle and Spa Fields Chapel*, ed. by Edwin Welch (London, 1975). See E. P. Crow, "John Wesley's Conflict with Antinomianism in Relation to the Moravians and the Calvinists" (Ph.D. thesis, University of Manchester, 1964).

particular.[21] Universalism, too, had leaders like James Relly (1722-1778) and Elhanan Winchester (1751-1797) who were step-children of the revival, and led some Methodists to abandon their original revivalism.

Structural tensions added fuel to the fire. The original revival bodies—the little societies and the itinerancies—were open in outlook. This made them vulnerable, and some seceded to sects like the New Jerusalem Church. The tightening controls of the Wesleyan Methodist Connexion were necessary, but resentment of these also resulted in schisms. On the Calvinist side, there were additional problems. No effective Calvinist connexion existed. Several loose associations of churches and preachers developed, including the Countess of Huntingdon's Connexion and the Rodborough Connexion. David Thompson and Deryck Lovegrove have shown that these were typical of many small non-exclusive networks of itinerant Calvinist Methodist preachers throughout the country. In the early nineteenth century, many of these small itinerancies, and the congregations they coaxed into existence, were consolidated into a new Dissent, which was based on the principle of a union of Independents (either Congregational or Baptist).[22] Since Nonconformity had lost the catholicity of old Dissent, it provoked sectarianism. Congregations and itinerancies rejecting denominationalism were forced to define the basis of their exclusiveness. The Countess of Huntingdon's Connexion declared its alignment with the Church of England. William Huntington S[inner] S[aved] (d. 1813) formed an exclusive group of antinomian nonbaptising churches in the South. Non-Calvinist Baptist itinerancies were unable to develop a strong structure until they were accepted into the Baptist Union at the end of the century. Thus, some old Evangelical societies were obliged to develop sectarian organization. The orthodox sects left over from the tidy-up of the Evangelical Revival did not prosper in the nineteenth century, and many members drifted towards the Evangelical denominations, or towards more extreme doctrinal positions. Thus the Methodist revival, while anti-sectarian in outlook, helped the formation of a range of more exclusive bodies.

The foundation of Essex Street Chapel, London, in 1774, signalled a new form of religious Dissent, not directly derived from old Dissent, al-

---

[21] See D. F. Clarke, "Benjamin Ingham (1712-1772), with Special Reference to his Relations with the Churches of his Time" (M.Phil. thesis, University of Leeds, 1971). *Historical Sketches of the Rise of the Scots Old Independent and Inghamite Churches* (Colne, 1814). For an interesting example see A. Brockett, *Nonconformity in Exeter 1650-1875* (Manchester, 1962), 160-71.

[22] Deryck Lovegrove, *Established Church, Sectarian People: Itinerancy and the Transformation of English Dissent, 1780-1830* (Cambridge, 1988); David Thompson, *Denominationalism and Dissent, 1795-1835: A Question of Identity* (London, 1985).

though eventually the Rational Dissenters aligned to it. But this Unitarian tradition developed different patterns at a popular level, including a sect of Methodist Unitarians. Methodism encouraged poor laypeople to form their own religious associations, and all sorts of religious traditions did so, including religions hostile to the revival. The latter are a very interesting group. By 1794, the writings of Thomas Paine had made many people conscious of the intellectual problems of traditional Christianity and the Established Church. Self-taught advocates of rational reform set out to form groups that, to varying degrees, were either anti-Freethought, fellow-travellers with Freethought, or (more usually) a little of each. Thus, there grew up a distinct congruence between some Protestant sectarianism and infidelity. These new religious movements were what sociologists call cults, for they lacked exclusiveness, were constantly changing in their views, and tended to embrace whatever new ideas were circulating in the secular world. Often the distinctive doctrines of Christianity were abandoned in favor of a vaguer theism or deism. Iain McCalman has shown how Deist churches were established by working-class Spenceans in London, partly because religious organization was familiar to people raised in the world of Methodism and Dissent.[23] In the North there were similar movements, including the mythological Deism of Robert Taylor's (1784-1844) Christian Evidence Society, and the rationalist Deism that Rowland Detroisier preached at Brinksway Chapel in Stockport. Sometimes (if not always) members of these cults had a deep religious earnestness, although there was little sense of the exclusivity of sect membership, and people changed movements easily, inspired more by the ethic of the bootstrap than by any particular doctrines.[24] Members of some working-class heterodox sects like the Methodist Unitarian Movement and the New Jerusalem Church were also sometimes attracted by Freethinking views, although their sects were tenaciously opposed to it.[25]

By the 1850s, working-class radicalism was spawning less sectarianism, since tolerance had become a dogma of the age, and trades unions had become the normal "association" for workers. Continued intolerance of heretical teaching by the churches (e.g., the heresy trial of the Rev. Charles Voysey [1828-1912]) encouraged the formation of small liberal sects based on the principle of toleration. South Place Chapel, which had been formed as a Universalist chapel under Elhanan Winchester and became a Unita-

[23] Iain McCalman, *Radical Underworld: Prophets, Revolutionaries and Pornographers in London, 1795-1840* (Cambridge, 1988).

[24] *Biographical Dictionary of Modern British Radicals,* ed. by J. O. Baylen and N. J. Gossman, 4 vols. (Hassocks, 1979-88), 1, 467-70; G. A. Williams, *Rowland Detroisier, a Working Class Infidel* (York, 1965) 4, 14, 24-32; McCalman, *Radical Underworld*, 188-90.

[25] See Lineham, "English Swedenborgians," 345-46.

rian church under W. J. Fox (1786-1864), then found a preacher in the American Moncure Conway (1832-1907), who replaced prayer with devotional exercises, and avoided commitment to any particular religion. South Place sat on the border between a religious and a secular cult.[26] Other groups in this uneasy "quasi-church" category included the Positivists at Newton Hall, the Church of Humanity, and the Fellowship of the New Life. At a working-class, level the Labour Churches founded by John Trevor at the end of the century tried to avoid dogma. While, in some respects, these groups were simply substitutes for churches for those who had lost faith but wanted a church, there were religious trends evident among them, and Spiritualism and Theosophy attracted support among members of such groups who hungered for a rational form of the supernatural. The desire to be part of a congregation was thus significant. These groups were nonexclusive sects, and they were very Protestant in their outlook.

The fascination with the biblical prophecies within nineteenth-century Protestantism is now generally recognized. It was a period when interpretations of the millennium shifted profoundly. Yet, the relationship of debates over the millennium in various contexts has still not been established. Distinctions between "millenarian" and "millennial" seem very unconvincing. In fact, the terminology of the whole discussion is due for an overhaul. Although the term "Millennialist" was the historic term that focused the debate over many generations, after Joseph Mede's interpretation had spread in the eighteenth century, the debate over the timing and order of the final events in world history that was all-important, rather than mere interest in the millennium. The factor that united those divided over interpretation of the prophecies and set them against other church people, was their "eschatological expectation." This was a common factor in many movements in Britain in the period. They deserve careful comparison. Scholars have compared the views of Edward Irving (1792-1834) about the millennium with those of Joanna Southcott (1750-1814), but there has been a failure to relate these to the various views canvassed among the Plymouth Brethen, although these views proved quite crucial in later prophetic interpretations, and probably were more influential than American Millerism.[27]

Why was eschatological expectation so vital an aspect of nineteenth-century society? No doubt the level of change that was taking place excited interest in the divine descriptions of the future of the world. Furthermore, Mede's views forced consideration of the issue of the manner of the return of Christ to earth. Excited anticipation at the fulfillment of the biblical

[26] S. K. Ratcliffe, *The Story of South Place* (London, 1955).

[27] See S. E. Orchard, "English Evangelical Eschatology" (Ph.D. thesis, University of Cambridge, 1969), 61-90.

prophecies of the end of time provoked some strong reactions at various levels of society. Interest in biblical eschatology was not confined to sectaries, and it is important to understand why only certain prophetic views were related to sectarianism. In the new interpretation of the prophecies, the significance of the church's purity was emphasized, and this excited a sectarian search for purity. Moreover, a heightened expectation of the near fulfillment of God's final work provides a very significant inducement to be absolutist in one's approach to church life. Furthermore, eschatological interest drew together people of common mind and isolated them from other members of the Established Church and Nonconformity.

The questions posed by the apocalyptic writers were often similar. Moreover, they often reflected secular issues, for example, the interpretation of the French Revolution. Indeed, the French Revolution persuaded many preachers to resort to apocalyptic images, although they did not agree on their interpretations. There was also constant debate between supporters of the different interpretations of the prophecies, and many people changed their interpretation several times in their lifetime. There was sometimes a cycle of excitement and disappointment. Yet, if the questions raised were sometimes similar, the answers given by the different movements were not, and nothing was potentially more sectarian than strong convictions about the correct interpretation of biblical eschatology. Such convictions were not always sectarian, but they did insulate people against the social tone of the age. Gradually, most Evangelicals in the Church of England adopted a premillennial perspective in this period. It made them more pessimistic in their attitude to society. Although only a small minority decided to leave the Established Church, it was a crucial factor for some. The sectarian impetus of eschatological interpretations in the era of the French Revolution may have concerned the nature of authority, as David Hempton has suggested,[28] but this ignores the background of attitudes to popular apocalypticism.

Popular apocalypticism was a very important factor in the social character of religion in the period, as J.F.C. Harrison has shown.[29] In many ways it represented the most disturbing aspect of popular English religion in the eyes of the Established Church, for it was biblicist, anticlerical, radical in its interpretation of the status quo, and open to occult forces. It was not essentially sectarian; Joanna Southcott was eager for the support of Anglican bishops. Yet, it expressed so all-encompassing a view of the world that it was bound to produce divisions. Sectarianism was also the only way to preserve hope and loyalty in the Southcottian faith in the painful years after Joanna's death at what should have been the moment of the birth of Shiloh. Messianism was inevitably sectarian. This is also

[28] D. N. Hempton, "Evangelicalism and Eschatology," *JEH* 31 (1980), 179-94.
[29] Harrison, *Second Coming*, 57ff.

evident in the effect of the messianic pretensions of "Sir William Courte-
ney" (John Nichols Tom, 1799-1838), the leader of the farmhands' rebellion in Kent in the 1830s, and in the extraordinary story of the Agapemone
of Somerset, in which the Rev. J. H. Prince (1811-1899), and his successor,
the Rev. J. H. Smyth-Pigott (d. 1927), both of whom declared themselves
to be God on earth, left their Anglican curacies for a private
community.[30]

Popular apocalypticism was not new. It had an historical genesis in
James Naylor, the Quaker messiah, and in the French prophets who came
to England in 1709. Although Methodist doctrine avoided eschatological
issues, many Methodists remained interested in them, and they were drawn
to radical quietist and mystical accounts of the future and
Swedenborgianism's promise of an age of fulfillment. The clarion call of
Richard Brothers (1757-1824) to British people to restore Israel gained
such attention that the government had him locked away as insane. Many
of his followers were attracted to Southcottianism. Irvingite apocalypticism
drew, to some extent, on the same market as well as on a fashionable audience, and some progressed from Irving's interpretation into one of the
Southcottian groups.[31] Irving's emphatic advocacy of this issue forced
many people to consider the issue, although not necessarily to accept his
answer. Prophetic conferences at Albury inspired intense discussion. The
early Plymouth Brethren were influenced by these discussions and by
conferences of their own where the issues were debated, and ultimately the
sect had to decide on what its view of prophecy was to be, and thus to
expel Benjamin Willis Newton, the rival to J. N. Darby (1800-1882).[32]

These remarkable movements are curiously different from American
apocalypticism at the same period. The Latter-Day Saints at an early stage
placed a strong emphasis on the millennial concerns, and the first magazine
of the Churches of Christ in Britain was, like its American counterpart,
called the *Millenial Harbinger*. There was some excited interest in William
Miller's expectation of the return of Christ in 1844, and the issue was the
subject of lively debate in the Churches of Christ at a early stage. As a result, Dr. John Thomas seceded to form the Christadelphians and ex-Mil-
lerites formed the Seventh-day Adventist and Watchtower movements.[33]

[30] Ronald Matthews, *English Messiahs: Studies of Six English Religious Pre-
tenders, 1656-1927* (London, 1936), 127-95.

[31] Harrison, *Second Coming*, 57-85, 86-134, 213-15; W. A. Smith, *"Shepherd"
Smith the Universalist: The Story of a Mind* (London, 1892), 34-43.

[32] H. H. Rowdon, *The Origins of the Brethren* (London and Glasgow, 1967),
12-17, 50-53, 230-33.

[33] David Thompson, *Let Sects and Parties Fall: A Short History of the Association of Churches of Christ in Great Britain and Ireland* (London, 1980), 38;
Louis Billington, "The Millerite Adventists in Great Britain, 1840-50," *Journal*

By the end of the century there was probably more debate about personal eschatology than about the future of the world. The Seventh-Day Adventists were identified as supporters of the doctrine of conditional immortality. This was a very sensitive issue in later-Victorian Britain, as Geoffrey Rowell has shown, although rarely the cause of major splits.[34] It is significant that the character of personal immortality was not the cause of more sectarian tensions in the period, for the question was one of heightened ethical sensitivity and could be argued by both Broad Churchmen and biblicists.

But biblicism and tensions over doctrinal orthodoxy were less causes of sectarianism in England than in America. The social subservience of many Church people kept them loyal to the Establishment. Some biblicists felt the need to fight for true doctrines, but few saw any need to part company with the Church, unless they were forced out. The classic case is the Countess of Huntingdon's Connexion, which would have remained a private team of preachers within the Church of England, but for the determination of the Bishop of London in 1780 to bring such bodies under discipline.[35] In the Church of England, the gradual acceptance of the Oxford Movement outraged some Evangelicals, and severe provocation by the Bishop of Exeter led to the secession of the founders of the Free Church of England, but its success was limited. Schismatic religious groups experienced "the dissidence of dissent," which was often endlessly divisive. In Oxford itself a group of University men, including Henry B. Bulteel (1800-1866), J. H. Philpot (d. 1869), F. W. Newman (1805-1897), and Benjamin Wills Newton (1807-1899) seceded in the ultra-Evangelical direction at the same time as J. H. Newman and Pusey were moving in the Catholic direction.[36] These men took varied final religious stances, including the Gospel Standard Baptists, the Brethren, the Catholic Apostolic

of American Studies 1 (1967), 191-212; Louis Billington, "The Churches of Christ," Journal of Religious History 8 (1974-75), 24-26; Ernest R. Sandeen, The Roots of Fundamentalism: British and American Millenarianism, 1800-1930 (Chicago, 1970).

[34] Geoffrey Rowell, Hell and the Victorians: A Study of the Nineteenth-Century Theological Controversies concerning Eternal Punishment and the Future Life (Oxford, 1974).

[35] A.C.H. Seymour, The Life and Times of Selina, Countess of Huntingdon (London, 1844); J. B. Figgis, The Countess of Huntingdon and Her Connexion (London, 1891); Edwin Welch, "Lady Huntingdon's Plans," Guildhall Studies in London History 2 (1975), 31-40; Edwin Welch, "Lady Huntingdon and Spa Fields Chapel," Guildhall Miscellany 4 (1972), 175-83; Welch, Two Calvinist Methodist Chapels.

[36] See The Seceders (1829-1869): The Story of a Spiritual Awakening As Told in the Letters of Joseph Charles Philpot and William Tiptaft, ed. by J. H. Philpot

Church, and Freethought, for schism for negative reasons is never enough, but horror at the corruption of the Church was necessary to start them on their journey. Curiously, a schismatic group left the Free Church of England to form the Reformed Episcopal Church when those who maintained that the Anglican Church as originally constituted was God-ordained were horrified by a tract entitled *Are There Romanising Germs in the Prayer Book?*[37]

Within the Evangelical Dissenting churches, doctrinal issues were a key cause of tension, particularly in the Baptist Church, where the shift from the traditional hyper-Calvinist position towards Fullerite Calvinism led, on the one hand, to the formation of a broadly based Baptist Union, but led, on the other hand, to the formation of various groups of Strict Baptists, most notably the Gospel Standard Baptists. When the New Connexion General Baptists were brought into the Union, and there were other signs of greater doctrinal tolerance, Charles Haddon Spurgeon attempted to stir up a "Downgrade" controversy, but few people were willing to secede for this reason. In Scotland, Presbyterianism was constantly splitting over purity of doctrine and organization, but in England doctrinal purity and traditionalism were less significant. The community was not nearly so sensitive to doctrinal issues as Scotland. Church polity was a more potent source of schism in the age of constitutional debate, for example, in Methodism. The century certainly threw up many significant issues on which the denominations were forced to change and accommodate the new world, but this did not create a sharp enough issue for a simple schism.

The sects of the nineteenth century were sometimes the product of ministerial secessions, although, on the whole, men like Charles Voysey, who seceded over accusations of heresy, did not prove capable of leading new movements, and simply gathered a single congregation of sympathizers. Others, like J. C. Philpot and William Tiptaft (d. 1864), joined existing sects. In the new Catholic Apostolic Church, Irving, the cause of the division, played a curiously retiring role. But sects emerged primarily from strong lay movements, which often drew on the incipient anticlericalism of English people. Indeed, some movements like the Brethren strongly resisted the organization of a new clerical hierarchy, and most groups (with the striking exception of the Catholic Apostolic Church) emphasized the kind of intimate and exclusive fellowship that inhibited the development of a clerical elite. The formation of a ministerial elite and ministerial training colleges in both the Churches of Christ and the New Jerusalem

(London, 1930); Rowdon, *Origins of the Brethren*, 64-69; T.C.F. Stunt, "John Henry Newman and the Evangelicals," *JEH* 21 (1970), 65-74.

[37] See *A History of the Free Church of England, Otherwise Called the Reformed Episcopal Church*, 2nd ed. (London and Lancaster, 1960), 50, 157-70.

Church was as tense a matter as it was in the various Methodist groups.[38] Leaders of sects were recognized for their charismatic qualities. Yet, sects had to decide how they were to perpetuate themselves, and groups with tight organization, like the Latter-Day Saints, prospered.

If the charismatic quality of sectarian leadership was important for men, it was far more so for women. For from the formation of the Quakers in the seventeenth century, there existed sects that recognized women with a calling to preach. Those women who sensed an inner calling usually found some sect that would recognize it. Moreover, many men were prepared to join sects formed around revelations received by women. The Southcottians are the obvious example, but another example is the Children of God (the "Walworth Jumpers," who later moved to a house at Hordle, Hampshire); the latter believed that Mary Ann Girling (d. 1886), was a female incarnation of Christ.[39] In its early days, Methodism had offered opportunities for women to minister in the domestic context characteristic of village preaching. As Methodism became more public and more formal, women who wanted to minister were forced to consider the sectarian option. The Female Revivalists of Leeds came into existence as Wesleyan controls on the local societies became tighter and inhibited women.[40] Deborah Valenze has described how Ann Mason (1791-1826) parted company with the Bible Christians, even though they permitted women preachers, because she rejected their authoritarianism.[41] The role of Catherine Booth (1829-1890) in forcing her husband William (1829-1912) to secede from the Wesleyan New Connexion is another classic example.[42] Women often played a prominent role in revivalist congregations, following the example of Phoebe Palmer, the American holiness preacher. Women seem to have had far more openings in the American religious world, and those sects open to an American influence were therefore freer to permit women's ministry. Another key factor was how leadership was defined within sects, for few sects were prepared to give women an institutional role. Sects like the Swedenborgians, which carefully defined the patterns of ministry, were quite traditional in their view of female ministries. An informal doctrine of ministry did not necessarily lead to liberty for women to preach, as is evident in the case of the Plymouth Brethren.

[38] Billington, "Churches of Christ," 30-36.

[39] W.H.G. Armytage, *Heavens Below: Utopian Experiments in England, 1560-1960* (London, 1961), 282-84; Davies, *Unorthodox London*, 89-108.

[40] Deborah M. Valenze, *Prophetic Sons and Daughters: Female Preaching and Popular Religion in Industrial England* (Princeton, 1985), 187-204.

[41] Ibid., 140-58.

[42] Robert Sandall and Arch R. Wiggins, *The History of the Salvation Army*, 7 vols. (London, 1947-1986), I, 10.

Another crucial theme was the desire for the church to return to its character in the days of the apostles (which went one step further than the Oxford Movement's focus on the Fathers). We are accustomed today to the Fundamentalist emphasis on obedience to the Bible in doctrinal, social, and individual spheres. In the nineteenth century, the concept of biblicism was much broader. Many new sects were motivated by an intense desire to recover the lost blessings and experiences of the early church by restoring it to its original structure. Some groups, like the Catholic Apostolic Church, placed their emphasis on the restoration of the gifts of prophecy and tongues. Others, like the Johnsonians, wanted to recover the radical communitarianism of early Christianity. The Quakers and the early Latter-Day Saints called for "primitive Christianity."[43]

This desire to restore the experience of the early church was reflected by a fascination with the simplicity of the biblical organization of the church. (Perhaps different factors were operating in the case of the Catholic Apostolic Church.) The context of this desire was the growing organizational hierarchy of Nonconformity, evident in both its denominational structures and the interdenominational missions. These religious organizations were seen as bureaucratic, worldly-wise, and too tolerant of social divisions. Purists believed that apostolic blessings would only be experienced when the church returned to what it was meant to be. The Sandemanian churches were early examples of this approach.[44] A further factor was a deep desire to return to the departed days early in the revival, when "vital" Christians experienced a close unity with one another. While one may talk about the nineteenth century as an age of Evangelical unity, there is a significant rise in the period of formal definition of differences. So sects often began, paradoxically, by seeking to bring about unity. This was critical to the motivation of the Churches of Christ and the Plymouth Brethren, as well as the Sandemanian groups and the Walkerites (followers of a former Fellow of Trinity College, Dublin).[45] Because the polity of many sects was congregational, it was possible for them to maintain at least a nominal openness to others.

In the 1820s and 1830s this viewpoint had wide currency. The tensions within the Establishment led to a demand for a more radical Evangelical-

[43] See E. P. Thompson, *English Working Class*, 129-30; S. Mews, "Reason and Emotion in Working-Class Religion, 1794-1824," *SCH* 9 (1972), 367-68; Davies, *Heterodox London*, 1, 245.

[44] See Harry Escott, *A History of Scottish Congregationalism* (Glasgow, 1960), 7-42.

[45] See R. H. Martin, *Evangelicals United: Ecumenical Stirrings in Pre-Victorian Britain, 1795-1830* (Metuchen, N.J., 1983); H. H. Rowden, "Secession from the Established Church in the Early Nineteenth Century," *Vox Evangelica*, III (1964), 77-78; Billington, "Churches of Christ," 22-23.

ism, and the example of the Haldane brothers was influential. Millennial excitement provided some of the context for the desire to create the church after God's intention. Darby, a key leader of the Brethren, believed that a day of ruin had driven the church and its ministry into apostasy, and believers who wanted to prepare for the coming of Christ must separate from the ruins of Christendom. These views have some precedents. There was a tradition of Restorationist separatism, which included the Scotch Baptists, the Quakers, and, to a lesser extent, the Walkerites. The Brethren's views were the most radical case for Restorationism, and "Plymouthism" was contagious, affecting ideas of ministry in many other orthodox sects, including the Churches of Christ.[46]

But the Brethren's position did not dominate in one aspect that some saw as the ultimate of Restorationism, the formation of communities on the New Testament pattern, where life could be lived in sectarian purity. This viewpoint attracted some interest, although the high price of land and the extent to which agricultural production was commercialized inhibited its development to the extent to which the Shakers and others spread it in the United States. The Moravians were the earliest Evangelical communitarians and they had settlements at Gracehill in Ireland, at Fulneck in Leeds, and at Dukinfield in Manchester. Small rural sects like the Cokelers at Loxwood in Sussex and the Children of God at Hordle, Hampshire, represented a primitive species of this aspiration, while the Agapemone at Somerset lived in an exotic community of sexual experimentation, and the Transcendentalists of Ham Common sought to develop a Freethinking mysticism. A number of Southcottian groups formed communities, including the Christian Israelites, followers of John Wroe (1782-1863) at Ashton-under-Lyne, and next at Wakefield, while the Jezreelites (the New and Latter House of Israel) built a great tower at Gillingham in Kent. Extreme sectarians were almost forced to found exclusive communities.[47] Owenite socialism drew inspiration from such sects, and for its part, early socialism colored the views of some of the sectaries.[48]

Scholars sometimes have ignored how mystical, occult, and transcendentalist beliefs also encouraged sectarianism. Although writers like James Obelkevich and Keith Thomas have rediscovered the role that traditional

[46] Stunt, "Newman and the Evangelicals," 65-74; Escott, *Scottish Congregationalism*, 45 ff.; T.C.F. Stunt, *Early Brethren and the Society of Friends*, Christian Brethren Research Fellowship Occasional Paper No. 3 (1970); D. Thompson, *Let Sects and Parties Fall*, 53.

[47] Armytage, *Heavens Below*, 47-57, 171-83, 272-86; Dennis Hardy, *Alternative Communities in Nineteenth-Century England* (London, 1979), 120-54; P. G. Rogers, *The Sixth Trumpeter; the Story of Jezreel and his Tower* (London, 1963).

[48] See J.F.C. Harrison, *Robert Owen and the Owenites in Britain and America: the Quest for the New Moral World* (London, 1969), 45-139.

religious ideas of magic and nature played in the intellectual equipment of the poor regardless of formal church commitment,[49] they have overlooked the tendency for these doctrines to stimulate sectarianism in the nineteenth century, when the culture of the rural poor was under threat from industrial society. Swedenborgianism's appeal lay in its defense of traditional ideas that nature and the Bible had deeper meanings under the surface. The East Lancashire weavers who were drawn into it saw it as a way to protect their traditions. In the nineteenth century, the Bible Christians of Salford split from the New Jerusalem Church because they believed that a vegetable diet was God's intended means to preserve the spiritual side of humans from corruption.[50] Traditional health remedies and healing rituals were common customs among the poor, and in Essex in 1837 a sect called the Peculiar People was gathered by James Banyard (1800-1863) on the basis of literal belief in the biblical injunction that the prayer of faith would heal the sick.[51] There was probably far more incipient sectarianism in the countryside than has ever been measured. In many respects, traditional prophetic beliefs drew the common people to Southcottianism.

By midcentury an additional factor was the new emphasis on the transcendental powers inherent in the human mind and the search for a rational basis of contact with the spiritual world. This is evident among the Transcendentalists of Ham Common and the Spiritualists. Disgruntled Swedenborgians joined many such groups.[52] In many ways, the elitist supporters of Theosophy shared something of the same motivation.[53]

The rise of revivalism in the mid-nineteenth century was a significant source of new religious institutions, but few had the character of exclusive sects. They were more open, for example, than the Methodist sects founded early in the century, the Bible Christians of Cornwall (the

---

[49] Keith Thomas, *Religion and the Decline of Magic* (London, 1971); James Obelkevich, *Religion and Rural Society: South Lindsey, 1825-1875* (Oxford, 1976).

[50] Lineham, "English Swedenborgians," 389 ff.; P. J. Lineham, "Restoring Man's Creative Power: The Theosophy of the Bible Christians of Salford," *SCH* 19 (1982), 207-23; and Paul A. Pickering and Alex Tyrrell, "'In the Thickest of the Fight': The Reverend James Scholefield (1790-1855) and the Bible Christians of Manchester and Salford," *Albion* 26 (1994), 461-82.

[51] M. Sorrell, *The Peculiar People* (Exeter, 1979), 21-29.

[52] Lineham, "English Swedenborgians," 389 ff.; Logie Barrow, "Socialism in Eternity: The Ideology of Plebeian Spiritualists, 1853-1913," *History Workshop Journal* 9 (1980), 37-69; Logie Barrow, *Independent Spirits: Spiritualism and English Plebeians, 1850-1910* (London, 1986).

[53] Bruce F. Campbell, *Ancient Wisdom Revived: A History of the Theosophical Movement* (Berkeley, 1980); Michael Gomes, *The Dawning of the Theosophical Movement* (Wheaton, Ill., 1987).

Bryanites), and the Primitive Methodists. The Evangelical community had an internal structural incoherence that allowed innumerable private initiatives, of which the greatest was the Salvation Army. The so-called 1859 revival produced no new denomination, and its supporters gloried in the fact: "It has been all prayer ... no sectarianism, no preachers, nothing, but prayer."[54] Sects like the Open Brethren benefited from the revival atmosphere and were drawn towards a more open stance. A stream of denominational and interdenominational revivalists followed the lead of Moody and Sankey in seeking opportunities for preaching outside the churches, and a plethora of mission halls opened, which in total attracted a significant proportion of church attendance in the London survey of 1902-3. A. D. Gilbert has suggested that these conversionist sects were especially significant at the end of the century, when main Evangelical denominations were in decline. The revivalist missions may be accused of undermining the structures of the church, but they also promoted a zeal for evangelism and spiritual transformation that the denominations could not contain.[55] They deserve comparison with the flourishing of independent fundamentalist groups in the United States, although the status of the Established Church did much to inhibit their growth. The Salvation Army is something of a special case, because its use of uniforms and bands gave it an exclusive atmosphere, and sociologists have recognized that in its demands on membership, its view of the sacraments, and its view of the world, it became increasingly sectarian.[56]

Revivalism also led to heterodox and experimental sectarianism in the United States, like Spiritualism and the Latter-Day Saints. To a degree, this phenomenon also is reflected in England, for example, in the Agapemone, the cult of Holy Love that began among spiritually zealous students at St. David's College, Lampeter, in the 1830s.[57] This is an unusual case. There were far fewer separatist holiness groups in England than in the United States at this stage. Spiritualism initially avoided sectarianism, and spiritualist churches were not established until the 1920s.

[54] J. E. Orr, *The Second Evangelical Awakening in Britain* (London and Edinburgh, 1949), 153.

[55] A. D. Gilbert, *Religion and Society in Industrial England: Church, Chapel and Social Change, 1740-1914* (London, 1976), 42-44, 221; Kent, *Holding the Fort*, 40, 304-5. See also E. A. Payne, *The Free Church Tradition in the Life of England* (London, 1944), 131.

[56] R. Robertson, "The Salvation Army: The Persistence of Sectarianism," *Patterns of Sectarianism*, ed. Wilson, 49-105; K. S. Inglis, *Churches and the Working Classes in Mid-Victorian England* (London, 1963), 175-214.

[57] C. Mander, *The Reverend Prince and his Abode of Love* (East Ardsley, Yorks, 1976), 43-54. For a more scholarly account, see Matthews, *English Messiahs*, 161-95; and Hardy, *Alternative Communities*, 134-39.

Sectarianism seems to attract much stronger support in some historical periods and community settings than in others. It was plainly an important social phenomenon in seventeenth-century England, and it is again in the present-day United States. The swing towards it in nineteenth-century Britain may not have been as intense as in these periods, but there was sufficient to require explanation. The themes of sectarianism that we have explored are significant enough to indicate that the new religious movements of the century reflect the general currents of English history in the period. W. R. Ward has shown how trends and tensions within Methodism and the Nonconformist churches reflect wider political trends in the period 1790 to 1850. The same approach could be extended to the formation of new religious movements. Sectarianism emerges out of a culture in which political and social issues were reflected and expressed in religious behavior. Arguably, there were moments in the changing social and political climate when the formation of new religious or social movements awoke strong interest. There was a major tide of support for sectarianism in the 1790s, another in the 1830s, and perhaps another more restrained tide in the 1860s. This does not mean that the sects sought popular support, or received it. Yet, in the end, they attracted attention because the denominations had become so political. John Kent's failure to recognize this distorts his interpretation of sectarianism.[58]

The French revolutionary wars increased the exclusiveness of new religious movements. J.F.C. Harrison has shown how popular excitement about the Second Coming heightened apocalypticism and separatism.[59] Political radicalism was quite compatible with religious sectarianism. When William Huntington knighted himself Sinner Saved, he was sneering at the higher reaches of society. The loyalism that developed after 1800 undermined support for the sects. The national organization of the New Jerusalem Church collapsed in the period 1800-15, and many middle-class Swedenborgian receivers returned to their parish churches.[60] Again after 1815, the repression of radicalism forced working-class movements to take refuge in sectarian contexts. Some of these were the radical and Deist sects well known to labor historians,[61] but the principal sect that took root at this period in the countryside in many Midlands counties was Primitive Methodism.[62]

The profound constitutional shift in England after 1827 promoted a new sectarianism, for it heightened fears and also excited sectarian aspirations. The attack on the standing of the Establishment certainly en-

[58] Kent, *Holding the Fort*, 304-7.

[59] Harrison, *Second Coming*.

[60] Lineham, "English Swedenborgians," 330-31.

[61] See McCalman, *Radical Underworld*, 128-51.

[62] See Obelkevich, *Religion and Rural Society*, 242-56.

couraged dissent, but anti-Liberalism and fear of democracy, the very forces that led to the Oxford Movement, were surprisingly common among some sectarians. Their mental world was shaped by a biblicist culture, anticlericalism, and a stock of apocalyptic fears, particularly focused by the Catholic Emancipation Act and its impact on Protestantism in Ireland. Evangelicalism and Freethought faced each other at several levels in society, as studies of Chartism have shown, and studies of the middle class could also show.[63] As the search for respectability drove Evangelical leaders to form denominational organizations,[64] others, particularly laity, felt the appeal of sectarianism, for they were suspicious of the emerging Evangelical clerical elite. The old interdenominational societies had become clericalized or denominationalized.[65] Pioneers of the Brethren and the Churches of Christ represent an attempt to maintain the old lay Evangelical spirit.[66] Sectarianism is thus the logical concomitant of the growth and the denominationalisation of the Nonconformist and Methodist world. These issues were clouding the religious horizons of ordinary Nonconformists, although their clergy did not notice the fact. Thus, the development of sectarianism casts an interesting reflection on the religious politics of the age. The sects represented a minority opinion, it is true, but a minority opinion that many people considered. The research of T.C.F. Stunt indicates that another major factor was that while the Evangelical denominations were stabilizing, there were rising fears that in Ireland and in Europe the new wave of Evangelical advance was being stymied by authoritarian repression. Radical Restorationist Protestantism reacted to the news from Geneva and Dublin.[67] At this "moment," apocalypticism was combined very naturally with Restorationism.

In the 1860s and 1870s, a new phase of informal new religious movements occurred, with the growth of faith missions and holiness sects. These had a less militant theology (other than its anti-Catholicism and anti-infidelity), but the sense of struggle heightened their fervency. On the other side of the spectrum, the growing Victorian crisis of faith pushed others into mediating cults, like Charles Voysey's Church of the Future and Ro-

[63] See Eileen Yeo, "Christianity in Chartist Struggle, 1838-42," *Past and Present*, No. 91 (1981), 109; for Ireland, see Rowden, *Origins of the Brethren*, 1-12, 17-22.

[64] Lovegrove, *Established Church, Sectarian People*, 159-60.

[65] Martin, *Evangelicals United*, 195-98.

[66] D. Thompson, *Let Sects and Parties Fall*, 9; also his *Denominationalism and Dissent*, 23-25.

[67] T.C.F. Stunt, "Geneva and British Evangelicals in the Early Nineteenth Century," *JEH* 32 (1981), 35-46, esp. 44. I am grateful to Dr. Stunt for information on this point.

bert Elsmere's "New Brotherhood of Christ," although many of these were confined to the metropolis.[68]

Alongside these general factors we need to note the role of external influences on British religion and also factors that influenced the local environment. In the nineteenth century, established religious groups did not look kindly at religious influences from the United States. Methodist conferences refused to license Lorenzo Dow and James Caughey to minister in England. Their ministry was thus forced in non-Wesleyan directions. The Primitive Methodists were not the only beneficiaries of this attitude.[69] The undisciplined and charismatic American voices represented, to some British people, a model of what a truly Protestant England might be. Dr. John Thomas came back from America and founded the Christadelphians, and Moncure Conway took South Place Chapel in a new and distinctly secular direction. Curiously, these two movements were less successful in the United States.[70] The tastes and tolerances of the American and British communities were significantly different. Other American religious groups attracted a sectarian following in England, including the Latter-Day Saints (which had supporters in England from about 1840), the Seventh-day Adventists (which developed a following from 1878), the Campbellite Churches of Christ (which emerged in the 1830s from publicity about Campbell's ideas, although they were never a subordinate "British branch" of the movement), Spiritualism (which Mrs. Hayden brought across the Atlantic in 1852), and later the Jehovah's Witnesses (1881), Christian Science (1897), and the Church of the Nazarene (1915).

This transatlantic inspiration needs to be set alongside a European factor. In the eighteenth century, the radical Pietism of the Moravians and other groups directly influenced the first Evangelical revival,[71] and the French Quietists influenced the development of a mystical fraternity in England.[72] The occult tradition had strong European influences, and Swedenborgianism was shaped, in part, by French émigrés.[73] We have already mentioned the Continental influence on radical Evangelicalism in

[68] W. S. Smyth, *The London Heretics, 1870-1914* (London, 1967), 8-9, 23-24.

[69] See Kent, *Holding the Fort*, 9-70; Richard Carwardine, *Trans-Atlantic Revivalism: Popular Evangelicalism in Britain and America, 1790-1865* (Westport, Conn., 1978).

[70] See Charles H. Lippy, *The Christadelphians in North America* (Queenston, Ont., and Lewiston, N.Y., 1989).

[71] W. R. Ward, "Power and Piety: The Origins of Religious Revival in the Early Eighteenth Century," *Bulletin of the John Rylands University Library of Manchester* 83 (1980), 231-52.

[72] Desirée Hirst, *Hidden Riches: Traditional Symbolism from the Renaissance to Blake* (London, 1964), 180 ff.

[73] Lineham, "English Swedenborgians," 137-48.

the 1830s. Another important factor was the contribution of the Scots, Irish, and Welsh to English sectarianism. Scottish Presbyterians were a direct influence on the growth of Evangelical Nonconformity in the North of England, and consequently Glas and Sandeman influenced the Inghamites and London Baptists in the antinomian direction, and the Haldane brothers inspired revivalists to abandon the Establishment.[74] Welsh influences were crucial for the Calvinist Methodists and it was James Relly, a Welshman, who pioneered Universalism in England. Irish Protestants were the strongest exponents of apocalyptic fear of Rome, which helped the emergence of the Brethren.[75]

Environmental factors affected the scale of sectarianism in different districts. In a superb study of upstate New York, Whitney Cross long ago argued that the flourishing of sectarian religion follows in the aftermath of revival and large-scale enthusiastic religious movements.[76] The eighteenth-century revivals in England were focused in the West Riding of Yorkshire, Cornwall, Somerset, and, to a lesser extent, Lancashire and Gloucestershire. Primitive Methodist revivals touched Staffordshire and eastern Yorkshire. Although the revival probably did not have as great an impact in England as in the United States, it nevertheless transformed several communities. It is not easy to compare this on a sound statistical basis with sectarian distribution, for no single denomination encapsulated the impact of the revival, and it is a complex matter to use the 1851 census to compare sects and revival regions. Nevertheless, the regional concentrations of sectarianism do bear some relation to the centers of the eighteenth-century revival. The one variation from the focus of the eighteenth-century revival is the strong sectarian presence in London, reflecting the tendency of sects to take advantage of the freedoms and anonymity of a large city. But apart from this, the parallels are striking.

The New Jerusalem Church was focused in Lancashire and the West Riding, the Latter-Day Saints in Lancashire and the West Midlands, the Seventh-day Adventists in London, Birmingham, and Manchester, and Spiritualism in Lancashire and the West Riding. The Brethren were found in the West Country and the Northwest, and the Churches of Christ in Lancashire, Cheshire, and the East Midlands. Southcottians were concentrated at least initially in London, Yorkshire, Lancashire, Devon, and the

[74] R. Halley, *Lancashire: Its Puritanism and Nonconformity* (Manchester, 1872), 512, 515-18; Escott, *Scottish Congregationalism*, 17-42; Stunt, "Geneva and British Evangelicals," 35-46.

[75] Hempton, "Evangelicalism and Eschatology," 185.

[76] W. R. Cross, *The Burned-Over District: The Social and Intellectual History of Enthusiastic Religion in Western New York, 1800-1850* (Ithaca, N.Y., 1950).

Midlands.[77] Overall, there is a focus on London, the West Country, and the Northwest. One center of the earlier revival was the vicinity of Haworth in the West Riding, whose vicar, William Grimshaw (1708-1763), was one of the leading Church Methodists. Yet, many of his converts found their way into the Wesleyan Methodists, the Baptist chapel, and the antinomians. The neighboring village of Keighley became the major center of the New Jerusalem Church in the county, and in the 1860s, Spiritualism's British focus was in the same village, while Inghamite and Moravian chapels were not much further away.

We have focused on the emergence of sectarianism and seen how intertwined it was with the political and social circumstances of the day and changes in Dissent and the Established Church. Yet, to survive, sects had to find methods of continuing to recruit members and of securing their own internal stability. Those that failed to do this, including the radical Deists and the transcendentalist New Thought groups, soon collapsed. The methods used are extremely revealing. There were many parallels between sectarian methods and those of the denominations they had left. They primarily recruited from dissatisfied members of other denominations, and their methods included vigorous attacks on the denominations in debates, pamphlets, and sermons. They attracted people in existing churches who longed for the close fellowship and commitment that their denominations lacked. The split in the Wesleyan Methodist Connexion in 1848 benefited the sects to some extent. For example, J. B. Rotherham left the Wesleyans and joined the Churches of Christ, where he became an important leader.[78] Yet, simultaneously, both the Brethren and the Churches of Christ experienced their own major disruptions in the late 1840s, the Brethren splitting over the issue of sectarian structure and exclusiveness, and the Churches of Christ faced with the secession of more apocalyptic Christadelphians. The New Jerusalem Church also experienced a crisis at this time.[79]

Sects that gathered around charismatic leadership found it acutely difficult to develop a stable basis of life. The Brethren, the New Jerusalem Church, and the Southcottians were all repeatedly convulsed with leadership disputes. Some sects invested their charismatic leader with absolute authority. Others were doomed to remain small because they were led by small-minded figures who periodically expelled threats to the received tradition. In the New Jerusalem Church and the Churches of Christ, the so-

[77] Lineham, "English Swedenborgians," 453-54; Gay, *Geography of Religion*, 189-96; F. Roy Coad, *A History of the Brethren Movement: Its Origins, Its Worldwide Development, and Its Significance for the Present Day* (Exeter, 1968), 164-85; Billington, "Churches of Christ," 29; Harrison, *Second Coming*, 109-11.

[78] D. Thompson, *Let Sects and Parties Fall*, 48.

[79] Cf. ibid., 44, 62; Lineham, "English Swedenborgians," 355.

lution to the problem of order was clericalism. The Catholic Apostolic Church took this to an extreme and became an intensely liturgical body with large numbers of ordained clergy, although it remained dependent on its charismatically identified Twelve Apostles. Clericalism sometimes led clergy to move closer to the denominations in their attitudes. Other sects retained their intense isolationism and antimodernism, and sought to preserve their lifestyle and doctrines by formal and informal restrictions on worldliness and contact with other churches. The British Mormons achieved their separation by fleeing from Babylon to the Zion in America, whereas the Churches of Christ and the Exclusive Brethren did so by forbidding communion with unbaptised believers.[80] Even moral movements of the age, like the temperance movement and the campaign against the Contagious Diseases Acts, were suspect in the eyes of many, because of the contact they brought with the world.[81] Yet, if we examine the changing buildings of the sectarians and compare them with, say, the Methodists, it is striking how much the simple and unadorned, but respectable, buildings of established sects parallelled those of Nonconformity.

Sectarianism has sometimes been seen as a movement of the downtrodden, appealing primarily to the working-class poor. Sufficient evidence has now been accumulated to reject this theory. J.F.C. Harrison in his study of millenarian sects concludes that

> none of the millenarian movements we have looked at had any substantial following among the poor. There is little to suggest that the disinherited and outcasts of society found solace or hope in millenarian belief. Such evidence as we have points to support from artisans, small farmers, shopkeepers, tradesmen, domestic servants and women, together with an important minority of merchants, businessmen, clergy and members of the professions. Middle-class observers repeatedly expressed surprise that the followers of millenarian prophets were not the poorest members of the community, but on the contrary were people of modest social standing, people "who ought to have known better."[82]

With some qualifications, these remarks fit many other sects as well. There are differences within and between the sects, particularly when compared with the Nonconformist denominations, but it is important to compare sects and denominations in the same settings, since environmental factors explain some huge variations in the social character of religious movements in different locations. Hobsbawm, writing of the labor sects, argues

---

[80] See P.A.M. Taylor, *Expectations Westward: The Mormons and the Emigration of the British Converts in the Nineteenth Century* (Ithaca, N.Y., 1966), 26; D. Thompson, *Let Sects and Parties Fall*, 76-86.

[81] Billington, "Churches of Christ," 40-42; Coad, *History of the Brethren*, 263.

[82] Harrison, *Second Coming*, 221.

that they tended to attract the working class to a greater extent than the Nonconformists, although he qualifies his comments by noting that working-class sectarians separated themselves from the culture of their class, and often began to better themselves as a result.[83] Yet, the short life of these sects makes his argument problematic, and while there is no denying that many of the poor knew much more than the rich about the sects, they were reluctant to join them. Even the Salvation Army was relatively unsuccessful in the East End of London, and even Mormons must have been artisans, for they had to be readers.[84] On the whole, the working class remained impervious to sectarian attempts to convert them, although there were always some exceptions.[85] Sect membership often was focused in one particular artisan occupation, although it is difficult to establish precise reasons for this, other than the particular circumstances of the initial converts. Thus, the New Jerusalem Church had a very strong concentration of Lancashire weavers, and the early Brethren attracted large numbers of Northern and Scottish fishermen. In general, the Plymouth Brethren and the Catholic Apostolic Church had more supporters of high social status than other sects, and the Deist sects more of low status, but groups like the Christadelphians, the Churches of Christ, the New Jerusalem Church, and the Salvation Army always had a few wealthy people, who had a position of inordinate influence, and the usual range of lower-middle-class and artisan members, many of whom achieved a status and dignity in the sect that they did not know outside.[86]

A great deal more research is needed on the history of sectarianism in nineteenth-century England. While some sects have been carefully studied, a great many others have been neglected. In some cases, social interpretation has been neglected by ongoing research. In other cases, research needs to give more attention to the inner logic and working of the sects. The general theme of the rections of church leaders to the sects is neglected, although it bears comparison with the activities of present-day deprogrammers. One inhibition on research is the sects' attitude to their records. If any records are preserved, they often are protected in a truly sectarian fashion. While some groups, like the Brethren, the Moravians, and the

[83] E. J. Hobsbawm, *Primitive Rebels* (Manchester, 1959), 130-34.

[84] Taylor, *Expectations Westward*, 31.

[85] For two points of view, see Kent, *Holding the Fort*, 67; and Hugh McLeod, *Religion and the Working Class in Nineteenth Century Britain* (London, 1984), 49.

[86] See Lineham, "English Swedenborgians," 380-81, 386-88; Coad, *History of the Brethren*, 172-73; B. R. Wilson, "The Exclusive Brethren," *Patterns of Sectarianism*, 329-31; Rowdon, *Origins of the Brethren*, 137, 153; Billington, "Churches of Christ," 30-31, 44 fn. 112; D. Thompson, *Let Sects and Parties Fall*, 33-34.

New Jerusalem Church, have made their records available, and other records have drifted into public repositories, some remain in private hands. It is plain that research calls for a high level of tact and understanding. Yet, it has remarkable potential for contributing to an understanding of nineteenth-century religious patterns.[87] The sects were a small part of nineteenth-century life; they do not deserve equal treatment with the Methodists, the Nonconformists, and the Church of England. Yet, in many ways they created important borders and reflected important tensions in the larger denominations. Researchers should beware of what is, in fact, a sectarian attitude in themselves towards such groups.

[87] See, for example, O. Michael Friedman, *Origins of the British Israelites: The Lost Tribes* (San Francisco, 1993); Glenn K. Horridge, *The Salvation Army: Origins and Early Days, 1865-1900* (Godalming, Surrey, 1993); as well as the collection of essays in *Mormons in Early Victorian Britain*, ed. by Richard L. Jensen and Malcolm R. Thorp (Salt Lake City, Utah, 1989).

7

Freethought: The Religion of Irreligion

Edward Royle

DESPITE THE TOTAL rejection by nineteenth-century Freethinkers of the creeds of Christianity and all its various organizational forms, the history and historiography of irreligion in Britain have closely followed orthodox religious lines. In organizing to reject religion, Freethinkers behaved like one or more Christian denominations, and their historians have approached their subject in the same way as have the historians of religion. As a consequence, it is both possible and necessary for a chapter on irreligion to shadow closely those other chapters that are explicitly about religion; but because the forms of irreligion are less well known to most historians of religion than their own subject matter, there is need first in this chapter to define and examine the development of the topic under review.

"Freethinker" was, and is, the term generally preferred by those who, from a religious point of view, are usually referred to as "infidel" or irreligious. It has been applied to a variety of non-Christian positions, including Atheism, Deism, Rationalism, Secularism, Agnosticism, Ethicism, and even some forms of Positivism. In themselves, of course, all these labels apply to intellectual positions rather than organizations, but, during the course of the nineteenth century, adherents to these various views did gather in organizations for their mutual protection, encouragement, and development. Thus, the single word "Freethought," when applied to organization, is distinguished from the intellectual disposition to free thought. The claim of these Freethinkers was that they had no creeds. That is, their thoughts about life and eternity were not fettered by beliefs accepted from tradition or revelation, but were derived from, and tested by, reason according to the scientific method. Free thinking, it was assumed, would lead to Freethought.

The concept of Freethought was essentially a product of the scientific Enlightenment of the later seventeenth century, and the earliest usage of the word in English appears to have been in a letter from William Molyneux to John Locke (6 April 1697), in which John Toland (1670-1722) was described as a "candid freethinker."[1] Toland's *Christianity Not Mysterious* (1696) was one of the earliest publications in a debate about the truth of the Christian revelation that marked the early years of the eighteenth century and laid the foundations for later developments in Freethought. The origin of Freethought among "Commonwealthsmen" and republicans is significant, for there was always to be a strong political dimension to irreligion—a dimension recognized and reienforced by the Blasphemy Act of 1695, which excluded irreligion from the provisions of the Toleration Act of 1689, thus drawing a clear line between irreligion and Protestant Dissent. The legal position had first been set out in the common law, which, in the words of Chief Justice Hale in Taylor's Case (1675), stated that "to say religion is a cheat is to dissolve all those obligations whereby civil societies are preserved; and Christianity being parcel of the laws of England, therefore to reproach the Christian religion is to speak in subversion of the law"[2]

This attitude, which grew out of fears engendered by the English Civil War, served to keep "respectable" Freethought hidden behind the walls of the Latin language, ironic defences of Christianity, or highly priced volumes intended only for the libraries of gentlemen, until well into the nineteenth century. Matters were made worse when, in the aftermath of the French Revolution, fears about the connection between irreligion and political upheaval appeared to be confirmed by events in France and reactions to those events throughout Europe. For two generations between 1790 and 1850, organized irreligion was synonymous with extreme political radicalism. Its high priest was Thomas Paine (1737-1809), whose *Age of Reason* (1793-94) attacked the Bible and Christian revelation with that same merciless wit and journalistic skill he had earlier applied to the British Constitution, monarchy, and aristocracy in *Common Sense* (1776) and *Rights of Man* (1791-92).

This phenomenon of organized radical anti-Christianity was essentially British—and indeed English. Despite some French and American influences, themselves traceable to seventeenth-century writers like John Toland, Freethought belonged securely within the context of English working- and lower-middle-class Dissent, which then spread its influence to

[1] See Gordon Stein, "Freethought," in *The Encyclopedia of Unbelief*, ed. by Gordon Stein, 2 vols. (Buffalo, N.Y., 1985), 1, 247.

[2] Quoted from W. H. Wickwar, *The Struggle for Freedom of the Press, 1819-1832* (London, 1928), 25.

other parts of the English-speaking world, notably, the United States.[3] Not until the development of Positivism and Ethicism later in the nineteenth century, with their respective French and American origins, did forms of organized Freethought emerge in England that both owed something to other traditions and also appealed to a higher social class and to followers who included those of more conservative political opinions.

Radical Freethought developed in the nineteenth century in a self-conscious tradition, from the artisan reading clubs that met in the 1790s to discuss Paine's works, through the early nineteenth-century publishers of the so-called blasphemous and seditious press who reissued Paine and similar works—notably, Richard Carlile (1790-1843), who in the 1820s organized Zetetic or free enquiring societies to maintain his cause—to the rationalist followers of Robert Owen (1771-1858) and early secular mille-narian socialism, and thence with some Owenites led by George Jacob Holyoake (1817-1906) into Secularism. The latter reached its heyday in the 1880s, inspired by the formidable oratory of Charles Bradlaugh (1833-1891) and the blasphemously witty journalism of George W. Foote (1850-1915). From this central core, connections were established with sympathetic intellectuals like John Stuart Mill (1806-1873), and member-ships and aims overlapped with Positivist, Ethicist, and Rationalist groups, which coexisted with Secularist societies like separate denominations within a parallel—or indeed parody—of the Christian world. When assess-ing their influence and importance, though, the historian soon becomes aware that these irreligious groups differed from their Christian counter-parts in one major respect. Although, like the Christians, their "uncon-scious" following was always greater than their "conscious" following (to use the categories employed by Horace Mann in the 1851 Religious Cen-sus report), their committed memberships were never as large as any but the smallest of Christian denominations—a few thousand at the most.

The earliest studies of irreligion in its various forms were almost wholly in-house and denominational. In this respect, the historiography of Freethought follows the same path as that for orthodox Christianity. Nineteenth-century histories were mainly by sympathetic scholars explor-ing their own intellectual roots, notably, Leslie Stephen[4] and J. M. Ro-bertson.[5] Robertson (1856-1933), in particular, was a prolific writer from within the Secularist-Rationalist tradition, whose *A History of Freethought*

---

[3] For freethought in the United States, see G. A. Koch, *Republican Religion: The American Revolution and the Cult of Reason* (New York, 1933); Albert Post, *Popular Freethought in America, 1825-1850* (New York, 1943); and Sidney Warren, *American Freethought, 1860-1914* (New York, 1943).

[4] *History of English Thought in the Eighteenth Century*, 2 vols. (London, 1876).

[5] *A Short History of Freethought, Ancient and Modern* (London, 1899).

in the Nineteenth Century[6] remains the most wide-ranging survey of intellectual Freethought yet published, although only 10 pages out of over 600 were devoted directly to that branch of organized Freethought of which he was a prominent leader. The same, largely intellectual, approach was also adopted by other writers, such as A. W. Benn, who wrote from an Agnostic position.[7] The one major Christian contribution to the history of Freethought in this period was A. S. Farrar's 1862 Bampton Lectures, *A Critical History of Free Thought in Reference to the Christian Religion*, but this was a theological and intellectual review occasioned in part by, but not about, the expansion in organized popular unbelief.

The second major area of historical writing opened up by the later nineteenth-century Freethinkers themselves was biographical, the products of which were published in the Freethought periodicals of the time. Outstanding among these contributions were articles by J. M. Wheeler (1850-1898), which were collected, extended, and published as *A Biographical Dictionary of Freethinkers of All Ages and Nations*,[8] a work of reference of fundamental importance for any scholar and the basis of all future biographical dictionaries, including Joseph McCabe's *Biographical Dictionary of Modern Rationalists*.[9]

Much writing by and about nineteenth-century Freethinkers was polemical. One of the most prolific authors, G. J. Holyoake, was concerned to maintain through his autobiographical works his own view of the movement of which he was a founder and the centrality of his own importance within it. Thus, his *The History of the Last Trial by Jury for Atheism in England* (1850)[10] —a record of his own trial and sufferings in 1842—was a vindication and defense of his credentials to lead militant Freethought at a time when his increasing moderation was bringing criticism from rivals such as Charles Southwell (1814-1860), who had been imprisoned for blasphemy in 1841 and whose own delightfully racy *Confessions of a Freethinker* were also published in 1850. Holyoake's moderation in 1850 was about to lead to his launching of Secularism, a movement influenced by Owenite Rationalism, Utilitarianism, and Positivism, and intended to provide an ethical system based in the here and now that would provide a positive philosophy for those whose inability to accept

[6] 2 vols. (London, 1929).

[7] *The History of English Rationalism in the Nineteenth Century*, 2 vols. (London, 1906).

[8] (London, 1889).

[9] (London, 1920).

[10] Holyoake was, as usual, being both inaccurate and misleading. He was tried for blasphemy, not atheism, and there had been subsequent trials in Scotland for selling blasphemous literature (in 1843). The next trial in England was Pooley's Case (1857).

Christian theology had left them open to the charge of being immoral and unworthy of citizenship. This appeared to sidestep the issue of whether or not a God actually existed, moving from outright atheism towards what Thomas Huxley was later to call Agnosticism.

The theological debate about whether an atheist could or could not avow that God did not exist was to divide the Freethinkers as acutely as the debate over "the elect" divided Calvinist and Arminian Evangelicals, and it remains an important issue in the historiography. In general terms, Charles Bradlaugh denied the existence of any God whom any religion had sought to proclaim, and called this atheism; Holyoake thought such a denial speculative and irrelevant to the affairs of this world and resented Bradlaugh's ascendancy in the Secularist Movement from the 1860s. This produced a considerable literature of disputation, culminating in Holyoake's *The Warpath of Opinion* and *The Origin and Nature of Secularism* (both of 1896). The former was, in part, a response to a vindication of Bradlaugh against all who maligned him—whether Christian or fellow Secularist—written by his daughter, Hypatia Bradlaugh Bonner (1858-1934).[11] Much of the controversy was conducted in biographical form. Holyoake's own autoiography, written in the 1880s, was published in 1892 and was supplemented in 1905 with further volumes.[12] Holyoake's death the following year led in 1908 to a commemorative, scholarly, and highly favorable biography by Joseph McCabe (1867-1955), an ex-Jesuit Freethought lecturer who used the occasion to defend the moderate rationalist position embodied in the Rationalist Press Association and to attack the more extreme form of atheistic Secularism represented by Bradlaugh's creation, the National Secular Society, led after his death in 1891 by G. W. Foote.[13]

For many historians of nineteenth-century England until at least the 1960s, Atheism, Freethought, and Secularism meant either nothing at all or only what was embodied in the works of Bradlaugh Bonner, Holyoake, McCabe, and Robertson. Control over how the past was to be viewed had been achieved beyond the grave through accessible and readable autobiographical and biographical justifications. Even the historian who wished, or realized the need, to dig deeper would have found only more works of the same genre. The only major biographies of Richard Carlile were that

[11] *Charles Bradlaugh: A Record of His Life and Work, by His Daughter, with an Account of His Parliamentary Struggle, Politics, and Teachings, by John M. Robertson*, 2 vols. (London, 1894).

[12] G. J. Holyoake: *Sixty Years of an Agitator's Life*, 2 vols. (London, 1892); *Bygones Worth Remembering*, 2 vols. (London, 1905).

[13] J. McCabe, *Life and Letters of George Jacob Holyoake* (London, 1908).

written by his daughter, Theophila Carlile Campbell,[14] which includes the text of several letters and so is an invaluable primary source, and that by the anarcho-communist Guy Aldred (1886-1963), who was inclined to interpret Carlile as a predecessor worthy of himself.[15] Mrs. Bradlaugh Bonner put a great deal of effort into a volume about her father to commemorate the centenary of his birth, but this again should be used mainly as a primary source.[16] In turn, posthumous tribute was paid to Mrs. Bonner by her husband, Arthur, in his biography.[17]

The bias in this work does not undermine its value when used with caution, and not all publications of this period have lost all value as secondary histories. Much of Robertson's historical work has stood the test of time, as has the first major sympathetic *Life of Thomas Paine*,[18] written by Moncure Daniel Conway (1832-1907), the American-born minister of the Freethinking South Place Chapel in London. Conway also prepared the first definitive edition of the *Writings of Thomas Paine* (1894-96). The first move away from the biographical approach came with W. H. Wickwar, *The Struggle for the Freedom of the Press, 1819-1832*,[19] which was centered on the activities of Carlile, but was by no means exclusively devoted to them. This remained the best book on the period until the 1960s, but was something of an exception. Most studies dating from the first half of the twentieth century continued to be in-house and denominational, the only *History of the British Secularist Movement* being a short study by J. E. McGee, an American Freethinker, which was issued by Haldeman-Julius, a noted though minor American Freethought publisher, and is now extremely rare.[20]

The same comments can be applied to early histories of other branches of unbelief. Autobiographies, biographies, and denominational histories written by adherents continued to predominate until well into the twentieth century. Positivism was, for example, represented by Frederic Harrison's and Malcolm Quin's memoirs.[21] Again, the fullest history of the movement was by J. E. McGee, published by the English rationalist firm

[14] *The Battle for the Freedom of the Press as Told in the Story of the Life of Richard Carlile* (London, 1899).

[15] *Richard Carlile, Agitator: His Life and Times*, rev. ed. (Glasgow, 1941).

[16] *Champion of Liberty: Charles Bradlaugh*, ed. by J. P. Gilmour (London, 1933).

[17] A. Bonner and C. Bradlaugh Bonner, *Hypatia Bradlaugh Bonner: The Story of Her Life* (London, 1942).

[18] (New York, 1892).

[19] (London, 1928).

[20] (Girard, Kans., 1947).

[21] F. Harrison, *Autobiographic Memories*, 2 vols. (London, 1911); M. Quin, *Memoirs of a Positivist* (London, 1924).

of Watts in 1931.[22] Another prolific contemporary writing from within the movements was F. J. Gould (1855-1938), who was active in Secularism, Positivism, and Ethicism and who wrote an account of his own spiritual journey.[23] On parts of this journey, Gould was accompanied by Harry Snell (1865-1944), the first popular Freethought activist to reach the House of Lords (for political services to Labour).[24] Moncure Conway also remains his own best historian.[25] The *Story of South Place*, Conway's London chapel, which started in 1793 as a congregation of Universalists and subsequently passed through Unitarianism under W. J. Fox (1786-1864) to become an Ethical Society under Stanton Coit (1857-1944), was briefly written by one of its members in 1955, to commemorate the twenty-fifth anniversary of the society's move to Conway Hall where it still thrives.[26] Though better than many conventional chapel histories, the book is essentially of that genre, and the subject still awaits a fuller study. The same was true for many years of the Ethical Movement. Gustav Spiller's *The Ethical Movement in Great Britain* was no more than—in the author's own subtitle—*A Documentary History*, a source book rather than an historical study.[27] These comments can also be applied to the two principal works on the Rationalist Press Association. Gould's *Pioneers of Johnson's Court*[28] is a chronicle rather than the history it purports to be, while Whyte's *Story of the Rationalist Press Association*[29] is again a short—though very useful—denominational history, written with all the insights of the RPA's then vice chairman.

There is a sense, therefore, in which practically all the books written about the Freethought movement before about 1950 should be read as a part of its prehistory. Informative though some of these studies are, they are essentially primary sources for what they tell later historians about contemporary attitudes and self-perceptions. Freethought was scarcely noticed by those outside its walls, except when Christian opponents felt obliged to refer to or examine its progress, and these works rarely rose above polemic. Freethought played little part in general histories of the period. As with the history of orthodox religion, though, the publishing

[22] *A Crusade for Humanity: The History of Organized Positivism in England* (London, 1931).

[23] *The Life Story of a Humanist* (London, 1923).

[24] H. Snell, *Men, Movements, and Myself* (London, 1936).

[25] *Autobiography, Memories, and Experiences*, 2 vols. (London, 1904).

[26] S. K. Ratcliffe, *The Story of South Place* (London, 1955).

[27] (London, 1934).

[28] F. J. Gould, *The Pioneers of Johnson's Court: A History of the Rationalist Press Association from 1899 Onwards* (London, 1929; rev. ed., 1935).

[29] A. Gowans Whyte, *The Story of the Rationalist Press Association, 1899-1949* (London, 1949).

explosion and quest for new and different research topics that marked the 1960s produced a new interest in, and study of, the literature and organizations of Freethought.

The reasons for this can be traced, in part, to changes within Britain itself. With that decline in religious observance that has characterized much of the last 100 years, but became marked in cultural terms from the later 1950s, scholars may have felt able to detach themselves from polemic and view irreligion with indifference as a social phenomenon rather than as a position to be justified or as a supposed threat (notwithstanding the subsequent revival of blasphemy prosecutions in English courts of law).[30] Furthermore, the changing nature of historical studies, with the move away from a concentration on established structures in political and ecclesiastical life, also encouraged a revival of interest in what appeared to be a curious countercurrent in nineteenth-century history.

The first interest in the history of Freethought, though, came not from general historians of the nineteenth century, but from historians of ideas—theological, philosophical, and literary—and from sociologists of religion. Much of the early writing came not from within Britain itself, but from the United States, where several isolated, unpublished, and little-known theses were produced, in addition to some important published works.

The Freethinkers best known to the academic world were those eminent literary figures, the Victorian "honest doubters," and this is where most scholars have begun. In two volumes of biographical studies of nineteenth-century writers, Basil Willey[31] included sympathetic explorations of the minds of leading doubters such as John Stuart Mill, Charles Hennell, George Eliot, Francis Newman, and John Morley, while, in the United States, Walter Houghton explored similar territory thematically.[32] The implications of the ideas of these eminent doubters for the history of irreligion were first pointed out by H. R. Murphy in an article that argued that the rejection of Christianity was more a matter of ethical revulsion than of intellectual and scientific criticism.[33] The alleged tension between religion and science, which had been celebrated in such works as J. W.

---

[30] Following the successful prosecution of J. W. Gott for blasphemy in 1921, the offence of blasphemy was widely believed to be dead. The Blasphemy Act was repealed in 1969, but a private prosecution was successfully brought in 1977, which reaffirmed the illegality of blaspheming the Christian religion in England and Wales. The law in Scotland probably is dead.

[31] *Nineteenth-Century Studies: Coleridge to Matthew Arnold* (London, 1949); *More Nineteenth-Century Studies: A Group of Honest Doubters* (London, 1956).

[32] *The Victorian Frame of Mind, 1830-1870* (New Haven, 1957).

[33] H. R. Murphy, "The Ethical Revolt Against Christian Orthodoxy in Early Victorian England," *AHR* 60 (1955), 800-17.

Draper's *History of the Conflict between Religion and Science* (1874), was shown to be of secondary importance. At this point the literary and moral argument engaged with that derived from the history of science.[34] The debate became—and remains—a matter of whether and how far the rejection of religious beliefs in the nineteenth century was, in fact, the outcome of rationalism, freethinking, and science, as both propagandists and historians have often assumed.[35]

Literary historians continued to draw attention to Freethought throughout the 1960s. A.O.J. Cockshut's *The Unbelievers*[36] was another study of "honest doubt"—respectable agnostic thought in the later nineteenth century—in which Bradlaugh is mentioned only in passing and Holyoake scarcely at all. An interest in the writer George Bernard Shaw (1856-1950) brought W. S. Smith to study *The London Heretics, 1870-1914*.[37] Although this book drew attention in some detail to the Secularists, Positivists, and South Place, it still gave undue prominence to Shaw's distorted view of his own significance and failed to grasp the more popular and populist side of Freethought. Some of the best studies to be produced by American scholars in the 1960s were regrettably never published.[38] Of these, Nelson's thesis made full use of the Rationalist Press Association archives and library, for the first time exploiting the full potential of the pamphlet and periodical literature of Freethought. His interest, though, remained intellectual, a study of ideas such as social Darwinism rather than of social movements.

The approach to a study of Freethought through the history of ideas has been both natural and unavoidable in the case of work on that most intellectual wing of the movement—Positivism. In 1957, a thesis by Sidney Eisen, part of which was later published in article form, looked at the life

[34] C. C. Gillispie, *Genesis and Geology: A Study in the Relations of Scientific Thought, Natural Theology, and Social Opinion in Great Britain, 1790-1850* (Cambridge, Mass., 1951); J. C. Greene, *The Death of Adam: Evolution and its Impact on Western Thought* (Iowa City, 1959).

[35] John Kent, *From Darwin to Blatchford: The Role of Darwinism in Christian Apologetic, 1875-1910* (London, 1966); R. M. Young, "The Impact of Darwin on Conventional Thought," *The Victorian Crisis of Faith*, ed. by A. Symondson (London, 1970).

[36] *The Unbelievers: English Agnostic Thought, 1840-1890* (London, 1964).

[37] (London, 1967).

[38] W. D. Nelson, "British Rational Secularism: Unbelief from Bradlaugh to the Mid-Twentieth Century" (Ph.D. thesis, University of Washington, 1963); C. W. Krantz, "The British Secularist Movement: A Study in Militant Dissent" (Ph.D. thesis, University of Rochester, 1964).

and thought of Frederic Harrison.[39] W. M. Simon also produced an intellectual survey of European Positivism, supplemented by a more specialized article on the English followers of Comte.[40] In all these accounts, the center stage is held by Richard Congreve (1818-1899), founder of the London Positivist Society in 1867 and of the Positivist Church of Humanity in 1878, and his three pupils at Wadham College, Oxford—John Henry Bridges (1832-1906), Edward Spencer Beesly (1831-1915), and Frederic Harrison (1831-1923)—whose approach to Positivism was less priestly than Congreve's and depended less on specifically Christian forms. The impact of these people on Victorian thought and literature, or their involvement in the politics of the labor movement,[41] has—perhaps rightly—attracted historians more than a study of the reasons why four men, ten women, and two children attended worship at the Chapel Street Church of Humanity, in Holborn, London, one Sunday morning in 1903.[42]

The first interest in Freethought as organization and in Freethinkers as social groups came from sociologists of religion. Their insights have done a great deal to redress the imbalance implicit in the literary approach and to put Freethought securely within a religious interpretational context. It may be an indication of the state of historical studies of Freethought in the 1950s that the first brief historical survey of organized popular Freethought, by John Eros, was published not in a mainstream historical journal but in the *Sociological Review*.[43] This interest was taken up in the 1960s by Charles Krantz in the United States, in a thesis that sought to locate Secularism within the cultural framework of English Dissenting Protestantism,[44] and by two English sociologists, Colin Campbell and Susan Budd. In 1967, Budd contributed an article on "The Humanist Societies" to a collection of sociological essays edited by Bryan Wilson, in which

[39] S. Eisen, "Frederic Harrison: The Life and Thought of an English Positivist" (Ph.D. thesis, Johns Hopkins University, 1957); "Frederic Harrison and the Religion of Humanity," *South Atlantic Quarterly* 66 (1967), 574-90.

[40] *European Positivism in the Nineteenth Century: An Essay in Intellectual History* (Ithaca, N.Y., 1963); "Auguste Comte's English Disciples," *Victorian Studies* 8 (1963-64), 161-72.

[41] Royden Harrison, *Before the Socialists: Studies in Labour and Politics, 1861-1881* (London, 1965).

[42] Richard Mudie-Smith, *The Religious Life of London* (London, 1904), 182.

[43] "The Rise of Organized Freethought in Mid-Victorian England," 2 (1954), 98-120.

[44] Krantz, "British Secularist Movement."

she examined the consequences for Freethought organizations of a belief system that, in its rejection of authority, was antiorganizational.[45]

This raised important doubts about Krantz's approach. Should Freethought properly be regarded as a part of the religious scene? How far can the sociology of religion be used to understand a belief system that is opposed to religion? The problem of how to think, in sociological terms, about Freethought organizations was one to which Colin Campbell turned his attention in a series of conference papers and articles in the later 1960s and then in a fuller study.[46] In this work, Campbell addressed the question of whether irreligion should be seen as a negative, the obverse of religion, dependent upon it for interpretation and analysis, or whether it should be seen as a positive, open to sociological analysis in its own right. He concluded in support of the latter position, and then proceeded to discuss a variety of irreligious organizations both historically and sociologically. In analyzing Secularism, he suggested two different types. On the one hand, there was Bradlaugh, who can be categorized as an "eliminationist"—one who rejects and wishes to destroy that to which he is opposed; and on the other hand, there was Holyoake, who was a "substitutionist"—one who seeks to replace rejected religion because he recognizes the essential social function played by religion and who thus adopts a more open—even "religious"—approach.[47] This analysis makes clear the affinity between Holyoake's brand of Secularism, together with both Positivism and Ethicism, and religious systems, but provides an alternative way of thinking for those aspects of Freethought that cannot so easily be typed as "religious."

Also in 1967, Budd published an article on the reasons why the rank and file of the Secularist movement abandoned their faith.[48] For the first time, attention was diverted from the views and conversions of an intellectual elite to the rank-and-file membership of local Freethought societies. Budd's method was to analyze the minor autobiographies and biographies—especially obituary notices—published in the Freethought periodical press. Her findings largely confirmed the theory offered by Murphy,[49] that the rejection of Christianity was principally on ethical

[45] S. Budd, "The Humanist Societies: The Consequences of a Diffuse Belief System," *Patterns of Sectarianism: Organisation and Ideology in Social and Religious Movements*, ed. by B. R. Wilson (London, 1967), 377-405.

[46] *Toward a Sociology of Irreligion* (London, 1971).

[47] C. Campbell, "Analysing the Rejection of Religion," *Social Compass* 24 (1977), 339-46.

[48] S. Budd, "The Loss of Faith: Reasons for Unbelief Among Members of the Secular Movement in England, 1850-1950," *Past and Present* No. 36 (1967), 106-25.

[49] H. R. Murphy, "Ethical Revolt Against Christian Orthodoxy."

grounds, the Bible being the most significant book to stimulate the process of deconversion.

Susan Budd's complete thesis, which dealt not only with Secularism, but also with Rationalism, the Ethical Movement, and Humanism as it developed up to the 1960s, was revised and published some nine years after its completion.[50] Like many pioneering studies, it caused no great controversy, for most critics were not sufficiently informed to comment upon it, but it did help to put the study of Freethought more securely on the historical agenda. The principal criticisms came from within the National Secular Society itself, where some members objected to her too-ready alignment of Secularism with the working class and Rationalism with the middle class. All such attempts to use class categories in specific instances are fraught with danger, but it must have come somewhat as a surprise to an academic conditioned by the ethos of the 1960s, in which to be thought "working-class" was perceived as morally superior to being thought "middle-class," to find an organization proud of its *embourgeoisement*.

These insights derived from the sociological approach enriched the study of Freethought history in the 1970s. Not only did they draw attention to a dimension of Freethinking that literary scholars had ignored, but they also served as a corrective to those historians whose image of G. J. Holyoake was as "founder" of the cooperative movement, or whose sole—and often inaccurate—knowledge about Charles Bradlaugh was of his struggle to enter Parliament.

The latter provided Walter Arnstein with the subject of a monograph in 1965.[51] This work was important because, for the first time, it set out in a nonpartisan way the complicated events surrounding the refusal of the Speaker of the House of Commons to permit Bradlaugh to swear the oath of allegiance after his election for Northampton in 1880 and placed them securely in their political context. Although Arnstein did not at that time have access to the Bradlaugh Papers, he was nevertheless able, through a scrupulous use of a wide range of newspaper, manuscript, and official sources, to provide a valuable survey of one of the most misunderstood and misinterpreted causes célèbres of the later nineteenth century. But despite the insights provided by Arnstein into Bradlaugh as a Freethinker, his account was generally received as a contribution to the history of Gladstone's second ministry rather than to the history of Freethought, while the prejudiced and uninformed continued to believe that Bradlaugh

[50] *Varieties of Unbelief: Atheists and Agnostics in English Society, 1850-1960* (London, 1977).

[51] W. L. Arnstein, *The Bradlaugh Case* (Oxford, 1965).

was the monster of Christian propaganda or the paragon of his daughter's biography.[52]

The wider Freethought context in the 1960s still remained the province of the denominational historian. David Tribe, then president of the National Secular Society, in 1967 published a general history of Freethought to commemorate the centenary of his society's foundation in 1866.[53] As a Secularist activist, Tribe was well placed to appreciate the courage of Bradlaugh, the role of Freethought pressure groups, and the development of the modern humanist movement. His work therefore provides both a useful guide to Freethought history and a sourcebook for more recent developments, though it lacks some of that critical detachment that might have been expected of a scholarly work written in different circumstances.

With the notable exception of Wickwar's work,[54] very little attention had been paid before 1960 to the popular literature of Freethought and the role of the unstamped press. An early article by J. Holland Rose,[55] which was contemptuously dismissive, set the tone until a new appreciation of the part played by the blasphemous and seditious press was presented in Brian Simon's first volume of *Studies in the History of Education, 1780-1870*.[56] This was followed in 1963 by Edward Thompson's monumental *Making of the English Working Class*, which put Paineite republicanism and the popular press firmly in the mainstream of historical interpretations of the period between 1790 and 1832.[57] In the same year, a thesis examined some radical publishers and publications of early nineteenth-century London.[58] Nevertheless, as late as 1970, a collection of studies of *Popular Movements, 1830-1850*, edited by J. T. Ward, still lacked an entry on the blasphemous and seditious press, though two important studies were published just too late to influence the selection.[59] Through these works,

---

[52] The orthodox reception given to Arnstein's book partly resulted from the interpretation suggested by its subtitle, *A Study in Late Victorian Opinion and Politics*. The new edition was instead subtitled by its American publisher, *Atheism, Sex, and Politics among the Late Victorians* (Columbia, Mo., 1983).

[53] *100 Years of Freethought* (London, 1967).

[54] *The Struggle for the Freedom of the Press.*

[55] "The Unstamped Press, 1815-36," *EHR* 12 (1897), 711-26.

[56] (London, 1960).

[57] E. P. Thompson, *The Making of the English Working Class* (London, 1963).

[58] H. J. Luke, "Drams for the Vulgar: A Study of Some Radicals and Radical Publications of Early Nineteenth Century London" (Ph.D. thesis, University of Texas, 1963).

[59] Patricia Hollis, *The Pauper Press: A Study in Working-Class Radicalism in the 1830s* (Oxford, 1970); Joel H. Wiener, *The War of the Unstamped: The Movement to Repeal the British Newspaper Tax, 1830-1836* (Ithaca, N.Y., 1969).

an understanding of the radical culture out of which popular Freethought grew was greatly extended.

The most important and influential study of the nature of that radical culture that nurtured popular Freethought came in 1969, with the publication of the first attempt to come to grips with the organization and mind of popular Owenism—J.F.C. Harrison's *Robert Owen and the Owenites*.[60] In this book, Harrison combined the insights of an historian of education, radicalism, and religion to remove the Owenite story from its position as prologue to histories of the the Fabian Socialist, trade-union, or co-operative movements to which it had been relegated (not least by the writings of G. J. Holyoake[61]) and to place it back in its contemporary religious context. In so doing, he prepared the way for further studies of both latter-day Owenism and Secularism.

Encouragement for this came in the unlikely form of G. Kitson Clark, a conservative Anglican whose good-humoured disparagement of "infidelity" was more than matched by his unprejudiced curiosity to understand all aspects of Victorian life. In a *festschrift* presented to Kitson Clark in 1967 by his former pupils, F. B. Smith published the first general survey since Eros of what he termed "the Atheist Mission," a study of organized popular Freethought from the Owenite dissidents of 1840 such as Charles Southwell and G.J. Holyoake through to the end of the Bradlaugh years.[62] Smith's interest had, in fact, originally been aroused by the presence of followers of Secularism in his native Australia, who not only were organized very much as in Britain, but whose journals were full of news and reports from back home.[63] Meanwhile, Kitson Clark was also encouraging another student, Edward Royle, to investigate Secularism more thoroughly as an aspect of the religious history of Victorian Britain.

Working with a narrower focus than Susan Budd's, Royle exploited the pamphlets and periodicals of early Victorian Freethought to produce a thesis[64] on the development of Secularism out of Owenism under Holyoake's leadership between 1841 and 1861. Most of the sources had

---

[60] *Robert Owen and the Owenites in Britain and America: The Quest for the New Moral World* (London, 1969); the American edition reverses title and subtitle.

[61] Especially Holyoake's *History of Co-operation*, 2 vols. (London, 1906).

[62] "The Atheist Mission, 1840-1900," *Ideas and Institutions of Victorian Britain: Essays in Honour of George Kitson Clark*, ed. by Robert Robson (London, 1967), 205-35.

[63] F. B. Smith, "Religion and Freethought in Melbourne, 1870-1890" (M.A. thesis, University of Melbourne, 1960). Similar emigrant sources led to M. Francis, "British Secularism, 1840-1885" (M.A. thesis, University of Toronto, 1969).

[64] Edward Royle, "George Jacob Holyoake and the Secularist Movement in Britain, 1841-1861" (Ph.D. thesis, University of Cambridge, 1968).

previously been greatly underused. Holyoake's letters, which had been deposited with the Co-operative Union at Holyoake House in Manchester, had been forgotten and almost lost during the Second World War and since then had been only dipped into, mainly by Co-operative scholars.[65] With the assistance of the Co-operative Union, Royle was able to prepare a comprehensive descriptive index of the Holyoake Correspondence and, after extending his doctoral research, produced a general survey of nineteenth-century radical Freethought,[66] a collection of primary sources,[67] and a monograph that covered the years 1791 to 1866.[68] A subsequent monograph, using similar sources, the Bradlaugh Papers, and the National Secular Society archives, extended this survey to 1915.[69]

While attempting to place Freethought within its intellectual context, these works were primarily concerned with Secularism as a political and religious movement—an aspect of that alliance of Liberal radicalism and chapel culture that was such a feature of nineteenth-century Britain. To some extent, Royle's works still conformed to the model of denominational history, though this time written by an outsider, and their aim was, in part, to supply that need already met in many areas of orthodox religious history for a framework within which other, more detailed, and often local studies could be located. His interpretation of Secularism as an irreligious denomination was substantially in agreement with those of Krantz and F. B. Smith, although he also emphasized the role of Secularism as a radical political grouping, in keeping with the general trend among historians of nineteenth-century politics to show a new appreciation of the religious dimension to political activity.[70] However, in using a study of midnineteenth century Secularism to expand a view of post-Chartist radicalism, Royle was in more controversial territory. By emphasizing the

[65] Susan Budd was probably the first scholar to realize the potential of the collection for the history of Freethought. It does not appear to have been used in the rather slight article by Angus McLaren, "George Jacob Holyoake and the Secular Society: British Popular Freethought, 1851-1858," *Canadian Journal of History* 7 (1972), 235-51.

[66] *Radical Politics, 1790-1900: Religion and Unbelief* (London, 1971).

[67] *The Infidel Tradition from Paine to Bradlaugh* (London, 1976).

[68] *Victorian Infidels: The Origins of the British Secularist Movement, 1791-1866* (Manchester, 1974).

[69] *Radicals, Secularists, and Republicans: Popular Freethought in Britain, 1866-1915* (Manchester, 1980).

[70] Eileen Yeo, "Robert Owen and Radical Culture," *Robert Owen, Prophet of the Poor*, ed. by Sidney Pollard and John Salt (London, 1971), 84-114; E. Yeo, "Christianity in Chartist Struggle," *Past and Present* No. 91 (1981), 109-39; Stephen Yeo, "A New Life: The Religion of Socialism in Britain, 1883-1896," *History Workshop Journal* 4 (1977), 5-56.

continuities in Freethought ideas and even organization from the 1790s to the 1890s and the centrality within that of the Paine-Carlile tradition of radical infidelity, he was implicitly challenging that view of radical history that saw a distinct break around midcentury between those increasingly class-conscious politics that reached their climax in Chartism and the moderation of popular Liberalism in the mid-Victorian years.[71]

By 1980, after approximately two decades during which new perspectives were opened up in British social history, the history of Freethought could be said to have emerged from the shadows of denominationalism, partisanship, and Victorian obscurity. This did not mean that the subject was exhausted, but that the basic features of the major themes had now been explored in thesis and monographic form. Budd's study of the years after 1850 was an indispensable starting point, along with Stein's descriptive bibliography.[72] Royle's two volumes on Secularism gave much of the general background to the more "popular" expression of militant Freethought.

In the next few years the Ethical Movement was studied further by MacKillop,[73] although his primary interest in the intellectual side of Ethicism led him to neglect some of the connections between the Ethical Movement and other political, religious, and Freethought organizations. Positivism was also the subject of new studies that build upon the work of Eisen and W. M. Simon to extend an understanding of the impact of Comte's leading English followers on ideas and politics in the second half of the nineteenth century. Christopher Kent studied the relationship between the elitism of Comtist philosophy and the democratic politics of some of Comte's leading English disciples;[74] Martha Vogeler provided a biographical study of Frederic Harrison's Positivist career,[75] and T. R.

[71] See J. H. Wiener, "Collaborators of a Sort: Thomas Paine and Richard Carlile," *Citizen of the World: Essays on Thomas Paine*, ed. by Ian Dyck (London, 1987), 105; and John Belchem, *"Orator Hunt": Henry Hunt and English Working-Class Radicalism* (Oxford, 1985), for the view that postwar radicalism had played itself out by 1848. Carlile and Hunt were, of course, great rivals, and the historiography, to some extent, reflects each man's assessment of his own importance in shaping and defining the "true" radical tradition.

[72] *Freethought in the United Kingdom and Commonwealth: A Descriptive Bibliography* (Westport, Conn., 1981).

[73] I. D. MacKillop, *The British Ethical Societies* (Cambridge, 1986).

[74] C. Kent, *Brains and Numbers: Elitism, Comtism, and Democracy in Mid-Victorian England* (Toronto, 1978).

[75] M. S. Vogeler, *Frederic Harrison: The Vocation of a Positivist* (Oxford, 1985).

Wright placed Congreve, Harrison, and their friends within the wider context of the Victorian literary, intellectual, and critical world.[76]

Detailed studies were also written that used the insights gained since the 1960s to explore further the nature of religious unbelief in the nineteenth century and the connections between Freethought and other aspects of Victorian life and thought. Banks, for example, reexamined the question of the spread of birth-control information and practices from the time of the Bradlaugh-Besant Trial of 1877 and concluded that Secularism and declining religious belief had very little to do with the falling size of families in later Victorian England.[77] Mullen began the process of questioning and interpreting the earlier work of Budd and Royle, examining the paradox of the Secularists as a militantly antireligious group constrained to play out in religious terms an increasingly obsolete role within a rapidly secularizing society.[78] She explained the peculiar religiosity of atheism as a product of the cultural background of the participants, a point made earlier by the Secularist leader, Chapman Cohen, who, as a Jew, did not carry with him the burdens of a rejected Christian past.[79] The Secularists and their like have also been located more precisely within the broader culture of working-class life and religion by Hugh McLeod.[80]

If the working class did not regularly attend church or chapel, religious feelings among them nevertheless remained strong, often assuming unorthodox forms that verged at times on Freethought. A literature has developed to explore the forms that this took within the labour movement, later nineteenth-century Socialism, and the early Labour Party. Some of this material was published in the 1960s in works by K. S. Inglis on the Labour Church movement[81] and by F. Reid on the Socialist Sunday schools,[82] although a major thesis on the Labour Churches remains unpublished.[83] Subsequently, Stephen Yeo drew new attention to the religion of socialism

[76] T. R. Wright, *The Religion of Humanity: The Impact of Comtean Positivism on Victorian Britain* (Cambridge, 1986).

[77] J. A. Banks, *Victorian Values: Secularism and the Size of Families* (London, 1981).

[78] Shirley A. Mullen, *Organized Freethought: The Religion of Unbelief in Victorian England* (New York, 1987).

[79] Royle, *Radicals, Secularists, and Republicans*, 121.

[80] H. McLeod, *Class and Religion in the Late Victorian City* (London, 1974).

[81] *Churches and the Working Classes in Victorian England* (London, 1963).

[82] "Socialist Sunday Schools in Britain, 1892-1939," *International Review of Social History* 11 (1966), 18-47.

[83] D. F. Summers, "The Labour Church and Allied Movements of the Late Nineteenth and Early Twentieth Centuries" (Ph.D. thesis, University of Edinburgh, 1958).

in the later nineteenth century,[84] and an unpublished thesis by G. J. Mayhew explored the ethical and religious foundations of socialist politics in Britain between 1884 and 1931.[85] The Labour leader, J. Ramsay MacDonald, after all, moved in the same circles for a time as Stanton Coit, J. M. Robertson, and F. J. Gould. The Labour Party may have owed more to Methodism than to Marx, but it also owed something to Ethicism. Gould's part in this was explored by David Nash.[86]

The two most important works to suggest fruitful new directions for study in the 1980s were Iain McCalman's *Radical Underworld*, which attempted to take some of the shine off the self-proclaimed idealism of the blasphemous and seditious press and further broke down the artificial barriers erected by historians between various forms of religious, social, and political activity,[87] and Logie Barrow's *Independent Spirits*, a study of plebeian spiritualism in the second half of the nineteenth century.[88] Barrow rightly criticized Royle for emphasizing the Secularist inheritance from Owenism and plebeian radicalism whilst ignoring the spiritualist tradition that also came out of Owenism, which shared much of the same mental world and which acted as a rival and even threat to Secularist organization. Much more work of this kind remains to be done.

There is also need for historians of Freethought to emulate those who study Christianity and to undertake more local studies. An appeal along these lines was made by a Freethinking ex-clergyman, F. H. Amphlett-Micklewright, in 1969, but few have as yet followed his suggestion.[89] Apart from two undergraduate dissertations that looked at Leicester and Birmingham, the only local study of Secularism so far is by David Nash on

[84] S. Yeo, "Religion of Socialism."

[85] "The Ethical and Religious Foundations of Socialist Politics in Britain, 1884-1931" (Ph.D. thesis, University of York, 1980).

[86] "F. J. Gould and the Leicester Secular Society: A Positivist Commonwealth in Edwardian Politics," *Midland History* 16 (1991), 126-40.

[87] *Radical Underworld: Prophets, Revolutionaries, and Pornographers in London, 1795-1840* (Cambridge, 1988). See also McCalman's "Unrespectable Radicalism: Infidels and Pornography in Early Nineteenth-Century London," *Past and Present*, No. 104 (1984), 74-110; and his "Popular Irreligion in Early Victorian England: Infidel Preachers and Radical Theatricality in 1830s London," *Religion and Irreligion in Victorian Society: Essays in Honour of R. K. Webb* (London, 1992), 51-67.

[88] *Independent Spirits: Spiritualism and English Plebeians, 1850-1910* (London, 1986).

[89] "The Local History of Victorian Secularism," *Local Historian* 7 (1969), 221-27.

Leicester, using the records of the still-extant society there.[90] Nash's approach, based, in part, on that adopted by Stephen Yeo in his study of the churches in Reading,[91] was to consider Secularism in the context of the changing and increasingly competitive leisure market of the later nineteenth century. He also interpreted Secularism as a local social support system, analogous to that provided for religious believers by their chapels. He thus—in common with some recent historians of religious denominations—drew on the insights of both the sociology of religion and the sociology of leisure. Other areas still remain to be studied, although the local sources have not survived to the same extent as at Leicester. The village of Failsworth, to which Amphlett-Micklewright drew attention and where a Secularist Sunday school remained until 1958, would certainly repay detailed investigation, as would the activities of Freethinkers in Bradford and Leeds at the end of the nineteenth century, when an independent Secularist movement touched the boundaries of socialism, anarchism, and libertarianism under the leadership of J.W. Gott, the last man in England to be imprisoned for blasphemy.[92]

The biographical approach enjoyed something of a revival among historians in the 1980s. The life of Annie Besant (1847-1933) had already been written at length in two volumes by A. H. Nethercot, in which he emphasized the discontinuities in her "nine lives."[93] However, this extraordinarily talented woman has continued to fascinate biographers, and Nethercot's work came too early to take full advantage of the research being undertaken from often newly available sources in the 1960s. A new life by Anne Taylor, using, among other sources, unpublished biographical notes compiled by Hypatia Bradlaugh Bonner, has supplied this deficiency.[94] David Tribe was the first to use this source when Mrs. Bonner's descendants gave him access to the Bradlaugh Papers to produce a biography that, for the first time, explored aspects of his life, particularly his

[90] Rosamund Billington, "The Leicester Secular Society, 1862-1920: A Study in Radicalism and Respectability" (B.A. dissertation, University of Leicester, 1968); Christine Stephens, "The Secularist Movement in Birmingham and District, 1850-1885" (B.A. dissertation, University of Birmingham, 1972); D. Nash, *Secularism, Art, and Freedom* (Leicester, 1992).

[91] *Religion and Voluntary Organisations in Crisis* (London, 1976).

[92] See Royle, *Radicals, Secularists, and Republicans*, 62-63, 277-83, 323-24, 327; and E. Royle, "Owenism and the Secularist Tradition: The Huddersfield Secular Society and Sunday School," *Learning and Living: Essays in Honour of John Harrison*, ed. by M. Chase and I. McCalman (London, 1996).

[93] *The First Five Lives of Annie Besant* (London, 1961); *The Last Four Lives of Annie Besant* (London, 1963).

[94] *Annie Besant: A Biography* (Oxford, 1992).

business dealings, which were avoided by his daughter in her biography.[95] Meanwhile, Fergus D'Arcy wrote a doctoral thesis on the political side of Bradlaugh's activities.[96] Also in the 1970s, Lee Grugel and Barbara Jean Blaszak completed theses on G. J. Holyoake. Part of Grugel's work on Holyoake as a radical Gladstonian was subsequently published.[97] About the same time, J. W. Nott produced a thesis on Richard Carlile as an agitator, and Joel Wiener followed this in 1983 with a rather more narrowly focused biography and a short essay on Paine and Carlile.[98]

But many other figures are still to be studied. Brief biographies of some of the lesser leaders of Freethought have appeared in recent works of reference,[99] but neither of Bradlaugh's principal successors as president of the

[95] D. Tribe, *President Charles Bradlaugh, M.P.* (London, 1971).

[96] "Charles Bradlaugh and the World of Popular Radicalism, 1833-1891" (Ph.D. thesis, University of Hull, 1979).

[97] L. E. Grugel, "George Jacob Holyoake: A Study in the Progress of Labor and the British Reform Tradition in the Nineteenth Century" (Ph.D. thesis, University of Chicago, 1971); L. E. Grugel, *George Jacob Holyoake: A Study in the Evolution of a Victorian Radical* (Philadelphia, 1976); B. J. Blaszak, "George Jacob Holyoake: An Attitudinal Study" (Ph.D. thesis, State University of New York at Buffalo, 1978).

[98] J. W. Nott, "The Artisan as Agitator: Richard Carlile, 1816-1843" (Ph.D. thesis, University of Wisconsin, 1970); J. H. Wiener, *Radicalism and Freethought in Nineteenth-Century Great Britain: The Life of Richard Carlile* (Westport, Conn., 1983); J. H. Wiener, "Collaborators of a Sort."

[99] *Dictionary of Labour Biography*, ed. by Joyce Bellamy and John Saville, 8 vols. (London, 1972-87): 1 (1972) for Henry Hetherington (1792-1849), radical and Freethought publisher; Austin Holyoake (1826-1874), Freethought printer and brother of G. J. Holyoake; 2 (1974) for Robert Cooper (1819-1868), Owenite and Freethought leader; Frederic Harrison; 4 (1977) for Annie Besant; 5 (1979) for Harriet Law (1831-1897), independent Secularist editor and lecturer; 6 (1982) for Richard Carlile, Emma Martin (1812-1851), Owenite and Freethought lecturer; Robert Owen; 7 (1984) for Charles Bradlaugh. *Biographical Dictionary of Modern British Radicals*, ed. by J. O. Baylen and N. J. Gossman, 4 vols. (Brighton, 1979-88): 1 (1979) for Richard Carlile; Robert Owen; W. T. Sherwin (1799-?); Robert Taylor (1784-1844), Freethought clergyman, "the Devil's Chaplain"; 2 (1984) for Joseph Barker (1806-1875), one-time Secularist; Elizabeth Sharples Carlile (1803-1861), Freethought lecturer and "common-law" wife of Richard Carlile; Charles Cattell (1830-1910), Birmingham Secularist; Richard Congreve; Rowland Detroisier (ca. 1800-1834), Freethinking radical; W. J. Fox; Henry Hetherington; Austin Holyoake; G. J. Holyoake; Charles Southwell; 3 (1988) for Guy Aldred; Annie Besant; Charles Bradlaugh; J. H. Bridges; Stanton Coit; G. W. Foote; Frederic Harrison; W. Stewart Ross; Charles Watts; C. A. Watts. See also *Encyclopedia of Unbelief*, ed. G. Stein, passim. For Barker, also see Betty

National Secular Society—G. W. Foote (1850-1915) and Chapman Cohen (1868-1954)—has as yet been done justice. Foote was the subject of a short unpublished biography by Herbert Cutner, a Freethinker, but that manuscript appears to have been lost; there are no Foote papers, and he left no autobiography. Cohen, the first prominent Jew in the British Freethought movement, published what he modestly called *Almost an Autobiography* in 1940, but nothing else major has been written about him.[100] The same applies to such prominent persons as Charles Watts (1836-1906) and his son, Charles Albert Watts (1858-1946), founder of the Rationalist Press Association; William Stewart Ross (1844-1906), editor of the *Agnostic Journal*, whose idiosyncracies linked him with both the agnostic Marquess of Queensberry and Guy Aldred; Stanton Coit (1857-1944), the American founder of the British Ethical Movement, who fought Wakefield at the 1906 General Election as the only official non-working-class Labour candidate, beating the Liberals into third place. F. J. Gould (1855-1938), Secularist, Positivist, Ethicist, and Moral Education campaigner, has received some attention from Nash, but much more could be said in a fuller study.[101] Even John Mackinnon Robertson, the most distinguished Freethinker to maintain contacts with all branches of the movement and its first member to enter government, has received scant attention—one unpublished thesis, a brief booklet, and a collection of essays do less than justice to a man of Robertson's importance.[102]

Historians of irreligion should also follow historians of orthodoxy into studying the place of women in Freethought. Little biographical work has been done apart from the studies of Besant and short contributions to various biographical dictionaries on Elizabeth Sharples Carlile, Emma Martin, and Harriet Law. One important monograph includes a study of Owenism and women,[103] but there is practically nothing on the mid- and

Fladeland, *Abolitionists and Working-Class Problems in the Age of Industrialization* (Baton Rouge, 1984), 132-70.

[100] C. Cohen, *Almost an Autobiography: The Confessions of a Freethinker* (London, 1940). Richard F. Stratton is working on a Life of Cohen—see *Free Inquiry* (Buffalo, N.Y.), 15 (1994), 41-42.

[101] *Secularism, Art, and Freedom*; "F. J. Gould and the Leicester Secular Society."

[102] J. C. Kaczkowski, "John Mackinnon Robertson: Freethinker and Radical" (Ph.D. thesis, St. Louis University, 1964); Martin Page, *Britain's Unknown Genius: An Introduction to the Life-Work of John Mackinnon Robertson* (London, 1984); *J. M. Robertson (1856-1933): Liberal, Rationalist, and Scholar*, ed. by G. A. Wells (London, 1987).

[103] B. Taylor, *Eve and the New Jerusalem: Socialism and Feminism in the Nineteenth Century* (London, 1983).

late-century periods, and the sociology of gender in irreligion is even less developed than in religious studies.

The sources for such local, personal, and gender studies are scattered and difficult, though some have been made more easily accessible by recent microfilming projects. The Holyoake Correspondence is located mainly at the Co-operative Union in Manchester, though his diaries (disappointingly thin after the early years) and notebooks, together with some letters, are at the Bishopsgate Institute in London.[104] The Bradlaugh Papers, originally entrusted by the Bradlaugh family to the National Secular Society, have now also been deposited with the Bishopsgate Institute for safekeeping.[105] The papers of the Positivist leader Richard Congreve are in the British Library, London, and the Bodleian Library, Oxford; the E. S. Beesley Papers are at University College, London; and the Frederic Harrison Papers are at the London School of Economics. There are some Richard Carlile Papers in the Huntington Library, San Marino, California; and some Holyoake letters at Duke University, Durham, North Carolina. The major collections of institutional records on public deposit are the Owenite Societies Minute Books (1835-45) at the International Institute for Social History in Amsterdam;[106] the Leicester Secular Society minute books and other papers are at the Leicester County Record Office.[107] The records of the British Humanist Association, the National Secular Society, the Rationalist Press Association, and the South Place Ethical Society are all held at their respective headquarters in London.

Much of the history of the Freethought movement is contained in the weekly and monthly periodicals put out over the years by the various leaders and their rivals in the different branches of the movement. The earliest use of the periodical form by Freethinking radicals dates from immediately after the end of the Napoleonic Wars, with W. T. Sherwin's *Weekly Political Register* (1817-19). Over fifty such papers were produced during the course of the nineteenth century, including long runs of Holyoake's *Reasoner* series (1846-72), Bradlaugh's *National Reformer* (1860-93), and G. W. Foote's *Freethinker* (1881-present),[108] as well as short

---

[104] Microfilms and Index available from Microform Ltd., Wakefield, Yorkshire, U.K.

[105] Microfilms and Index (hard copy) available from Microform Ltd.

[106] Available from Research Publications, Reading, U.K., and Woodbridge, Conn.

[107] *The Records of the Leicester Secular Society, 1852-1943*, introduced by E. Royle, Wakefield, Microform Ltd., 1981. These papers were originally collected by F. J. Gould, when the society employed him as its organizer; see his *The History of the Leicester Secular Society* (Leicester, 1900).

[108] for which see Jim Herrick, *Vision and Realism: A Hundred Years of "The Freethinker"* (London, 1982).

runs of minor papers such as Charles Southwell's *Investigator* (1843) or the anonymously edited (perhaps by George Standring) *Secular Work* (1896-97), in addition to ephemeral spoofs like W. J. Ramsey's *Jerusalem Star* (1895-96). Some of these papers are extremely rare in the original, but have been rescued by various microfilming projects.[109] In this way, Southwell's *Lancashire Beacon* (1849-50) has again been made available from a private collector's copy where no complete run was otherwise available;[110] the Owenite *Herald of Progress*, of which copies were extremely rare,[111] is now more widely available to scholars; while the eccentrically and intermittently published Bradford *Truthseeker* (1894-1915) has been pieced together from several different locations in as complete a set as can probably now be reassembled.[112] In Britain, the most useful libraries to visit in search of these periodicals, apart from the British Library, are the Bishopsgate Institute (which houses Holyoake's own collection of almost all his publications)[113] and the major provincial public libraries, especially Manchester.[114]

Most of these periodicals, issued either weekly or monthly, were small, cheap papers published in octavo, quarto, or foolscap. Rarely were they full-scale newspapers, and those that began in this format, such as the

[109] The bulk of these periodicals from the 1830s is available from Microform Ltd., *Religion, Radicalism, and Freethought in Victorian and Edwardian Britain: Collection of Periodicals*, introduced by Royle (Wakefield, 1981). The major exception is the *National Reformer*, available from Datamatics, Inc., New York. Carlile's *Republican* and the Owenite *New Moral World* have been reprinted by the Greenwood Press.

[110] The copy once listed in the Manchester Central Reference Library Catalogue apparently disappeared over half a century ago, and the only other copy listed in the U.K., at the Bodelian Library, Oxford, is incomplete. No copies are listed in the Union List of Serials.

[111] The only known copy in the U.K. is in the Manchester Central Reference Library. Copies are listed in the Union List of Serials at Yale; the Forbes Public Library, Northampton, Mass.; and Columbia University.

[112] The microfilm edition uses the copies in the British Library, the National Secular Society, and private hands. Fragments of runs before 1905 are listed in the Union List of Serials at Columbia University and the New York Public Library.

[113] Holyoake's library was given to the Bishopsgate Institute by his daughter, Mrs. Holyoake Marsh, and a complete descriptive listing was undertaken at the time by the then librarian, C.W.F. Goss, *A Descriptive Bibliography of the Writings of George Jacob Holyoake, with a Brief Sketch of His Life* (London, 1908).

[114] The first Manchester Public Library (1851) was housed in the former Owenite Hall of Science, shortly after Southwell's occupancy of the hall, and thus appears to have inherited a number of works from the Freethought library there.

National Reformer, soon reverted to the smaller and cheaper size. They are useful as denominational magazines, for announcements and reports of meetings, obituaries and portraits of leading figures, correspondence, controversies, ideas, and opinions. Their drawback is that they are often introverted, give only the views of the editor and his clique, and encourage the historian to neglect wider questions of context and significance.[115]

The other major published source for Freethought is the pamphlet literature that it generated. Many of the leaders were prolific writers who sought to give a wider currency to their message through tracts and pamphlets, sometimes in conscious imitation of the religious tract societies. Some of these pamphlets, like the periodicals, have recently been made more widely available through reprints and microfilming. John Saville edited selections of both Charles Bradlaugh's and Annie Besant's pamphlets,[116] while the complete Holyoake collection, from his own library at the Bishopsgate Institute and at the Co-operative Union in Manchester, was microfilmed in 1981.[117] Anthologies of Freethought writings have also been published,[118] but other obscure and rare material still remains to be reprinted—not least the sensationalist *Confessions* of Charles Southwell and the illuminating *Random Recollections* of Sydney Gimson of Leicester, whose list of public acquaintances reads like a roll call of advanced thinkers in later-nineteenth century England.[119]

The temptation is to read and study this mass of still relatively neglected material simply because it is there, but historians of orthodox, mainstream denominations might wish to suggest that the former neglect of Freethought is all it deserved. Of what significance for an understanding of Victorian England are studies of tiny clusters of people, at best a few thousand strong?

Apart from the response that minorities, no less than majorities, have always been legitimate subjects for historical enquiry, two further answers might be given, one political and one religious.

[115] Some examples are discussed in E. Royle, "Newspapers and Periodicals in Historical Research," *Investigating Journalism: The Press in the Nineteenth Century*, ed. by L. Blake, A. Jones, and L. Madden (London, 1990), 48-59.

[116] *A Selection of the Political Pamphlets of Charles Bradlaugh*, ed. by J. Saville (New York, 1970); *A Selection of the Social and Political Pamphlets of Annie Besant*, ed. by J. Saville (New York, 1970).

[117] *Selected Pamphlets by G. J. Holyoake, 1841-1904*, introduced by E. Royle, Microform Ltd., Wakefield.

[118] *Classics of Freethought*, ed. by P. Blanchard (Buffalo, N.Y., 1977); *An Anthology of Atheism and Rationalism*, ed. by Gordon Stein (Buffalo, N.Y., 1980).

[119] Edited reprints of these works are in preparation by Royle and Nash, respectively.

The political answer, couched in terms of John Stuart Mill's essay *On Liberty*, is that minorities have their rights as well as majorities. Indeed, the worth of a society might well be measured in terms of how the majority regards its minorities, especially a minority that exists to challenge some of the most basic assumptions of the society that the majority dominates. Just as Western democrats in the second half of the twentieth century assessed Soviet society in the light of its treatment of its dissident—often religious—minorities, so the historian might look afresh at nineteenth-century English liberal and Christian society through the eyes of its Freethought dissidents.

This point also holds true for the religious justification for studying Freethought in the nineteenth century. The Freethinkers were very much a part of the religious scene, both in their organizational forms as "chapels" with hymns, preachers, tracts, and ceremonies and in the role that they played in provoking and challenging the orthodoxly religious. The Freethinkers loomed much larger on the Christian horizon—and were thus a far more significant part of the nineteenth-century religious scene—than their numbers alone would appear to have warranted. One cannot understand the way in which many Christians reacted to the threat of "infidelity" in the Victorian age without knowing who those infidels were. Equally, an understanding of the Christian reaction to Freethought can serve as a salutary reminder in current controversies[120] of the fleeting nature of human values and historical judgements. To study the past is to hold up the mirror of the future to one's own face.

As further work is undertaken on the history of Freethought,[121] some of the assumptions of the past thirty years will be subjected to renewed questioning. First, is it sufficient to regard unbelief as possessing that same degree of coherence as may be attributed to the Christian system? That is, should the religious services of the Positivist Churches or Ethical Societies be thought of as belonging to the same system as Secularist debating so-

[120] Despite changes in public opinion since the nineteenth century, pronouncements of liberal theology still arouse antagonism in the United Kingdom (for instance when voiced by Dr. David Jenkins, Bishop of Durham), while the science versus religion issue with regard to evolution is still a matter of concern in some parts of the United States. In 1989, the question of blasphemy and freedom of expression was raised worldwide with the publication of Salman Rushdie's novel, *The Satanic Verses*, which some Muslims thought offensive to their faith. For the history of blasphemy in Britain, see Nicholas Walter, *Blasphemy Ancient and Modern* (London, 1990).

[121] The most recent general survey of the topics covered in this chapter is E. Royle, "Secularists and Rationalists, 1800-1940," *A History of Religion in Britain: Practice and Belief from Pre-Roman Times to the Present*, ed. by S. Gilley and W. J. Sheils (Oxford, 1994), 406-22.

cieties? It is true that the Freethinkers were inclined to define themselves collectively in relation to Christianity, that there were overlaps in membership, influences, and ideals among the various Freethinking groups, and that the Freethinkers themselves did debate the function of their activities not between but within their various organizations. Nevertheless, there is a danger that a view of Freethought that starts with a Christian norm from which there are irreligious deviations will not sufficiently discriminate between, or appreciate, those "deviations." Freethought cannot be written about in the singular. The Freethinkers' incoherence may have been no more than that of divided Christendom, but it was certainly no less.

Second, there remains the question, Should Freethought be seen as dependent upon its opposite or as something quite different, perhaps less akin to a church than to a mechanics' institute, political pressure group, or football club? The prevailing interpretation to date has been that Freethought is best seen as standing in form and function at the extremities of religious dissent, not a contribution towards the secularization of society but a victim of that process. But is to describe Freethought as "the religion of irreligion" a mistake, arising out of a confusion between form and content? Just because the form assumed by irreligion in the nineteenth century was that of a religious organization, does that mean such a form was indispensable to the organization of the content?

The decline and virtual disappearance of organized Freethought in the twentieth century might suggest that content (Freethought) was heavily dependent upon form (religious organization). Was it the failure of the form that undermined the validity of the content or vice versa? Such questions could well be asked by students investigating the meaning of the secularization concept. In a curious way, they will no doubt once more need to examine one of the major paradoxes in that nineteenth-century debate between Holyoake and Bradlaugh. The former, asserting the irrelevance of the "religion" question to secular life, expressed himself in religious terms; the latter, engaging in a crusade that took its language and points of controversy from religion, sought to destroy all religion and to create a truly secular society. Which contributed most to secularization?

The question should also be asked, Could Freethought have been organized other than as "the religion of irreligion"? This is not idle speculation, for the Rationalist Press Association did suggest a new model based on the subscription book club, but as a consequence was denied charitable status in Britain on the grounds that it was a propagandist body and a commercial publisher rather than a religious organization. Historians of religion might pause to consider in a world of multifarious, million-dollar sects what the distinguishing characteristics of a religious organization might be. The question of when a church is not a church remains a potent and divisive one.

8

The Missionary Movement

Jeffrey Cox

THE NINETEENTH-CENTURY MISSIONARY movement is part of a much broader transformation of religion in the modern world. Stories of the missionary movement have been told, in outline and in detail, many times. Between 1945 and 1981, doctoral students in North America completed 943 dissertations on missionary work.[1] Despite much very interesting detailed research, however, among historians the broad conceptual framework has advanced very little beyond the multi-volume histories of Kenneth Scott Latourette.[2] Scholarship on missions remains, for the most part, a story of Christian expansion and church growth despite many acknowledged failures along the way. Although by no means uncritical of the missionary past, missionary scholarship is dominated by a rhetoric of celebration.

The celebratory tone is difficult to reconcile with the dominant language of more general scholarship on religion in the modern world. There we encounter not a rhetoric of celebration but a rhetoric of decline. Scholarly argument continues to be dominated by the assumption that religion is marginal in the modern world or, if not marginal, then an archaic and therefore surprising survival. These assumptions are built into much modern discourse, including journalism and everyday language as well as more formal inquiry. The dominant metaphor, whether explicitly recognized or not, is a graph with a line sloping sharply downward, reflecting the declining importance of religion in the modern world.

[1] Theodore Bachman, "North American Doctoral Dissertations on Mission, 1945-1981," *International Bulletin of Missionary Research* 7 (1983), 98.
[2] *A History of the Expansion of Christianity*, 7 vols., (New York, 1937-45); *Christianity in a Revolutionary Age*, 5 vols., (New York, 1957-61).

It is true that many thinkers have recently learned to be cautious about deploying sweeping explicit theories of secularization and modernization. We are now less likely to see boldly written assertions such as Kingsley Martin's "Rationalism has argued the church out of existence"[3] or the materialist version that flourished during the heyday of social history in the 1970s, Peter Burke's "Secularization may have spread with chemical fertilizer."[4]

But the rhetorical problem is broader than the choice or rejection of an explicit theory of intellectual or social change. In many discussions of religion, unimportance is presumed, and importance is treated as exceptional. As long as words such as "decline," "unimportant," "marginal," "survival," and "surprising" dominate our discussions of religion, it will be difficult to escape the confines of secularization theory. Even those who explicitly reject theories of secularization will be reduced to dealing with religion in discrete historical circumstances, without being able to set modern religion or the missionary movement in a broader context. The great story of religion in the modern world is the story of secularization, a story that marginalizes religion in general and with it the missionary movement. Peter Burke began his article on religion in *The New Cambridge Modern History* by making fun of the simplicities of secularization theory, only to conclude that "[t]he simple picture with which we started was not radically wrong, but lacking in nuances."[5]

Because the scholarly interpretation of religion is dominated by a rhetoric of decline, missionary scholarship has been isolated by its sharply different, celebratory tone. In his essay, "Failure of a Mission: Christianity outside Europe," John Kent goes to the other extreme by importing into church history the venerable verdict of the external critics of missions and declaring the entire enterprise a failure.[6] He combines the approach of the decline-and-fall school of Western historians of religion, who argue that the churches are doomed to inevitable and hopeless failure in Europe, with the approach of secular historians of the non-Western world who treat missions as an epiphenomenon of Western political and commercial expansion. The entire missionary movement becomes, in Kent's view, an attempt to salvage the churches from declining influence at home by identifying with Western imperial power abroad.

---

[3] Kingsley Martin, *Critic's London Diary: From the New Statesman, 1931-1956* (London, 1960), 130.

[4] *The New Cambridge Modern History*, 13, Companion Volume (Cambridge, 1979), 312.

[5] Ibid., 316.

[6] *The Unacceptable Face: The Modern Church in the Eyes of the Historian* (London, 1987).

Kent introduces another dimension of the missionary story, its relationship to the great drama of Western expansion and resistance to that
expansion known as imperialism. Stories of imperialism have been either
pro-imperialist or anti-imperialist, but, like the theory of secularization,
both kinds of story marginalize missionaries.[7] The grand tradition of imperialist historiography echoes Sydney Smith's comments in his widely
read *Edinburgh Review* essay of 1808, where he described missionaries in
India as "little detachments of maniacs."[8] British imperial administrators,
unless they were concerned solely with the security of empire, regarded
themselves as agents of progress and modernity. Imperial administrators
who regarded religion as agents of progress and modernity have been exceptions, such as the more extreme Evangelicals of the Punjab School,
who wished to use state schools for religious propaganda. On ecclesiastical
issues, they found themselves marginalized or defeated politically.[9] In the
imperial enterprise, missionaries were most likely to be treated as marginal
eccentrics (as in Kipling) or dangerous threats to imperial security. That
attitude dominated imperial historiography as well, where missionaries are,
for the most part, treated as marginal figures or are not treated at all.

That attitude to missionaries may also be found in anti-imperialist
historiography, in the nationalist anti-imperialist histories of nations once
under direct colonial rule, and in the unmasking rhetoric of Saidian studies
of the culture of imperialism.[10] Except by scholars who are committed in
some way to the missionary enterprise, missionary work has often been
ignored, dismissed as a minor and ephemeral aspect of colonial domi-
nation, or simply written off as a failure. Even in the history of Africa,
where missionary work probably had its greatest influence, the burgeoning
field of African religion has emphasized the overwhelming importance of
the African contribution at the expense of the European or American
missionary contribution to African religious history.[11] Missionary enter-

---

[7] I deal with this problem in greater detail in "Audience and Exclusion at the
Margins of Imperial History," *Women's History Review* 3 (1994), 501-14.

[8] "Indian Missions," 12 (April 1808), 179.

[9] See Stanley Elwood Brush, "Protestants in the Punjab: Religion and Social
change in an Indian Province in the Nineteenth Century" (Ph.D. thesis, University
of California at Berkeley, 1964).

[10] See for example Gauri Viswanathan, *Masks of Conquest: Literary Study and
British Rule in India* (New York: Columbia University Press, 1989), who treats
missionaries as imperial functionaries.

[11] On this topic see Norman Etherington, "Missionaries and the Intellectual
History of Africa: A Historiographical Survey," *Itinerario* (The Journal of the
Centre for the History of European Expansion, University of Leiden), 7:2 (1982),
116-43.

prise is treated as marginal to the histories of both sending and receiving nations, and left stranded between national histories.

Despite the very large amount of writing about missionaries, this is obviously a topic that cries out for a new approach. In order to understand the missionary movement, it is necessary first to set mission work in the context of broader changes that have transformed religion in the West during the last 300 years. What is radically different about religion in the modern world is its context. The most decisive aspect of that context for religion is not science, or technology, or modernization, or urbanization, but state power.

The missionaries who began successful modern missionary work in the late eighteenth and early nineteenth centuries recognized that a religion enforced by state power is fundamentally different from one that must operate in a free market in institutions and ideas. A religion enforced by state power (as opposed to one merely aided by the state) may be rejected or ignored by large sections of the population—but it is unlikely to be unimportant. The emergence of the religiously neutral state or the antireligious state makes religion not unimportant but problematic. Under such conditions it becomes possible for religion to be unimportant, marginal, archaic, or a survival. As soon as it becomes possible for religion to become unimportant, it is likely in some particular circumstances actually to become unimportant.

Unimportance is not inevitable, however, and the emergence of a world in which religion is universally unimportant or marginal is highly unlikely. I now understand much better Harold Perkin's comment that religion became both more and less important in the Industrial Revolution, a comment that I once cited as an example of the confusion caused by secularization theory.[12] Religion has become less important in the last 200 years, and that is part of the story. But less important is not the same thing as unimportant. Furthermore, the standards for judging importance and unimportance have changed. Religion has not only declined; it has been transformed. In some ways, religion as it appears today, in forms unimaginable in the late seventeenth century, is more important now than it was 250 years ago.

The free market in religion has produced a great variety of patterns of adaptation to circumstances, patterns that themselves have changed rapidly in the wake of intellectual changes, such as the advent of biblical criticism in the nineteenth century, or social and economic changes, such as the advent of the automobile. Religion can be very important, as it is in Ireland, Poland, Iran, or the United States. It can be widely ignored, as in

[12] Harold Perkin, *The Origins of Modern English Society 1780-1880* (London, 1969), 203; Jeffrey Cox, *The English Churches in a Secular Society: Lambeth, 1870-1930* (New York, 1982), 11.

Great Britain and France. It can be virtually suppressed by the exercise of
state power, as the Communist government of Albania came close to de-
monstrating.

The free-market metaphor is a useful alternative way to think about
religion in Europe and North America. But however appropriate the free-
market metaphor might be in Western countries, it breaks down in an
imperialist context. Imperialism is about power. Edward Said has taught
us that power is not merely a question of military force, litigation, and
prison, but also a question of apparently benign aspects of imperialism
such as scholarship and, by implication, religion. It is that question of the
relationship between missionary persuasion and imperial power, that the
bulk of celebratory scholarship on missionaries fails to address directly or
in a satisfactory way.

One notable recent exception is Brian Stanley's *The Bible and the
Flag*.[13] Stanley argues that missionaries were not imperialists in the ordinary sense of the word because their motives were entirely different from
those of imperial functionaries and apologists. For missionaries, the British
Empire, like the Roman Empire, was ephemeral and the Kingdom of God
eternal. The British Empire might be providential, but it was also doomed,
and the missionary task was to promote an ecclesiastical empire that would
survive when the British Empire was dead and forgotten.

Stanley makes a very strong argument for the complexity of the missionary relationship to imperialism and for the enormous variety of missionary responses to the imperial setting. But his absolution of missionaries from the taint of imperial corruption leaves many questions
unanswered. Is it possible for persuasion to be politically neutral in an
imperialist setting? What are we to make of the many examples in practice
of missionary complicity with imperialism? How important are motives
anyway? If missionaries were not imperialists, perhaps they were even
worse: naive dupes of the imperialist enterprise. T. O. Beidelman's thorough and exemplary study of an East African mission led him to conclude
that "Christian missions represent the most naive and ethnocentric, and
therefore the most thoroughgoing facet of colonial life.... Missionaries in-
variably aimed at overall changes in the beliefs and actions of native peoples, at colonization of heart and mind as well as body. Pursuing this sustained policy of change, missionaries demonstrated a more radical and
morally intense commitment to rule than political administrators or business men."[14]

---

[13] *The Bible and the Flag: Protestant Missions and British Imperialism in the
Nineteenth and Twentieth Centuries* (Leicester, 1990).

[14] T. O. Beidelman, *Colonial Evangelism: A Socio-Historical Study of an East
African Mission at the Grassroots* (Bloomington, Indiana, 1982), 5-6.

These are some questions that should be kept in mind in telling a new story of the missionary movement, one mindful of the formal pluralism that religious men and women encountered in Europe and North America and the imperialist context in which religious persuasion occurred in the non-Western world, including parts of the world not under direct imperial control. One of the first English-language writers to face up to the situation of modern religion in the West was William Carey.[15] As a Baptist minister in late eighteenth-century England, he belonged to one branch of a denomination that in its earliest statements of faith in the seventeenth century declared voluntary religion to be the only true religion: "The magistrate is not by virtue of his office to meddle with religion."[16] By 1792, when he published his *Enquiry into the Obligations of Christians, to Use Means for the Conversion of the Heathens*,[17] Carey felt confident enough to argue that "the spread of civil and religious liberty" meant that for the gospel "a glorious door is opened, and is likely to be opened wider and wider."[18]

Carey recognized that he was up against the dead weight of public opinion. Although the European Christian world had been expanding for more than 300 years, the responsibility for the spread of Christianity was not even remotely considered to be a concern of the ordinary Christian laity or clergy. It was, instead, the responsibility either of government officials or of clergymen in the highest levels of the church hierarchy, who were, in turn, responsible for supervising specialists in religious expansion.

Because of the abolition of religious orders in Protestantism, purposeful Christian expansion outside the West before the eighteenth century had been almost entirely Roman Catholic. At a crucial time in the course of Western expansion, the Roman Catholic Church sanctioned an entirely new order of specialists in expansion, the Jesuits. Furthermore, Roman Catholicism became part of the official state ideology of two of the leading imperial powers, Spain and Portugal, which used the Jesuits and compet-

[15] William Carey (1761-1834), pioneer Baptist missionary to India. A small-town shoemaker in Northamptonshire, he later became a Baptist pastor in Leicester, helped found the Baptist Missionary Society, and established a Baptist mission in Bengal (1793). After receiving an appointment as Professor of Sanskrit in the East India Company's College at Fort William (1801), he prepared grammars and dictionaries in various Indian languages and published Bibles or portions of Scripture at the Baptist Press in Serampore.

[16] Cited in A. C. Underwood, *A History of the English Baptists* (London, 1947), 42.

[17] The full title is *An Enquiry into the Obligations of Christians, to Use Means for the Conversion of the Heathens in Which the Religious State of the Different Nations of the World, the Success of Former Undertakings, and the Practicability of Further Undertakings, Are Considered* (Leicester, 1792).

[18] Ibid., 79.

ing church orders to promote ecclesiastical expansion. For both bureaucratic and ideological reasons, Roman Catholicism had a head start in
non-European church growth, a fact that Carey lamented at length in his
Enquiry.

For the Protestant imperial powers, Great Britain and the Netherlands,
the relationship between state power and religion was much more ambiguous than in Catholic Spain and Portugal. Neither country had at its
disposal a group of religious specialists who could be deployed for purposes of expansion. The Dutch were willing to use state power to force
conversions, but their efforts to do so in Sri Lanka were timid when
compared to those of the Portuguese in Goa. The expansion of the two
Protestant nations was carried out, in part, by religious and commercial
bodies one or two steps removed from the Crown. Although in both nations attempts were made to supply chaplains for their trading companies,
the bureaucratic difficulties turned out to be daunting, and it was never
clear exactly what the duties of these ministers were with respect to the
native populations, or even if they had any. The same confusion plagued
the (Anglican) Society for the Propagation of the Gospel in Foreign Parts,
founded in 1701 primarily to minister to Englishmen abroad or at least
those who were willing to accept Anglican ministrations.

Both German Pietism and the English and American Evangelical Revival produced committed Christians concerned about the salvation of
those beyond the confines of Christendom. But they confronted officials
of both church and state who would neither deal with the matter of
Christian expansion nor encourage anyone else to deal with it. With no
German Lutheran imperial state to support them, Pietists from Halle persuaded the Danish court to allow them to do missionary work in Danish
possessions on the Coromandel coast. Later, this mission gained additional
support from the Anglican Society for the Promotion of Christian
Knowledge, whose primary purpose was the dissemination of Christian
literature. By the end of the eighteenth century, however, only the Moravians had achieved much independent success in missionary activity, and
they had achieved it by acting independently of the state, as a voluntary
society.

That was the essential point, which Carey grasped clearly and explained
to his readers. The voluntary society, funded by voluntary contributions
and thus ultimately dependent on persuasion rather than force or law, was
the basic and new unit of religion in the Evangelical Revival. In order to
extend the logic of voluntary religion abroad, serious-minded Christians
would have to abandon their faith in the meddling magistrate, the venal
trading company, and the indifferent church hierarchy. Instead, "suppose
a company of serious Christians, ministers and private persons, were to

form themselves into a society."[19] Such a society might receive contributions, recruit missionaries, and support them abroad. "If congregations
were to open subscriptions of *one penny* or more per week, according to
their circumstances, and deposit it as a fund for the propagation of the
gospel, much might be raised in this way."[20]

That is exactly what happened. Carey's optimism about the prospects
for successful voluntary organization in Britain was fully justified. The
logic of voluntarism worked against the major excuse for ignoring the
problem of overseas expansion, which was that God would, in his own
good time, see to the conversion of the heathen. This was the theological
counterpart to the view that taking care of religion was the responsibility
of someone else, a meddling magistrate, East India Company bureaucrat,
or worldly bishop. Evangelical Protestants had rejected this view decisively
at home, and it was only a matter of time before they rejected it in their
thinking about foreign parts of the world.

What they needed was a new bureaucratic mechanism, and Carey
supplied the model. He played a crucial role in founding the Baptist Society for Propagating the Gospel among the Heathen in 1792, which was
followed by the interdenominational (later Congregational) London Missionary Society in 1795, the Evangelical Anglican Society for Missions to
Africa and the East (later known as the Church Missionary Society) in
1799, and the Wesleyan Missionary Society in 1813. With the gradual
transformation in the early nineteenth century of the Society for the Propagation of the Gospel into an ordinary missionary society representing
the interests of High Church Anglicans, the three major Nonconformist
denominations and two major Anglican church tendencies each had an
efficient bureaucratic machine for raising money and supporting foreign
missionaries. After England ceased to be a mission field itself for Roman
Catholics, English Catholics raised the money to establish their own foreign missionary college in 1866, St. Joseph's in Mill Hill. Lesser societies
flourished with specialized appeals to a home constituency, such as High
Church Anglicans who wished to create a celibate religious order for missionary work in Africa or women who wanted to do something about the
plight of Indian widows. These voluntary societies became the characteristic form of Protestant ecclesiastical organization at home and abroad in
the nineteenth and twentieth centuries.

Once Carey supplied an organizational model, many English men and
women could be persuaded that mission work was both desirable and
possible. If popish missionaries can do it, and the Moravian Brethren, why
not English Baptists? If trading companies can send people abroad, and
slave traders, why not Evangelical Anglicans? If Captain Cook can sail to

[19] Ibid., 82.
[20] Ibid., 85.

Tahiti, why not Congregationalists? Setting up a voluntary society and raising money to support other people to go abroad turned out to be relatively easy. Finding people willing to go was another matter.

Carey developed a new form of organization, but a new class of specialists in overseas church expansion did not yet exist in a well-defined form in the Protestant world. Carey assumed that ordinary ministers would be called by God to conduct their ministry abroad. But not every English minister was as committed as Carey, who left for Bengal in 1793 to begin an interesting career as a distinguished grammarian, translator, and printer of Bibles in various Indian languages.[21]

Carey's description of what awaited a minister abroad gives a hint of the difficulties the mission societies faced in recruitment: "It is inconsistent for ministers to please themselves with thoughts of a numerous auditory, cordial friends, a civilized country, legal protection, affluence, splendor, or even a competency." Instead, the object of their expectation should be "gloomy prisons, and tortures, the society of barbarians of uncouth speech, miserable accommodations in wretched wildernesses, hunger, and thirst, nakedness, weariness, and painfulness, hard work, and but little worldly encouragement."[22] The missionary societies had to set aside this talk of deprivation and replace it with the promise of admiration and heroism. In the early nineteenth century, they created a new kind of professional, the missionary, who received his compensation in the form of special honor, admiration, and respect from his Christian peers.

The rhetoric of missionary professionalism was plagued from the first by contradictions. In order to elicit contributions, the missionary societies portrayed foreign peoples as sunk in barbarism and suffering. The demands of missionary rhetoric produced depictions of foreign cultures that exacerbated an ignorant and fearful attitude at home toward the non-Western world. Africans were cannibals and polygamists, Indians were hook swingers and widow burners. This made donors less reluctant to give but ministers of religion more reluctant to leave home.

Furthermore, the professional missionary posed a danger to the status of the clergy in Anglicanism. Although some missionary recruits came from professional and clerical families, others were of lower standing and chose to be missionaries rather than artisans, clerks, or schoolteachers.[23]

[21] On early Baptist work in Bengal see E. D. Potts, *British Baptist Missionaries in India, 1793-1837: The History of Serampore and Its Missions* (Cambridge, 1967); Kenneth Ingham, *Reformers in India, 1793-1837: An Account of the Work of Christian Missionaries on Behalf of Social Reform* (Cambridge, 1956).

[22] *Enquiry*, 72.

[23] See S. C. Potter, "The Social Origins and Recruitment of English Protestant Missionaries in the Nineteenth Century" (Ph.D. thesis, University of London, 1974); C. P. Williams, "The Recruitment and Training of Overseas Missionaries

The Nonconformist denominations were accustomed to variable standards for their ministry, but the Church of England required a university degree, which provided a guarantee of the social standing of the graduate. In its first public statement, the Church Missionary Society (CMS) pointed out that a man "dwelling among savages rude and illiterate does not require the same kind of talents, manners, and learning, as are necessary in an officiating minister in England." Nonetheless, "He who is once episcopally ordained, though with a sole view of acting as a missionary to the heathen, would possess the power of officiating, and holding any benefice to which he might be presented, in the English church.... What security can be offered, that a person of inferior status, offering himself ... for orders, is not influenced by the desire of a more elevated rank in society?"[24] The society was sufficiently worried about diluting the social standing of the clergy to propose a separate status for missionaries, that of catechist, which would prevent their exercising clerical duties at home. In the end, the CMS was forced to establish systematic nonuniversity training for its recruits and have them ordained, but the presence of clergymen without degrees caused anxiety inside the organization and tension in the mission field.[25]

A missionary recruit who could withstand clerical snobbery inside the church might nonetheless be deterred by a barrage of ridicule from external critics of the missionary enterprise. Sydney Smith's attack on missionaries was only the most celebrated of many attacks that questioned the missionary's sanity. Furthermore, the horrendous losses from disease that struck early missionaries in Africa were impossible to keep a secret. Between 1809 and 1825, the CMS sent 89 men and women to West Africa. Fifty-four died, and 14 returned home ill.[26] The dangers of going abroad and the social stigma attached to the missionary made recruitment a slow business. By 1851, there were 228 ordained British missionaries at work in India, which represents considerable growth from the days of Carey but a small number to Christianize a subcontinent.[27]

in England Between 1850 and 1900," (M.Litt. thesis, University of Bristol, 1976); Stuart Piggin, *Making Evangelical Missionaries, 1789-1858: The Social Background, Motives and Training of British Protestant Missionaries to India* (Abingdon, 1984).

[24] *Account of a Society for Mission to Africa and the East instituted by Members of the Established Church* (London, 1799), 8.

[25] See C. P. Williams, "'Not Quite Gentlemen': An Examination of 'Middling Class' Protestant Missionaries from Britain, 1850-1900," *JEH* 31 (1980), 310-315.

[26] See *Report of the Medical Committee Appointed in 1825 by the General Committee of the CMS* (London, 1825), 8-9.

[27] See G. A. Oddie, "India and Missionary Motives c. 1850-1900," *JEH* 25 (1974), 61.

After midcentury, recruitment became more successful. The steamship made foreign travel seem less like permanent exile, and the expansion of European administrative control abroad made life overseas more familiar to the middle classes. The Baptist *Manual for Missionaries to the Congo*, published in 1890, took a matter-of-fact approach to life in Africa, claiming that missionaries would be healthy if they took care to get enough rest. Missionaries were sternly warned not to expect a breakdown in health before their first furlough in three years; "such anticipations work through the nerves upon the system, and are very likely to be realised."[28] Confident of missionary survival, the manual's author devoted considerable attention to matters of etiquette, ranging from the dangers of boring the captain on the outward passage to spoiling native servants after arrival.

The rhetoric of missionary heroism also became more refined, and the institutional growth of the churches provided a broader potential audience for missionary propaganda. Eugene Stock,[29] the official historian of the CMS, complained of the difficulties he faced when he began his work in the 1850s. At that time, many of the strongest Evangelical centers were not regular parishes, but proprietary chapels with "no schools attached to them, still less the modern 'parish room' or 'mission hall' for mission meetings."[30] By the end of the century, he could cite many contrasting examples, such as a village near Tunbridge Wells with "its wonderful mission meeting of 500 villagers, and its missionary boxes producing £300 a year."[31]

Broader networks of missionary support in the churches provided more work for Victorian Mrs. Jellybys, who recruited women and children in large numbers into missionary support organizations. By 1900, children provided a substantial amount of financial support for missions.[32] For children and adults, the nineteenth century missionary movement produced heroes such as David Livingstone and martyrs such as Bishop

[28] Baptist Missionary Society, *Manual for Missionaries to the Congo: Outfitting, Constitution of Mission, Travelling, etc.*, 2nd ed. (London, 1890), 103.

[29] Eugene Stock (1836-1928), a voluntary lay supporter of mission work and prolific writer and editor who became editorial secretary of the CMS (1873-1902) and secretary "without portfolio" (1902-6). A defender of Keswick theology, he wrote a useful history of the CMS that reflects the official downgrading of Henry Venn's enthusiasm for rapid progress toward self-government in the non-Western churches: *The History of the Church Missionary Society: Its Environment, Its Men, and Its Work*, 4 vols. (London, 1899, 1916).

[30] Eugene Stock, *My Recollections* (London, 1909), 54.

[31] Ibid., 315.

[32] On children in the missionary movement, see Frank Prochaska, "'Little Vessels': Children in the Nineteenth-Century English Missionary Movement," *Journal of Imperial and Commonwealth History* 6 (1978), 103-18.

Hannington, killed in East Africa in 1886. at the universities a missionary clerical subculture emerged, especially at Cambridge, where the Regius Professor of Divinity, B. F. Westcott, helped found the Cambridge Mission to Delhi (1876). Another High Church Mission, the Universities Mission to Central Africa (1860), revived earlier abortive Anglican attempts to follow in Livingstone's footsteps. The Evangelicals at Cambridge received more attention than their High Church rivals, however, for, in 1884, the captain of the Cambridge Eleven and the stroke oar on the Cambridge boat announced that they were going out as missionaries. Eventually they joined five others, the "Cambridge Seven," as missionaries with the nondenominational China Inland Mission (1862), an Evangelical "faith mission" founded to protest the cumbersome professionalism of existing missionary societies. The Anglican Church Missionary Society responded to this challenge to leadership within the world of Evangelical missions with their own "Cambridge Eight."

More important than celebrities or heroes were the ordinary recruits from families where missionary work, now a recognized profession, became a family tradition. Henry Wright, secretary of the Church Missionary Society from 1872 to 1880, sent four of his eleven children as missionaries. His successor, F. E. Wigram, saw five of his seven children volunteer.[33] Bishop Westcott not only helped found the Cambridge Mission to Delhi but was father to five sons, four of whom became missionaries to India. It would be possible to use missionary literature to identify dozens of more obscure clerical families, such as that of the Rev. J. E. Sampson of York and Barrow, described in the CMS official history as the "ideal leader of a Parochial Missionary Association in a poor district," and father of four daughters given to mission work in India.[34]

Buoyed by enthusiasm for empire and by the theological perfectionism emanating from the yearly Keswick Convention, the mission societies recruited record numbers in the 1880s and 1890s. The British branch of the American Student Volunteer Movement, which had adopted as its slogan "the evangelization of the world in this generation," claimed to have persuaded 1,621 students to a sign a declaration of intent to be a missionary between 1892 and 1899; 506 were said actually to have sailed.[35] What is more certain is that the CMS sent out 1,000 missionaries in the first eight decades of the nineteenth century and an equal number in the last two decades.[36] By one estimate, in the first decade of the twentieth century,

[33] Stock, *Recollections*, 277.
[34] Eugene Stock, *History of the Church Missionary Society*, 3, 797.
[35] Ibid., 691.
[36] Ibid., 704-5.

Great Britain supplied more Protestant missionaries than any other nation, with a total of over 6,000 in all fields by 1907.[37]

By far the most important boost to missionary recruitment came with the enlistment of large numbers of single women. Carey mentioned women only once: "the women, and even the children, would be necessary for domestic purposes; and a few articles of stock, as a cow or two, and a bull."[38] But middle-class women joined others who were excluded from the ministry and took advantage of the opportunities offered by missionary service. Their ideology was one of separate spheres. Women were needed for work that men could not do, notably, teaching Indian women in their homes. The Zenana Bible and Medical Mission was founded in 1861, the Church of England Zenana Missionary Society in 1880. Shortly afterwards, the other denominations went through varying degrees of bureaucratic contortion to make accommodation for single women. According to one estimate, in 1890, there were 2,343 male Protestant missionaries from Great Britain and 1,193 women, counting both wives and "other women."[39] In my own research I have identified more than 300 single Anglican women who served as missionaries of the Society for the Propagation of the Gospel in the cities of Delhi and Lahore alone between 1857 and 1947, most of them between 1870 and 1930.[40] By 1907, single women

[37] E. M. Bliss, *Encyclopaedia of Missions* (New York, 1891), 2, 606, gives a total of 3,536 male and female Protestant missionaries from England, Scotland, and Ireland in 1890. James Shepard Dennis's thorough but highly optimistic *Centennial Survey of Foreign Missions* (New York, 1902), 257-58, estimates the number of Protestant foreign missionaries from all countries in 1899 as as 17,254 with the largest number, 9,014, from Great Britain and Ireland. A more cautious article on missions, in the 11th ed. of the *Encyclopedia Britannica* (Vol. 8, 598), gives the following numbers for Protestant missionaries in 1907, but does not identify sources or explain the method of compilation: Britain—6,050, United States—3,973, Germany—1,250, Other—1,651. Other atlases and encyclopedias of missions published after the turn of the century organize missionary statistics by receiving, rather than sending, nation. See, for instance, Edwin Munsell Bliss, H. Allen Tupper, and Henry Otis Dwight, *The Encyclopedia of Missions*, 2nd ed. (New York, 1904); *Statistical Atlas of Christian Missions* (Edinburgh, 1910); and James Dennis, Harlan Beach, and Charles Fahs, *World Atlas of Christian Missions* (New York, 1911). Roman Catholic missionaries are even more difficult to count because of problems of definition. All of these statistics deserve further skeptical attention.

[38] *Enquiry*, 74.

[39] Bliss, *Encyclopaedia of Missions*, 606.

[40] See "Independent English Women in Delhi and Lahore," *Religion and Irreligion in Victorian Society: Essays in Honour of R. K. Webb*, ed. by R. W. Davis and R. J. Helmstadter (London, 1992).

missionaries in all fields outnumbered ordained missionaries 2,332 to 1,980.[41] Feminist scholarship on the British missionary movement is relatively undeveloped, although Martha Vicinus has some interesting comments on Anglican women's sisterhoods in the late nineteenth century.[42]

If the wives of missionaries were consistently included in the statistical tables as missionaries, as they were in the reports of some societies, the feminization of the missionary movement would be made even clearer. By the early twentieth century, it appears that well over 50 percent of all missionaries were women, although it is very difficult to be precise because of the undercounting of women in standard statistical sources. Their numerical dominance is not evident in the standard celebratory histories or statistical atlases of the missionary movement, which were for the most part written by authors who were ordained and therefore male.[43]

The missionary movement succeeded at creating organizations and recruiting missionaries. But the very success of missionary recruitment sharpened the problem of what missionaries should do when they arrived. In order to think about that problem at all, it was necessary to think about the relationship between Christianity and culture and the differences between Christian Western culture and non-Christian, non-Western culture. It is possible to discern even in Carey's early work the outlines of a set of ideas about the relationship between Christianity and culture that dominated most of the British Protestant missions in the nineteenth century.

Missionary theorists, from the first, resolutely opposed any concessions to biological racism: "Barbarous as these poor heathens are, they appear to be as capable of knowledge as we are; and in many places, at least, have discovered uncommon genius and tractableness."[44] Carey devoted considerable attention to persuading his readers that missionaries would not be

[41] Figures from the *Encyclopedia Britannica*; ordained missionaries—1,980; Laymen—1,738, Unmarried women—2,332.

[42] *Independent Women: Work and Community for Single Women, 1850-1920* (Chicago, 1985); cf. Helen Vreugdenhill, (University of Toronto), "Missionaries and Africans: British Anglican Women in East Africa, 1880-1920," paper presented to the annual conference of the North American Conference on British Studies, Montreal, 1993.

[43] The undercounting of women in statistical tables can be seen in the summaries in Dennis's *Centennial Survey*, 257, which lists a total of 5,599 men and 3,450 women missionaries from Great Britain and Ireland in 1902. Only 1,757 of those women are listed as married, leaving 3842 out of 5,599 male missionaries who appear in these tables as celibate. But a majority of male Protestant missionaries were married, and those who were widowed often remarried.

[44] *Enquiry*, 63. By "biological racism," I mean the view that other races have fundamental physical characteristics that make them permanently inferior to Europeans.

killed at once: "I greatly questions whether most of the barbarities prac-
tised by them, have not originated in some real or supposed affront, and
are therefore, more properly, acts of self-defence, than proofs of inhuman
and blood-thirsty dispositions."[45] The heathen, he argued, are just like us,
and it is not unlikely that they have been wronged by us.

The second missionary principle, discernible throughout the nineteenth
century despite great confusion in its application, was the primacy of
Christianity over civilization. This did not involve a rejection of the value
of Western civilization. Missionaries used the idea of civilization to interpret social and cultural difference and believed that societies could be
ranked on a hierarchy of civilizations. Much nineteenth-century missionary ethnocentrism and racism was based not upon biological racism, but
upon the idea of a hierarchy of civilizations. Hinduism, in particular, appeared in nineteenth-century missionary ideology as a debased and immoral religion when judged purely by its social consequences. Christianity,
on the other hand, had desirable moral and social consequences, and insofar as Western civilization was superior to other civilizations, Christianity could take the credit.

However, Christianity and civilization were not identical, and Christianizing the heathen and civilizing them were two distinct tasks. Missionaries would have rejected the argument that they were simply export-
ing Western values to non-Western cultures. They were keenly aware of
the sinfulness of all civilizations and the sins of many who called themselves Christians. Most Protestant missionaries would have agreed with
Carey that "[p]apists are in general ignorant of divine things.... Nor do the
bulk of the church of England much exceed them, either in knowledge or
holiness; and many errors, and much looseness of conduct, are to be found
amongst dissenters of all denominations."[46]

Instead of portraying themselves as participants in a generally beneficial
expansion of Western civilization, missionaries usually described Western
expansion as a race between the good and the evil aspects of Western
culture. On the one hand, according to Carey's reading of Isaiah lx.9,
"commerce shall subserve the spread of the gospel."[47] On the other hand,
"the vices of Europeans have been communicated wherever they themselves have been; so that the religious state of even heathens has been
rendered worse by intercourse with them!"[48]

A good deal of missionary practice becomes intelligible only on the
assumption that missionaries often unwittingly confused Christianity and
Western civilization while responding to changing definitions of what was

[45] Ibid., 64.
[46] Ibid., 65.
[47] Ibid., 69.
[48] Ibid., 64.

distinctively Christian and what was distinctively Western. Successive generations of missionaries complained that their predecessors Westernized instead of Christianized, even though the previous generation of missionaries had no intention of making that mistake. As they searched for an effective missionary strategy, some missionaries were prepared to argue that the work of civilization was a preparation for conversion and that civilized non-Christians were more likely to become Christians. Alexander Duff promoted Western-style higher education as a means of preparing the way for Christianity in Calcutta, and David Livingstone prescribed commerce for Central Africa.[49] But their arguments, if pressed very far, contradicted the clear theological egalitarianism of the New Testament, not to mention Western images of the noble, uncorrupted savage willing to receive the gospel. Despite confusion and contradiction on this point, in missionary rhetoric the ultimate task of the missionary remained Christianizing non-Christians, not civilizing barbarians.

At the Wolverhampton Church Congress of 1887, Canon Isaac Taylor suggested that Islam might be better suited than Christianity to the lower level of civilization in Africa.[50] The two major Anglican missionary societies rejected his views unequivocally. More was at stake than the Christian response to the growth of a newly aggressive Islam in Africa. The missionary societies rejected in principle Canon Taylor's explicit acceptance of the argument that Christianity was suited only to individuals at a certain level of sophistication. Occasionally in the late nineteenth century, more openly racist voices were raised against the missionary enterprise, on the grounds that Africans were too barbarous, backward, or uncivilized to be Christianized, but missionaries, for the most part, decisively rejected these views.

The debate about the precise relationship between Christianity and those aspects of Western culture that were also defined as beneficial, including commerce, stable government, and education, ebbed and flowed in the nineteenth century. Although missionaries were not primarily civilizers, they nonetheless believed in the potential blessings of Western civilization. But it is important to remember their ambiguous attitude to Western civilization. The spread of Western civilization was a providential opportunity, but it was an opportunity that Christians had to exploit vig-

[49] On one aspect of this debate see Brian Stanley, "'Commerce and Christianity': Providence Theory, the Missionary Movement, and the Imperialism of Free Trade, 1842-1860," *HJ* 26 (1983), 71-94. See Andrew Porter's response in "Commerce and Christianity: The Rise and Fall of a Nineteenth-Century Missionary Slogan," *HJ* 28 (1985), 597-621.

[50] Isaac Taylor, "Mohammedanism," *The Official Report of the Church Congress, 1887* (London, 1887).

orously in order to prevent un-Christian influences in the west from corrupting the heathen.

This ambivalent analysis of Western civilization provided one of the most effective arguments for missionary recruitment and fund-raising in the nineteenth century, and it was used both at home and abroad. There was little doubt in the minds of most British missionaries that conversion to Christianity set the former heathen on the road to a higher level of healthy civilization, whatever the level from which he began. While Christianizing the un-Christian, the missionary distributed, as a by-product, the blessings of civilization, too: "Would not the spread of the gospel be the most effectual means of their civilization? Would not that make them useful members of society?" Carey asked.[51]

Philanthropically minded English men and women who were skeptical of the value of Christianizing the heathen could at least raise their level of civilization and, in particular, improve the condition of women, by supporting the missionary movement, just as they could take steps to elevate the condition of the working classes at home by supporting the building of urban churches. Furthermore, this appeal was urgent because of the danger that unsavory agents of Western civilization would reach the heathen first, selling guns and alcohol and spreading Western diseases. Christians should give now before it is too late. This argument might be effective with both those who agonized over the prospect of millions dying and going to hell and those concerned with the material well-being for their fellow humans everywhere.

Many missionaries thought seriously about the relationship of Christianity and Western civilization. But only a minority of missionaries and missionary theorists directly confronted the anti-imperialist critique that emerged in the nineteenth century and that portrayed the entire missionary movement as intrinsically nothing more than a cultural projection of Western culture into the non-Western world.[52] Although anticipating, in some respects, the nineteenth century missionary analysis of Christianity and civilization, Carey failed entirely to address the relationship between Christian persuasion and imperial power or to foresee the problems that would arise in defining the relationship between relatively powerful Western missionaries and relatively powerless Christian converts.

The most influential British thinker on these problems was the chief administrator of the mid-Victorian Church Missionary Society, Henry Venn.[53] Under Henry Venn's leadership as honorary secretary from 1841

[51] *Enquiry*, 70.

[52] Stanley's *The Bible and the Flag* has a good account of the origins of this point of view.

[53] Henry Venn (1796-1873), the son of one of the founders of the Church Missionary Society, John Venn (1759-1813).

to 1872, the CMS became the leading Protestant missionary society in nineteenth-century England, and Venn's ideal of promoting self-government in the native church became the professed goal of most Protestant societies until the 1890s, when some of Venn's successors began to treat his ideas as unrealistically optimistic. Like Carey, Venn understood that religion was operating under a new set of rules. Unlike Carey, he understood something of the coercive nature of relationships between Western and non-Western peoples and the implications of imperialism for the long-term success of the missionary enterprise. From an Evangelical Protestant point of view, colonial religion was no true religion at all if it were entirely dependent upon state power or undue state influence. Furthermore if religion were nothing more than colonial rule in a religious form, then it would not survive without state power, and the missionary movement would fail in the long run.

Venn encouraged missionaries to devote their full attention to the creation of an indigenous "native" church that would be "self-supporting, self-governing, and self-extending." Optimistic about the prospects for creating an indigenous church in the foreseeable future, he looked forward to "the euthanasia of the mission" as the goal of the entire missionary movement.[54] Most nineteenth-century British missionary societies professed a similar goal when pressed for statements of their strategy, although there were disagreements about what constituted a reasonable timetable for ecclesiastical self-government.

In practice, Venn's prescription proved inadequate to control missionary practice. Although genuinely committed to the creation of an indigenous church controlled by non-Western Christians, Venn had little practical grasp of the way in which imperial power, even in noncolonized parts of the world, made it difficult for missionaries to act as anything other than religious specialists in the Western imperial establishment. Missionary and imperial interests frequently converged in practice. Furthermore, the imbalance in power and wealth between missionaries and Christian converts infected all attempts to encourage and promote ecclesiastical self-government. Beidelman's study of the relationship between CMS missionaries and Christian converts in East Africa is perhaps an extreme example, but it demonstrates clearly the extent to which missionaries could be seduced by the lure of power over others. Beidelman's comments could be extended to examples of missionary enterprise in many parts of the world.

[54] Wilbert R. Shenk, *Henry Venn, Missionary Statesman* (Maryknoll, N.Y., 1983), has a good bibliography of writings by and about Venn; a thorough analysis of Venn's struggle against missionary paternalism may be found in C. Peter Williams, *The Ideal of the Self-Governing Church: A Study in Victorian Missionary Strategy* (New York, 1990).

Brian Stanley is right to remind us of the complexity of the missionary story. It is important to keep in mind the independent origins of the missionary movement in the Evangelical Revival, the great variety of missionary tactics and the even greater variety of circumstances in which missionaries worked, the ways in which Christian converts reshaped Christianity for their own purposes with or without the cooperation of missionaries, and the potential for missionaries to become adversaries of Western colonial powers or traders and defenders of "native rights." Missionary rhetoric sometimes depicted the heathen as suffering from either barbarism or religious error, at other times as innocent victims of the wrong kind of Western expansion. Bishop Colenso of Natal was acting very much within the ideological limits of the missionary tradition in his extremely unpopular defense of Zulu rights.[55] C. F. Andrews acted within that same tradition as associate of, and publicist for, Gandhi, as have lesser missionaries who acted in defense of the rights not only of their converts but of others suffering from Western injustice.[56]

But it is also important to remember that Colenso, Andrews, and other critics of the missionary movement from within the Christian world were very much aware of the extent to which Christianity had been co-opted and seduced by imperialism and incorporated into the imperialist enterprise. If missionaries cannot be reduced to imperialists and nothing more, neither can they be portrayed primarily as humanitarian social reformers.[57] The origins of the nineteenth-century missionary movement were theological and Western. Christian expansion in one form or another was always its primary goal. Missionaries tried almost everything in pursuit of that goal: trading operations, schools, government service, publishing and translation, street preaching, exploration, politics, social reform, and irregular military operations.[58] The missionary ideologies of Carey, Venn, and others provided little practical guidance to missionaries once they arrived in the mission field. The missionary movement solved its problems

[55] See the excellent study by Jeff Guy, *The Heretic: A Study of the Life of John William Colenso, 1814-1883* (Pietermaritzburg, 1983).

[56] On Andrews, see Hugh Tinker, *The Ordeal of Love: C. F. Andrews and India* (Delhi, 1979); Daniel O'Connor, *Gospel, Raj and Swaraj: The Missionary Years of C. F. Andrews 1904-14* (Bern, 1990); Jeffrey Cox, "C. F. Andrews and the Failure of the Modern Missionary Movement," *Modern Religions Rebels: Essays in Honour of John Kent,* ed. by Stuart Mews (London, 1993).

[57] For examples of this genre, see Ingham, *Reformers in India*; G. A. Oddie, *Social Protest in India: British Protestant Missionaries and Social Reform, 1850-1900* (New Delhi, 1979).

[58] For a good sample, see the articles in *Missionary Ideologies in the Imperialist Era: 1880-1920,* ed. by Torben Christensen and William R. Hutchison (Copenhagen, 1982).

of organization and recruitment at home, but failed to develop any practical or effective theories of church growth or non-Western church organization.

Left to their own devices in the field, most missionaries eventually tried to adapt the model of clerical professionalism to local circumstances. Clergymen at home, they behaved like clergymen abroad. Wives and, later, teachers and nurses at home, missionary women behaved like wives, teachers, and nurses abroad. If missionaries were not primarily agents of imperialism, except where their interests converged with the state, or social reformers, except where their interests diverged from those of the state or local elites, they were almost everywhere institution builders. They created churches, theological training colleges, hospitals, clinics, and schools of every variety and staffed them to the highest professional standards possible. They behaved this way even while debates raged in missionary circles about the relative merits of institution building versus evangelism. Some of the strongest critics of institution building were themselves institution builders when making decisions in the field. Their conscious and unconscious institutional orientation helps explain their tenacious defense of educational work as an evangelistic tool even in contexts where it was obviously an evangelistic failure. It also accounts for their readiness to adopt medical mission work without noticing how inefficient it was in terms of church growth or self-government.

Professionalism was not an efficient path toward a self-supporting, self-governing, and self-extending church. Even within the CMS, where missionaries and missionary administrators made good-faith efforts to put Venn's ideas into practice, missionaries failed in the nineteenth century to develop a practical way to foster the growth of self-governing churches within a short period. This failure has been attributed to the rise of racist, imperialist thinking within the missionary community in the late nineteenth century or, alternatively, to the influence of the Evangelical perfectionism of the Keswick convention.[59]

Our view of nineteenth-century racism is shaped by the twentieth-century experiences of straightforward moral struggle against racial segregation in the American South, apartheid in South Africa, and, most important of all, the war against Nazi brutality. Nineteenth-century missionary thought on racial difference is, by way of contrast, extremely diffuse and complex. Missionaries appear to have been largely indifferent to theories of inherent physical differences based on race, which were becoming more popular in the late nineteenth century. Even conservative Anglican mis-

[59] See E. A. Ayandele, *The Missionary Impact on Modern Nigeria, 1842-1914: A Political and Social Analysis* (London, 1966); cf. Andrew Porter, "Cambridge, Keswick, and late Nineteenth-Century Attitudes to Africa," *Journal of Imperial and Commonwealth History* 5 (1976), 5-34.

sionaries in India complained privately about the new prevalence of racial thinking in the 1890s, but those same missionaries in other contexts used racially charged rhetoric based on theories of cultural hierarchy and difference that are very shocking today.[60] It is clear that some missionaries absorbed some of the new enthusiasm for overt imperialism that swept Britain in the 1880s and 1990s. From the point of view of someone who is defined as inferior, it may not matter whether the inferiority is based on cultural or physical difference. Theological perfectionism in Evangelical circles obviously had an additional influence on missionary relationships with their converts in Nigeria, India, and elsewhere. Christian egalitarianism and more specific missionary theories designed to promote equality between non-Western Christians and Western missionaries were usually overpowered by the massive, pervasive inequality between Europeans and non-Europeans in an imperialist context.

But that is not to say that missionary intentions never made a difference. The problem of creating a self-supporting, self-governing, and self-extending church existed before and after the high imperial phase of missionary expansion between 1880 and 1920, and some missionary difficulties were rooted in the specific character of missionary theory. Venn not only failed to explain how a voluntary society like the CMS could foster the growth of an episcopal church; he and other missionary theorists never provided a practical institutional model that would facilitate the development of an independent, non-Western Christian church of any ecclesiastical variety as long as non-Western clergymen were expected to conform to Western models of clerical professionalism. Furthermore, the institutional emphasis produced missions centered around schools and hospitals which were funded largely from abroad, and missionaries were understandably unable or unwilling to divorce funding from control. Mission funds remained under mission control even when non-Western clergymen with inferior educations were given equal rights in the local church.

The same problem, the lack of a realistic model of how to proceed, plagued missionary efforts to achieve church growth. The missionary history of the nineteenth and early twentieth centuries contains many examples of missed opportunities and wasted effort. Lack of numerical success, and the inevitable use of the word "failure" by critics of missions generated a prominent line of argument in the nineteenth century, one that was essential in order to explain to contributors at home that their money was not being wasted. We are sowing the seed, missionaries argued, in obedience to Christ's command. At some time in the future, the church would grow. If it did not, that was God's responsibility.

[60] I deal with some of these issues in "A Bishop in Search of a Church: George Alfred Lefroy," *After the Victorians: Private Conscience and Public Duty in Modern Britain*, ed. by Susan Pedersen and Peter Mandler (London, 1994).

Missionaries used this argument in contexts where opportunities for conversions were, in fact, limited, such as Kashmir or Syria, and in contexts where subsequent experience has demonstrated that they were ignoring opportunities all around them. As a practical matter, sowing the seed meant building institutions. Regardless of the ebb and flow of argument at home about the relative merits of institutional and evangelistic approaches, they continued to build churches, parsonages, schools, and other institutions. Medical mission work was a particularly useful investment in institution building from the missionary point of view, since it provided practical benefits in the form of medical care to the missionaries themselves. Although medical work was even less efficient in generating church growth than educational work, it was easier to justify theologically. The New Testament records are embarrassingly silent on the subject of higher education, but Christ's specific injunction to heal the sick could be used to silence the numerous critics of missionary institution building.

The institutional approach to missions led to the most serious of all criticisms from the missionary point of view, since it came from within the churches at home. From the early nineteenth century, there was periodic unease in Britain about luxurious living by missionaries, who usually maintained Western standards of living when those around them were living in relative poverty. Missionaries themselves often felt anxious about their standard of living, and almost all of the major missionary societies went through periodic controversies and crises about opulence in the mission field.[61] The missionary standard of living created barriers to evangelism, critics argued, and cautious bureaucratic methods at home shackled the workings of the Holy Spirit. Those sentiments and a revival of millennarian expectations among Evangelicals created the impetus for new "faith missions" in the late nineteenth century. The best known was the China Inland Mission, which sent out missionaries without having the money to support them as an act of faith that the money would subsequently appear. Almost every mission field, and some of the mainstream mission societies, felt the influence of this movement. The ideal "faith" missionary was neither an institution builder nor a social reformer, but an itinerant evangelist in native dress.[62]

The implicit or explicit institution-building approach of the major nineteenth-century missionary societies meant that church growth was largely accidental rather than the product of an effective missionary strategy. Churches grew because indigenous individuals or social groups found

[61] For a thorough account of one such crisis in Wesleyan Methodism, see *The Missionary Controversy: Discussion, Evidence and Report, 1890* (London, 1890).

[62] For an account of millennarian influence in Africa and its consequences for the Baptist Missionary Society among others, see Ruth M. Slade, *English Speaking Missions in the Congo Independent State (1878-1908)* (Brussels, 1959).

Christianity useful for their own purposes, not because missionaries knew how to recruit new members for their churches. The dominant model of clerical education, with its ideal curriculum of Hebrew, Greek, and church history, was a serious barrier to the development of indigenous forms of Christianity. Indigenous forms of Christian piety began to develop under missionary tutelage, but a truly self-supporting, self-governing, and self-extending church emerged only when Christian converts began to remake the church in their own image and to their own ends. This was true even in cases where missionaries made strenuous, good-faith efforts to foster ecclesiastical self-government with indigenous Christian forms.[63] As a practical matter, self-supporting, self-governing, and self-extending churches could develop only when Christian converts were practically beyond the control of the missionary because of geographical or cultural distance or as a result of schism. In many cases, self-government occurred only after the missionaries either left or were forced into a subordinate role by political circumstances.

By 1900, however, missionaries were beginning to see the first signs of the broader movements that have transformed the missionary movement in the twentieth century. The emergence of liberal theology, for instance, created ecumenical enthusiasm within the missionary community and was responsible for the subsequent reinterpretation of mission history in the service of the ecumenical movement. With its emphasis on service rather than conversion, liberal theology provided a new and useful theological justification for the nineteenth-century institutional strategy and allowed institution-building to continue within the liberal Protestant denominations under the banner of the social gospel. Liberal theology also prepared the way for the displacement of the mainstream Protestant missionary societies by Pentecostal and Evangelical groups in the mid-twentieth century.

Even more important, however, in terms of the broader significance of the nineteenth-century missionary movement was the evidence by 1900 of the beginning in some countries of large-scale church growth. In different parts of the world, individuals and groups found Christianity attractive or useful for their own good reasons and were undeterred by the inability of the Western churches to provide a model for instant indigenous self-governing Christianity in the mission field. The course of church growth in the twentieth century has been documented in an overstated but nonetheless systematic and impressive way in David Barrett's monumental

[63] For one example of this, see Jeffrey Cox, "On Re-defining Crisis: The Victorian Crisis of Faith in the Punjab, 1880-1900," *Victorian Faith in Crisis*, ed. by R. Helmstadter and B. Lightman (Stanford, 1990).

World Christian Encyclopedia.[64] In ways that they had not anticipated, nineteenth-century missionaries were right when they argued that they were sowing the seed. The nineteenth-century missionary movement was both a success and a failure. To treat it as an unambiguous success story in the celebratory tradition of Kenneth Scott Latourette or Barrett is to miss a large part of the story, including the political failure of Christianity in China, the miserable failure to develop anything of interest to say to Muslims and caste Hindus, and the inability of missionaries to respond effectively to the anti-imperialist critique.

But to treat the missionary movement as simply a failure fails to take into account at least two ways in which the missionary movement has been and is important in world history. Individual missionaries played influential roles in their adopted countries as social reformers, language scholars, publishers, educators, physicians, medical administrators, and nurses. Furthermore, the often inadvertent success of the missionaries in sowing the seed has stimulated the development of self-supporting, self-governing, and self-extending churches in spite of clerical professionalism. In many parts of the world, including Korea, Indonesia, and much of Africa, Christian churches which are a direct or indirect legacy of the missionary movement are growing rapidly.

Africa is the most impressive example. Much of the church growth in Africa has been by churches that broke away from mission churches, or had independent origins with leaders trained in the missionary educational system. The recent historiography of African Christianity has rightly emphasized the importance of the African contribution and de-emphasized the importance of the missionary contribution, but it is difficult to believe that either William Carey or Henry Venn would object to that. Displacement is not the same thing as euthanasia, but the result is the same: self-supporting, self-governing, and self-extending African churches. The great importance of the missionary movement in beginning this process is undeniable, even if it is temporarily out of fashion to admit it or even analyze it. In the last 200 years Christianity has become a world religion rather than merely a European religion. The major contribution of the nineteenth-century missionary movement has been to ensure the continued importance of religion in a world where the rules governing religion have changed fundamentally.

Not Jet–it it last ch.

---

[64] David Barrett, *World Christian Encyclopedia: A Comparative Survey of Churches and Religions in the Modern World, A.D. 1900-2000* (Nairobi, 1982).

Selected Bibliography

Armytage, W.H.G. *Heavens Below: Utopian Experiments in England, 1560-1960*. London, 1961.

Arnstein, W.L. *The Bradlaugh Case: A Study in Late Victorian Opinion and Politics*. Oxford, 1965; 2nd ed. pub. with subtitle *Atheism, Sex, and Politics among the Late Victorians*. Columbia, Mo., 1983.

_____. *Protestant versus Catholic in Mid-Victorian England: Mr. Newdegate and the Nuns*. Columbia, Mo., 1982.

Barrow, Logie. *Independent Spirits: Spiritualism and English Plebeians, 1850-1910*. London, 1986.

Bebbington, D.W. *Evangelicalism in Modern Britain: A History from the 1730s to the 1980s*. London, 1989.

_____. *The Nonconformist Conscience: Chapel and Politics, 1870-1914*. London, 1982.

Binfield, Clyde. *So Down to Prayers: Studies in English Nonconformity, 1780-1920*. London, 1977.

Bossy, John. *The English Catholic Community, 1570-1850*. London, 1975.

Bowen, Desmond. *The Idea of the Victorian Church: A Study of the Church of England, 1833-1889*. Montreal, 1968.

Bradley, Ian. *The Call to Seriousness*. London, 1976.

The British: Their Religious Beliefs and Practices, 1800-1986. Ed. by Terence Thomas. London, 1988.

Brock, Peter. *The Quaker Peace Testimony, 1660 to 1914*. York, 1990.

Brose, Olive J. *Church and Parliament: The Reshaping of the Church of England, 1828-1860*. London, 1959.

Brown, Kenneth D. *A Social History of the Nonconformist Ministry in England and Wales, 1800-1930*. Oxford, 1988.

Budd, Susan. *Varieties of Unbelief: Atheists and Agnostics in English Society, 1850-1960*. London, 1977.

Campbell, Bruce F. *Ancient Wisdom Revived: A History of the Theosophical Movement*. Berkeley, 1980.

Richard Carwardine, *Trans-Atlantic Revivalism: Popular Evangelicalism in Britain and America, 1790-1865.* Westport, Conn., 1978.

Chadwick, Owen. *The Victorian Church.* Vol. 5 of *An Ecclesiastical History of England,* ed. by J. C. Dickinson. 2nd ed. London, 1970.

Clark, G. Kitson. *Churchmen and the Condition of England, 1832-1885.* London, 1973.

Clark, Kenneth. *The Gothic Revival: An Essay in the History of Taste.* London, 1962.

Cockshut, A.O.J. *The Unbelievers: English Agnostic Thought, 1840-1890.* London, 1964.

Coleman, B. I. *The Church of England in the Mid-Nineteenth Century: A Social Geography.* Historical Association Pamphlet, General Ser., No. 98. London, 1980.

Cox, Jeffrey. *The English Churches in a Secular Society: Lambeth, 1870-1930.* Oxford, 1982.

Currie, Robert, Alan Gilbert, and Lee Horsley. *Churches and Churchgoers: Patterns of Church Growth in the British Isles since 1700.* Oxford, 1977.

A Dictionary of Evangelical Biography. Ed. by Donald Lewis. Oxford, 1995.

Disciplines of Faith: Studies in Religion, Politics, and Patriarchy. Ed. by Jim Obelkevich, Lyndal Roper, and Raphael Samuel. London, 1987.

The English Presbyterians: From Elizabethan Puritanism to Modern Unitarianism. Ed. by C. G. Bolam *et al.* London, 1968.

Englishness: Politics and Culture, 1880-1920. Ed. by R. Colls and P. Dodd. London, 1986.

Enlightenment and Religion: Rational Dissent in Eighteenth-Century Britain. Ed. by Knud Haakonssen. Cambridge, forthcoming 1996.

Evangelicalism: Comparative Studies of Popular Protestantism in North America, the British Isles, and Beyond, 1700-1900. Ed. by Mark A. Noll, D. W. Bebbington, and George A. Rawlyk. New York, 1994.

Everitt, Alan M. *The Pattern of Rural Dissent: The Nineteenth Century.* Leicester, 1972.

Fielding, Steven. *Class and Ethnicity: Irish Catholics in England, 1880-1939.* Buckingham and Philadelphia, 1993.

Gay, John D. *The Geography of Religion in England.* London, 1971.

Gilbert, A.D. *Religion and Society in Industrial England: Church, Chapel and Social Change, 1740-1914.* London, 1976.

Gomes, Michael. *The Dawning of the Theosophical Movement.* Wheaton, Ill., 1987.

Halévy, Elie. *The Birth of Methodism in England.* Trans. and ed. by Bernard Semmel. Chicago, 1971.

_____. *A History of the English People in the Nineteenth Century.* 4 vols. London, 1949-51.

Hamer, D.A. *The Politics of Electoral Pressure: A Study in the History of Victorian Reform Agitations.* Hassocks, 1977.

Hardy, Dennis. *Alternative Communities in Nineteenth-Century England.* London, 1979.

Harrison, Brian. *Drink and the Victorians: The Temperance Question in England, 1815-1872*. London, 1971.

Harrison, J.F.C. *Robert Owen and the Owenites in Britain and America: The Quest for the New Moral World*. London, 1969.

_____. *The Second Coming: Popular Millenarianism, 1780-1850*. London, 1979.

Heeney, Brian. *A Different Kind of Gentleman: Parish Clergy as Professional Men in Early and Mid-Victorian England*. Hamden, Conn., 1976.

_____. *The Women's Movement in the Church of England, 1850-1930*. Oxford, 1988.

Hempton, David. *Methodism and Politics in British Society, 1750-1850*. London, 1984.

Hennell, M. *Sons of the Prophets: Evangelical Leaders of the Victorian Church*. London, 1979.

Hickman, M., and M. Hartigan, *The History of the Irish in Britain: A Bibliography*. London, 1986.

Hill, Michael. *The Religious Order: A Study of Virtuosi Religion and its Legitimation in the Nineteenth-Century Church of England*. London, 1973.

Hilton, Boyd. *The Age of Atonement: The Influence of Evangelicalism on Social and Economic Thought, 1795-1865*. Oxford, 1988.

A History of the Methodist Church in Great Britain. Ed. by Rupert Davies, A.R. George, and Gordon Rupp, 4 vols. London, 1965-88.

Holmes, J. Derek. *More Roman than Rome: English Catholicism in the Nineteenth Century*. Shepherdstown, W.Va., 1978.

Hurt, John. *Education in Evolution: Church, State, Society and Popular Education, 1800-1870*. London, 1971.

Inglis, K. S. *Churches and the Working Classes in Victorian England*. London, 1963.

The Irish in the Victorian City. Ed. by Roger Swift and Sheridan Gilley. London, 1985.

The Irish in Britain, 1815-1939. Ed. by Roger Swift and Sheridan Gilley. London, 1989.

Isichei, Elizabeth. *Victorian Quakers*. Oxford, 1970.

Jones, R. Tudur. *Congregationalism in England, 1662-1962*. London, 1962.

Kent, J.H.S. *Holding the Fort: Studies in Victorian Revivalism*. London, 1978.

_____. *The Unacceptable Face: The Modern Church in the Eyes of the Historian*. London, 1987.

Laqueur, T. W. *Religion and Respectability: Sunday Schools and Working-Class Culture, 1780-1850*. New Haven, 1976.

Latourette, Kenneth Scott. *Christianity in a Revolutionary Age*. 5 vols. New York, 1957-61.

_____. *A History of the Expansion of Christianity*. 7 vols. New York, 1937-45.

Lees, Lynn Hollen. *Exiles of Erin: Irish Migrants in Victorian London*. Manchester, 1979.

Little, Bryan. *Catholic Churches since 1623*. London, 1966.

Lovegrove, Deryck. *Established Church, Sectarian People: Itinerancy and the Transformation of English Dissent, 1780-1830*. Cambridge, 1988.

Machin, G.I.T. *The Catholic Question in English Politics, 1820 to 1830*. Oxford, 1964.

✓ ———. *Politics and the Churches in Great Britain, 1832 to 1868*. Oxford, 1977.

———. *Politics and the Churches in Great Britain, 1869-1921*. Oxford, 1987.

MacKillop, I. D. *The British Ethical Societies*. Cambridge, 1986.

McLeod, Hugh. *Class and Religion in the Late Victorian City*. London, 1974.

Mullen, Shirley A. *Organized Freethought: The Religion of Unbelief in Victorian England*. New York, 1987.

Neal, Frank. *Sectarian Violence: The Liverpool Experience, 1819-1914: An Aspect of Anglo-Irish History*. Manchester, 1988.

✓ Norman, Edward. *The English Catholic Church in the Nineteenth Century*. Oxford, 1984.

Obelkevich, James. *Religion and Rural Society: South Lindsey, 1825-1875*. Oxford, 1976.

Patriotism: The Making and Unmaking of British National Identity. Ed. by R. Samuel. London, 1989.

Patterns of Sectarianism: Organization and Ideology in Social and Religious Movements. Ed. by B. R. Wilson, London, 1967.

✓ Payne, Ernest A. *The Baptist Union: A Short History*. London, 1958.

Paz, D. G. *Popular Anti-Catholicism in Mid-Victorian England*. Stanford, 1992.

✓ Peel, Albert. *These Hundred Years: A History of the Congregational Union of England and Wales, 1831-1931*. London, 1931.

Prochaska, F.K. *Women and Philanthropy in Nineteenth-Century England*. Oxford, 1980.

✓ Reardon, B.M.G. *From Coleridge to Gore: A Century of Religious Thought in Britain*. London, 1971; 2nd ed., 1980, pub. as *Religious Thought in the Victorian Age*.

Religion and Irreligion in Victorian Society: Essays in Honour of R. K. Webb. Ed. by Richard W. Davis and Richard J. Helmstadter. London, 1992.

✓ *Religion in Victorian Britain*. Ed. by G. Parsons. 4 vols. Manchester, 1988.

Rosman, Doreen. *Evangelicals and Culture*. London, 1984.

Rowdon, H. H. *The Origins of the Brethren*. London and Glasgow, 1967.

Rowell, Geoffrey. *Hell and the Victorians: A Study of the Nineteenth-Century Theological Controversies Concerning Eternal Punishment and the Future Life*. Oxford, 1974.

✓ ———. *The Vision Glorious: Themes and Personalities of the Catholic Revival in Anglicanism*. Oxford, 1983.

Royle, Edward. *Radicals, Secularists, and Republicans: Popular Freethought in Britain, 1866-1915*. Manchester, 1980.

✓ ———. *Victorian Infidels: The Origins of the British Secularist Movement, 1791-1866*. Manchester, 1974.

Sandall, Robert, and Arch R. Wiggins. *The History of the Salvation Army*. 7 vols. London, 1947-1986.

Sandeen, Ernest R. *The Roots of Fundamentalism: British and American Millenarianism, 1800-1930*. Chicago, 1970.

✓ Sellers, Ian. *Nineteenth-Century Nonconformity*. London, 1977.

Shiman, Lilian Lewis. *Crusade Against Drink in Victorian England*. New York, 1988.

Soloway, R. A. *Prelates and People: Ecclesiastical Social Thought in England, 1783-1852*. London and Toronto, 1969.

Stanley, Brian. *The Bible and the Flag: Protestant Missions and British Imperialism in the Nineteenth and Twentieth Centuries*. Leicester, 1990.

Stewart, W. A. Campbell. *Quakers and Education, As Seen in Their Schools in England*. London, 1953; repr. Port Washington, N.Y., 1971.

Thompson, David. *Let Sects and Parties Fall: A Short History of the Association of Churches of Christ in Great Britain and Ireland*. London, 1980.

Tolles, Frederick B. *Quakers and the Atlantic Culture*. New York, 1960.

Underwood, A. C. *A History of the English Baptists*. London, 1947.

Valenze, Deborah M. *Prophetic Sons and Daughters: Female Preaching and Popular Religion in Industrial England*. Princeton, 1985.

Vann, Richard T. *Friends in Life and Death: The British and Irish Quakers in the Demographic Transition, 1650-1900*. New York, 1991.

Vicinus, Martha. *Independent Women: Work and Community for Single Women, 1850-1920*. Chicago, 1985.

Victorian Faith in Crisis: Essays on Continuity and Change in Nineteenth-Century Religious Belief. Ed. by Richard J. Helmstadter and Bernard Lightman. London and Stanford, 1990.

The View from the Pulpit: Victorian Ministers and Society. Ed. by P.T. Phillips. Toronto, 1978.

Viswanathan, Gauri. *Masks of Conquest: Literary Study and British Rule in India*. New York: Columbia University Press, 1989.

Ward, Bernard. *The Dawn of the Catholic Revival in England, 1781-1803*. 2 vols. London, 1909.

_____. *The Eve of Catholic Emancipation, 1803-1829*. 3 vols. London, 1911-12.

_____. *The Sequel to Catholic Emancipation, 1830-1850*. 2 vols. London, 1915.

Ward, R.W. *Religion and Society in England, 1790-1850*. London, 1972.

Werner, Julia Stuart. *The Primitive Methodist Connexion: Its Background and its Early History*. Madison, Wisc., 1984.

White, James F. *The Cambridge Movement: The Ecclesiologists and the Gothic Revival*. Cambridge, 1962.

Williams, C. Peter. *The Ideal of the Self-Governing Church: A Study in Victorian Missionary Strategy*. New York, 1990.

Wilson, B. R. *Sects and Society*. London 1961.

_____. *Religion in Secular Society*. London, 1966.

Wolffe, John. *The Protestant Crusade in Great Britain, 1829-60*. Oxford, 1991.

Wright, T.R. *The Religion of Humanity: The Impact of Comtean Positivism on Victorian Britain*. Cambridge, 1986.

Yates, Nigel. *Buildings, Faith, and Worship: The Liturgical Arrangement of Anglican Churches, 1600-1900*. Oxford, 1991.

This book is a most useful bibliographical tool.

Index

About the Contributors

Jeffrey Cox, Professor of History at the University of Iowa, published *The English Churches in a Secular Society: Lambeth, 1870-1930* (1982).

Sheridan Gilley, Reader in Theology at the University of Durham, published *The Irish in the Victorian City* (1985) and *The Irish in Britain, 1815-1939* (1989), both edited with Roger Swift; *Newman and His Age* (1990); and *A History of Religion in Britain: Practice and Belief from Pre-Roman Times to the Present* (1994), edited with W. J. Sheils.

Richard J. Helmstadter, Professor of History at the University of Toronto, is the co-author of *Religion and Victorian Society: A Sourcebook of Documents* (1985) with Paul T. Phillips, and co-edited *Victorian Faith in Crisis: Essays in Continuity and Change in Nineteenth-Century Religious Belief* (1990) with Bernard Lightman and *Religion and Irreligion in Victorian Society: Essays in Honour of R.K. Webb* (1992) with Richard W. Davis.

David Hempton, Professor of Modern History at the Queen's University of Belfast, is the author of *Methodism and Politics in British Society, 1750-1850* (1984), and, with Myrtle Hill, *Evangelical Protestantism in Ulster Society, 1740-1890* (1992).

Peter J. Lineham, Senior Lecturer in History at Massey University, has published on English religious history of the eighteenth and nineteenth centuries, and also on the religious history of New Zealand, including *There We Found Brethren* (1977), *No Ordinary Union* (1980), and *Transplanted Christianity* (1987) (with A. K. Davidson).

D. G. Paz, Professor of History at the University of North Texas, is the author of *The Politics of Working-Class Education in Britain, 1830-50* (1980), *The Priesthoods and Apostasies of Pierce Connelly: A Study of Victorian Conversion and Anticatholicism* (1986), and *Popular Anti-Catholicism in Mid-Victorian England* (1992).

Edward Royle, Reader in History at the University of York, has published on Freethought, on the religious history of Britain and on radical politics in the nineteenth century, as well as a general study, *Modern Britain: A Social History, 1750-1985* (1987).

R. K. Webb, Professor of History, Emeritus, at the University of Maryland Baltimore County, is the author of several books and articles as well as the general study, *Modern England: From the Eighteenth Century to the Present*, 2nd ed. (1980).

John Wolffe, Lecturer in Religious Studies and Sub-Dean of the Faculty of Arts at The Open University, is the author of *The Protestant Crusade in Great Britain, 1829-1860* (1991) and *God and Greater Britain: Religion and National Life in Britain and Ireland, 1843-1945* (1994).

ISBN 0-313-29476-3

9 780313 294761

90000>

EAN

HARDCOVER BAR CODE